W9-BLY-906

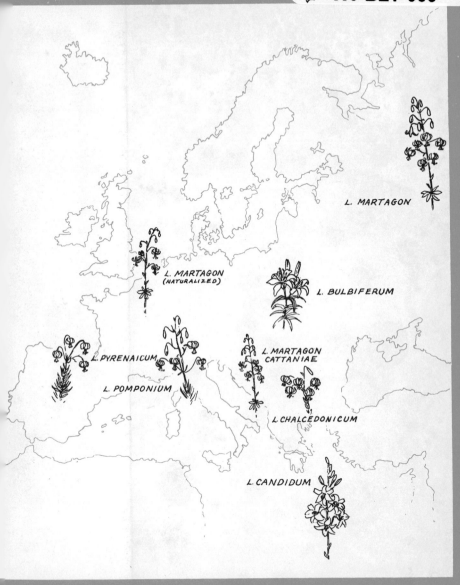

L. MARTAGON

L. MARTAGON
(NATURALIZED)

L. BULBIFERUM

L. PYRENAICUM

L. POMPONIUM

L. MARTAGON
CATTANIAE

L. CHALCEDONICUM

L. CANDIDUM

GROW WILD
EUROPE

Ana D. Thompson
August 1984

THE COMPLETE
BOOK OF LILIES

BY F. F. ROCKWELL
AND ESTHER C. GRAYSON

The Rockwells' NEW Complete Book of Flower Arrangement

10,000 Garden Questions Answered by 20 Experts (Editors)

The Rockwells' Complete Book of Roses

The Complete Book of Bulbs

The Complete Book of Lawns

The Complete Book of Annuals

Gardening Indoors

BY F. F. ROCKWELL

Around the Year in the Garden

The Treasury of American Gardens (with James Fitch)

The Book of Bulbs

The Home Garden Handbooks

BY JAN DE GRAAFF

The New Book of Lilies

THE
COMPLETE
BOOK
OF LILIES

F. F. Rockwell and Esther C. Grayson and Jan de Graaff

HOW TO SELECT, PLANT, CARE FOR,
EXHIBIT, AND PROPAGATE LILIES
OF ALL TYPES, WITH
ONE HUNDRED AND TEN PHOTOGRAPHS
THIRTY-ONE IN COLOR AND TWENTY-ONE
LINE DRAWINGS BY VIRGINIA HOWIE

AN AMERICAN GARDEN GUILD BOOK. DOUBLEDAY & COMPANY, INC.
GARDEN CITY, NEW YORK, 1961

To DR. SAMUEL L. EMSWELLER *of the Plant Industry Station, Beltsville, Maryland, who has accomplished so much in adding to the knowledge of lilies and lily culture, and in bringing them into more general use in the gardens of America.*

Library of Congress Catalog Card Number 61-6717
Copyright © 1961 by Fred F. Rockwell and Esther C. Grayson
All Rights Reserved
Printed in the United States of America

Foreword

It is now more than ten years since I wrote my *New Book of Lilies*. Ten springs went by, during which I saw the lilies emerging and was thrilled by vigorous young plants bursting through the ground; ten summers with the glory of acre upon acre of lily hybrids flowering in profusion, in a cloud of heavenly scent, on my ever-larger farms; ten autumns with the backbreaking work of lifting the bulbs, sorting and grading, packing and planting; and ten winters to speculate on things to come.

The first and second editions of my *New Book* are sold out. A third printing, a revised edition, was being considered. The lilies are different now; my outlook has changed; all of us here at the farms are older and, I believe, more experienced. New production methods have been tested and these provide much information of value to the gardener. New sprays and dusts have been introduced; new lily species have been discovered and described. New photographs have been made—too good to remain unpublished. It thus became obvious that a merely revised edition would not fill the need for an up-to-date book about lilies.

Apart from all this, there is a totally new selection of hybrid lilies. Many of them have been introduced since the *New Book* appeared; others that then were merely thought of are now a reality. Definite patterns and groupings can be discerned—we can now see an over-all picture of what is being done and of what may be expected in the lily hybrids of the future, and these add up to a fascinating, a thrilling prospect. To us, who live in this period, the rare privilege is granted of watching a beloved plant family evolve from its early beginnings as lilies of the field to the fine, colorful, beautifully shaped and balanced lilies of our gardens.

For the past ten years I had been gathering all new information. I realized that this led further and further along the path of highly technical developments—the preference of one chemical over another, the ability of one selective weed killer to do a better job than another, the genetic potential of certain lily species. In all this material I was beginning to lose sight of the home gardener, the hobby-greenhouse man and the use of the lily in home decoration. It was at this stage that I learned of the interest of Fred Rockwell and Esther Grayson Rockwell in these very matters. For years they had grown lilies—first in their beautiful garden at Van Houten Fields in West Nyack, New York, later in their new Grayrock Garden on Cape Cod.

Here was that rare combination of writer, gardener and flower arranger, photographer and keen student of nature, with all these qualifications tempered by years of experience. These qualities were exactly what I needed to reduce my book again to the essentials for the amateur lily grower, however expert or inexperienced he might be. In Esther and Fred Rockwell I found two green-thumb gardeners who had tried, successfully, I might add, to grow good lilies; who knew how to tell the story and to answer the questions that you would like to ask.

Out of this collaboration this book has come. It is, I believe, the first time a garden book has been written that reveals both complete commercial production techniques and definitive technical information and, at the same time, brings them down to their true perspective—their real worth to the home gardener. My technical data, leavened by a sharply critical, practical garden approach, reveal much that has previously been obscured. This book then puts the lily in its rightful place—as that of an easily grown, spectacularly beautiful garden plant for all gardens in the Northern Hemisphere.

In *The New Book of Lilies,* now out of print, acknowledgment was made to Earl Hornback, who has managed the world's largest lily farms and has looked after much of the detail of hybridizing done there ever since lilies became one of the main crops. Of late he has been ably assisted by Harold F. Comber and Kenneth Crutcher. All three have co-operated in the writing of this book. The authors are duly grateful to them for their assistance and advice, especially in the chapters devoted to culture, propagation, and classification.

To J. J. Grullemans of the Wayside Gardens, Mentor, Ohio, L. R. Sjulin of the Inter-State Nurseries, Hamburg, Iowa, and C. H. Perkins of Jackson & Perkins, Newark, New York, who, each in his own inimitable way, has done a yeoman job of bringing the lilies from the hands of the hybridizers to the not-always-eager hands of the American gardeners;

To Herman V. Wall and Jack Fields, who have given us of their best in illustrating the book, for a job well done, beyond the limits of the usual photographic assignment;

To Virginia Howie, whose delightful illustrations and amusing comments made our task easier and the book far more intelligible;

To Helen Kiester who did most of the typing and patiently deciphered the much-corrected copy submitted by three authors:

And to all the other people who have helped to put the lily on the map,

Our special thanks are due.

JAN DE GRAAFF

Gresham, Oregon
May 1961

Contents

PART III. THE LILY WORLD

Half-tone Illustrations

[PHOTOGRAPHS BY HERMAN V. WALL, EXCEPT AS NOTED]

Line Illustrations

[DRAWINGS BY VIRGINIA HOWIE]

Color Illustrations

[PHOTOGRAPHS BY HERMAN V. WALL, EXCEPT AS NOTED]

ERRATA
(*The Complete Book of Lilies*)

The titles of Plates 16 through 31 are incorrect; they should read as follows:

Introduction

My first interest in lilies dates back further than I can remember. There is a family story to the effect that I screamed and made a terribly embarrassing scene in church on the Easter Sunday when my nurse attempted to remove from my clutching hands the potted lily that had been presented to me at the close of the Easter service. During all the intervening years—or decades, I should say—my love of them has never lessened.

My first experiences in attempting to grow lilies, however, were anything but encouraging. Despite all the information I could get from books—which in those days laid much stress on the importance of "creating conditions as similar as possible to those in which they grow in the wild"—most of them disappeared within a year or two after transplanting.

Today the lily story is a very, very different one. A few days ago my partner and I had the pleasure of attending the second annual show of the New England section of the American Lily Society. The large central hall of the ancient and honorable Worcester Horticultural Society was filled to overflowing with excellent displays of lilies of every description, from rare and difficult species to the latest of the modern hybrids. Most interesting was the fact that many of these fine specimens had been grown by amateurs with small gardens and limited previous experience with lilies. Such enthusiasm at any special flower society show we had not seen since the early days of the dahlia and gladiolus societies.

Primarily the cause of the current upsurge in the interest in lilies is due to the long, long delayed breakthrough in getting the wild species to cross with each other, and give us, in lilies, man-made hybrids, such as gardeners have long enjoyed in hybrid roses, chrysanthemums, peonies, and scores of other flowers. These hybrid forms are not only much more varied, but also much easier to grow in gardens than are the various species from which they have been developed. The intriguing story of this long-delayed arrival of hybrid lilies is told elsewhere in this volume. When you have read it you will better understand why, in the history of ornamental horticulture, the present decade will be known as the era of the Lily.

It was with great pleasure that we accepted the opportunity to work with Jan de Graaff, whom we had known since he first came to America in those stormy days, still remembered by old gardeners, when a suddenly imposed bulb quarantine shut off the importation of most flower bulbs from Holland.

Mr. de Graaff has for years been recognized as the world's leading hybridizer and grower of lilies, and the knowledge which he has acquired in growing them cannot fail to be of great assistance to any gardener attempting to have lilies of his own.

As much of the information in this book is based upon personal experience, the first person pronoun "I" appears not infrequently. Our publishers have feared that this might be somewhat confusing but as Mr. de Graaff is located in Oregon, with lilies by the hundreds of thousands, and the Rockwells' gardening has been limited to the East Coast, on a purely personal basis, we feel that the reader will have, from the context, no difficulty in deciding who, at any given moment, is speaking.

As Mr. de Graaff's knowledge of lilies is based largely upon his own extensive work with them, it is natural, in fact inevitable, that much of the discussion on these pages should be built around his own creations. This is not meant to imply—and in fact he himself would be the last to wish to imply it—that other hybridizers are not achieving really remarkable results. His work, inspired by those who had worked in this field before him, has in turn encouraged many others to take it up, in widely separated sections of this country. New lily creations, covering many distinct new types, are appearing so rapidly that it has been impossible to discuss them all in this volume. The reader who has become, or may become interested in them, should by all means join his local group of the American Lily Society. The headquarters of regional societies are given on page 343.

And so we commend the reader to a new adventure in gardening—the discovery of the fascinating *new* world of lilies!

FREDERICK FRYE ROCKWELL

Grayrock-on-the-Cape,
Orleans, Mass.
July 15, 1960.

Part One

LILIES IN THE GARDEN

Until quite recently lilies were seldom seen except in large, professionally cared for gardens such as this one in England where Regal Lilies (a species from China) stand guard at an entrance gate.

CHAPTER *1. From Rare Species to plants for Everyman's Garden*

> *The deepest joy in life is to be creative. To find an undeveloped situation, to see the possibilities, to identify yourself with something worthwhile doing, put yourself into it, and stand for it—that is a satisfaction in comparison with which superficial pleasures are trivial.*
>
> ABRAHAM FLEXNER (1866–1959)
> *Head of Institute of Advanced Studies*
> *Princeton, N. J.*

Symbol of purity, perfection, and flawless beauty, striking in its variety of form, color, fragrance, and seasons of flowering, the lily is unique among all cultivated plants. In its almost endless variation it is rivaled only by the orchid. In its ease of culture, its endurance and vitality, it must be compared to the daffodil, the tulip, and the iris. All over America, all over Europe, in gardens new and old, lilies are flowering, year after year, with little or no care.

Who has not seen clumps of fine lilies—perhaps of the old Tiger Lily, the Candlestick Lily, or of the pure white Madonna Lily—in old farm gardens where they must have been at home for many years? Who among us has not driven along the highways of our country to be startled and arrested by the sight of some glowing yellow or orange flowers, lilies, shaped like toy balloons, like temple bells, swaying in the wind? Here they grow among grasses and low shrubs, under trees, in sunshine and shade. Here they live and multiply.

Why then have lilies been surrounded with an aura of exclusiveness? Why have they sometimes been marked with the stigma of ill temper, of being difficult to handle? Is it because they often have fallen into the hands of collectors rather than into the hands of practical gardeners? Is it because some experts rate rarity and exclusiveness as more important than general acceptance and use? Is it, perhaps, that we have not given the lily a fair trial? Or, is it rather that the cultural requirements of the lily have been misunderstood and that they have been incorrectly handled?

Probably all of these factors have contributed to the reputation of the lily, for good and for bad. Yet, its reported difficulties enhanced its fame, and those who succeeded with lilies could consider themselves expert gardeners and lily specialists. Its rarity has made many a gardener turn to it, intrigued by the challenge that these beautiful flowers offered. Its unique features, the fact that some species have only recently been discovered, and that, until recently, most of our garden lilies were still identical with the wild species—even though they may have been nursery-grown for centuries—induced many a scientist to devote his time and full attention to the lily.

Now, in laboratories and in greenhouses on university campuses and on college grounds all over the world, people are at work, studying the lily, its make-up and character. They are finding new facts. They are making discoveries. The life habits of the lily, its requirements and associations are being listed and tabulated for the first time. All of this adds up to a better understanding and to the more successful use of lilies in the gardens of our country. Failures there have been and failures there will be, but as stronger varieties of lilies are developed and fundamental conditions for culture better understood, success can be guaranteed as surely as with any other plant.

A BIT OF BACKGROUND

Let us look then at some of the essential facts that are known about the lily and that govern its culture. Lilies come from the Northern Hemisphere and are found in Asia, Europe, and North America. Most of those now in our gardens and commonly sold are identical with these wild lilies. In fact, we can still call them wild lilies, for they breed true from seed and to the botanist this is the earmark of a true species. In this characteristic the lilies are unique among our garden plants. Our daffodils and tulips, our iris and roses, our peonies and lilacs are all of hybrid origin. What gardener, except the inveterate collector or the student-specialist, would now plant a collection of wild roses or iris or poppies in his garden? Yet this is exactly what we have been asking gardeners to do with lilies.

Since the majority of the lilies we have known until recently are species (wild flowers identical with the lilies found in the wildernesses of Japan, China, India, Europe, and America), they are not especially adapted to garden use nor to frequent transplanting. Such rough handling and competition with other garden plants has not in the past been their lot.

One may ask why, among all flowers, lilies have stayed so aloof; and why they have not mixed with other lilies to provide us with stronger-growing, more adaptable hybrids. To answer this question we must look into several things. Where did our garden lilies come from? When did they reach our shores? What types or species are there; and under what circumstances can they be induced to mix or crossbreed?

THE GEOGRAPHIC DISTRIBUTION OF LILIES

Lilies grow only in the Northern Hemisphere, as far north as the Arctic Circle and as far south as the Philippine Islands. The latest information is that eighty-seven distinct species are recognized. Of these, forty-nine are from Asia, twenty-four from North America, twelve from Europe and two which appear both in Europe and in Asia. The great majority of lilies grow in the temperate zone.

From America

Let us first look at our American species. Their names suggest the open spaces, the plains and mountains where they grow: *L. washingtonianum,* white and purple; yellow *L. canadense; L. michiganense,* orange-yellow; *L. columbianum,* yellow to orange; *L. nevadense,* yellow to maroon. Then there are some that bear the names of famous botanists, of plant hunters and travelers: *L. hum-*

boldti, orange-red; *L. kelloggi,* mauve with maroon dots; *L. bolan-deri* and yellow *L. parryi.* There is that lovely orange lily of our Eastern seaboard so aptly named *L. superbum;* and another that is found both in the East and the Far West, *L. philadelphicum,* a rich orange-red. There is *L. pardalinum,* the orange to crimson Panther Lily that grows in western Oregon and California.

All of these, and a few more, will grow in your garden if conditions are just right; if healthy, strong bulbs are planted and left undisturbed. They have been used extensively by hybridizers and the resulting lilies are now on the market as *Bellingham Hybrids,* a strain of fine lilies far more adaptable to garden conditions than any of the original parent varieties. Most of the *Bellinghams* have nodding flowers ranging in color from light yellow through orange and red to deep maroon. More will be said about these in subsequent chapters.

From Asia

Then there are the Asiatic lilies. Of these the experts tell us that forty-nine distinct species are known. For convenience, let us separate the most important of them into the various flower-type groups.

With nodding flowers. We find that there are nine important species, all with nodding flowers, important either in themselves or for their hybrid offspring. They are: *Lilium cernuum,* a small soft lilac lily; *L. hansoni,* a substantial and stiff-looking yellow; *L. henryi,* a graceful and tall orange-yellow; *L. leichtlini maximowiczi;* and *L. davidi,* both good red lilies; *L. speciosum* and *L. auratum,* the gorgeously spotted species from Japan; *L. pumilum,* a tiny red; and finally the ubiquitous *L. tigrinum,* the Tiger Lily so well known in this country.

With upright flowers. There are two important wild lilies with upright flowers. One, *Lilium concolor,* has charming little star-shaped flowers, warmly tinted red—a real gem in flower arrangements. The other, *L. dauricum,* is a coarser but strongly growing upright, which comes in apricot or orange-red shades and also in yellow. It is from these two lilies that the European and Japanese gardeners have bred a number of hybrids which are being sold as varieties under the name of *L. maculatum.*

Nowadays even the finest of the newer lilies, such as Royal Gold (a pure yellow Regal) and White Regal, add their magic to hundreds of thousands of modest gardens in many lands.

With trumpets. Finally there are seven or eight varieties with trumpet-shaped flowers. Of these *Lilium regale* is already well known in this country. Other similar lilies are *L. leucanthum, L. sulphureum* and *L. sargentiae.* Then there are the pure white, such as *L. longiflorum,* our well-known Easter Lily, and the late-flowering *L. formosanum* and *L. philippinense.*

Rare Lilies.

So far we have considered eighteen lilies from Asia. This leaves thirty-one out of the forty-nine. For the greater part these are the really rare lilies of which there are only a few in the hands of experts, and which as yet do not play any role in our American gardens. For the curious reader we shall mention a few of them briefly.

There is *Lilium neilgherrense,* from India, with pale greenish-yellow, long trumpet flowers; *L. nepalense* from Nepal, also a trumpet lily with greenish white coloring and a deep purple-red throat; *L. lankongense* with soft lilac flowers attractively spotted with purple; and *L. ochraceum* from China and Upper Burma, with nodding, mustard-yellow flowers, often with a purple tinge and a deep maroon blotch in the center. Other Chinese species are pink *L. taliense;* orange *L. tsingtauense;* and finally *L. wardi,* a pink lily with nodding flowers from Tibet.

Some of these have been flowered in American nurseries; others are now being raised from seed. They are not difficult to grow nor difficult to acclimate, and while we feel sure that they will never play an important role in our American gardens, they may become quite popular with the specialists. They may also be important in hybridizing. There are still other Asiatic species to be tested and there may be some yet to be discovered. The ones listed here appear to be the most significant.

From Europe

Available to gardeners and hybridizers for several centuries or more, most of the European lilies are well known. They include *Lilium candidum,* the Madonna Lily; *L. chalcedonicum,* the "Scarlet Martagon of Constantinople" as older writers call it; the upright orange lilies, *L. bulbiferum* and its variety *croceum;* the charming *L. martagon* with either pink, purple or white nodding flowers; *L. monadelphum,* straw color to yellow; yellow *L. szovitsianum* from Russia; and *L. pomponium* from the Maritime Alps, with sealing-wax red, Turk's-cap blooms.

This very brief survey of the more important lilies will orient the reader. These are the species from which have come our new garden lilies, many already on the market, and others to be introduced in the near future.

The fact that some of them come from China, some from our own country, and others from Europe should not be a hindrance to their adaptation to our climate and soil conditions. Grown from seed, some individual plants will stand out for their ability to adjust themselves to their new surroundings. Others, raised from the seed of selected plants, demonstrate that their good qualities—such as resistance to drought and superior all-round performance—are to a very high degree transmittable. Continuous improvement of strains of species lilies is not only possible, but also commercially feasible and profitable.

Yet, on the basis of some thirty years' experience in raising lilies, we are convinced that our garden lilies of the future will not be the true species from foreign or domestic sources. They will not be the selected seedling strains of such species, even though those have proved to be distinctly better able to stand our average garden conditions. The new lilies for American gardens will be of hybrid origin, since thus, through judicious choice of types and qualities, we can bring out and strengthen the most desirable traits. We can accentuate hardiness, and emphasize color and refinement of form. Through hybridization, too, we can eliminate most, if not all, the poorer qualities—the weaknesses that might be inherent in some species native to other climates and used to other conditions.

Already in the hybrids of *Lilium henryi,* a tall orange-flowered lily, we have been able to introduce new colors, new forms and new habits of growth. We have done the same with many other lilies. In later chapters these hybrids will be described in more detail.

CHAPTER 2. *Modern Lilies*
for Modern Gardens

Have you seene but a bright Lillie grow,
Before rude hands have touched it?
Ha' you marked but the fall o' the Snow
Before the soyle hath smutched it?
        *   *   *
O so white! O so soft! O so sweet is she!

BEN JOHNSON (1573–1637)

Lilies have always been known as the prima donnas of the flower kingdom—wild, beautiful, enchanting, difficult, and unpredictable. In many respects this reputation was well merited. Species of *Lilium* are found in most sections of the Northern Hemisphere. In many instances they thrive under conditions which few other flowers of decorative value would tolerate. Yet, they succeeded in keeping themselves aloof, not only from man-made gardens, but—in most cases—even from one another. In their needs and in their tolerances they are, what we might call, specialized flowers.

It should be remembered that, nowadays, few of our popular garden flowers are still the original species. Run down the list—roses, iris, peonies, phlox, delphinium, poppies, gladiolus, marigolds, petunias, zinnias, tulips, daffodils, and shrubs such as lilacs and azaleas—in the forms which we use in our gardens, are the results of man-made crosses, hybrids bearing little resemblance to the original wild species from which they have been developed. This hybridizing process goes back, in most cases, through hundreds of years; in some, as with the rose, so far as to be lost in antiquity.

The process of "crossing" or intermarriage between natural species in the same family of plants varies greatly with the different families. Just why this should be so no one knows. In some cases no assistance from the hand of man, the plant breeder, is required. Nature, unaided, attends to the job. In the woods on Cape Cod, for instance, we can find a half-dozen distinct species of oak, interspersed with innumerable mongrel types which show, in varying degrees, the characteristics of the several parents. In a waterside grove of black gums, however, all are as alike as peas in the same pod.

It is a general characteristic of hybrid varieties that they are more vigorous, and grow satisfactorily under a wider range of conditions of soil and climate, than was the case with their parents. This is especially true of man-made or controlled hybrids developed during a long series of crosses, for the simple reason that the weak-growing and otherwise least satisfactory ones are constantly being discarded in the process; or—in the case of those which may show some unusual but desirable character, such as a new color or flower form—be retained merely for further breeding until the new color or form can be combined with a more vigorous strain.

"So what," the reader may ask, "has all this to do with the lily situation?"

It has a great deal! For centuries no attempts were made to get the natural species, the wild lilies, to cross. This was not due to the fact that members of the lily tribe were incompatible. It was, rather, that the natural species come into flower over a very wide period of time—early June to late September—thus reducing the range of possible artificial crosses. Now, with modern methods of preserving pollen by cool and dry storage, almost any two species may be crossed.

This recent breakthrough in lily hybridizing, however, has also been due to the fact that, although the natural species showed marked resistance to being crossed, their hybrid offspring did not. *They crossed readily not only with one another, but also back again with the natural species.*

In recent years, as a result, the flood gates to new lilies, and even to distinctly new *types* of lilies, have been opened. We now face the day when we shall have a plethora of new lilies.

Other hindrances. The difficulty, in the past, of creating new varieties of lilies was, however, not the only thing that interfered with their more general use in our gardens.

In addition there was the fact that, until quite recently, many species were imported from the Orient and from Europe. They spent weeks on shipboard between the time they were dug and the day they arrived, dried up and withered, to be planted in our gardens. Good, healthy lily bulbs remained rare and expensive.

A lily bulb, unlike a tulip, a daffodil, or a gladiolus corm does not go completely dormant. Such bulbs and tubers may—within reasonable limits—be handled and shipped like dry merchandise. Unlike them, the lily bulb has no protective parchment-like outer layers to provide protection and conserve moisture. When taken up for shipping, its fleshy roots, which normally would remain alive and plump through the winter, shrivel and dry up. The loose fleshy scales lose much of their moisture content. In handling they are easily knocked off or are injured and so become susceptible to disease. Small wonder then that in former days, after lily bulbs were in transit or storage for weeks or months, many of them failed to grow.

HOW THE PICTURE HAS CHANGED

How different is the prospect faced by the gardener who plants lilies today!

In the first place, most varieties are hybrids rather than original species. They possess hybrid vigor and, with few exceptions, will be much less insistent upon being provided with special conditions of soil, shade, drainage, depth of planting, and the like—conditions which their temperamental ancestors were likely to demand.

Then, too, *the bulbs will be received promptly after they are dug* —often in a matter of days instead of weeks or even months. Modern packaging in closed plastic bags, with light moist packing, insures uninjured scales and plump white roots instead of dried-out withered ones. Consequently, the bulbs are ready to re-establish themselves almost immediately in their new location.

Furthermore, and of equally great importance, is the fact that a

With the development, comparatively recent, of the breakthrough in the problem of hybridizing lilies, new and more vigorous forms resulted in their wider use by amateur gardeners. Here are some of the early Olympic Hybrids growing at Grayrock.

great many of the modern lilies are *grown from seed* and are thus free from diseases transmitted by vegetative propagation.

Lilies grown from seed are usually sold as "strains," instead of as named varieties. This means that, while all the flowers in a certain strain will be alike in general characteristics—type of flower, form, season of bloom, etc.—there will be some variation, especially in height, time of flowering, and depth of color.

While such variations might be a disadvantage to a commercial grower (who may want to get a uniform crop, with all blooms ready for cutting at one time), for the amateur or average home gardener a prolonged season of bloom is a decided advantage.

Slight variations in color or flower form really add interest to his planting. We ourselves feel this to be the case and most visitors to our garden express the same opinion.

For reasons that are obvious from the preceding pages, today's lilies can be enjoyed by everyone who can grow the average range of perennials. They are being grown so successfully that lily bulbs in variety are being sold not only by specialists, but are given generous space in most catalogs—even those of the big mail-order houses—and are distributed by garden centers. Local lily societies are being organized the country over, and many of these hold regional lily shows.

To the average homeowner the garden gate to the lovely world of lilydom is just beginning to open. To him and to her there is available a wealth of material in colors and flower forms scarcely dreamed of a few decades ago. Available in vigorous, healthy, strong-growing bulbs lilies are as sure to grow and give as much satisfaction as the other hardy plants he purchases. In fact, they require much less attention than many other garden favorites for they do not need constant spraying and special winter protection.

With some thought given to the selection of types and varieties, lilies may be enjoyed in constant succession for three months or more. They add greatly to the beauty of the garden and immeasurably increase its interest.

Let us then take a look at the ways in which the modern lilies may be used.

CHAPTER *3. Today's Lilies in Your Garden*

> *Go make thy garden fair as thou canst,*
> *Thou workest never alone;*
> *Perchance he whose plot is next to thine*
> *Will see it, and mend his own.*
>
> ELIZABETH RUNDLE CHARLES (1828–1896)

In the light of what has been said in the preceding chapter, it is not difficult to understand why lilies were sometimes not satisfactory for the small home garden.

Today any fairly competent gardener may enjoy the pleasures and rewards of lily growing. In fact, the point has been reached where one is not quite considered to *be* a competent gardener unless at least a small collection of lilies is found among his floral treasures.

We have never believed in "fad" gardens or gardening for—slightly to misquote Rudyard Kipling—"the things that we've learned from the yellow and brown can 'elp us a lot with the white." One need not become a lily specialist to profit from adding lilies to his general garden scheme. Indeed it is doubtful if there is any other one group of flowering plants that will add more interest and beauty to the over-all landscape effect than a collection of lilies. They may be had in bloom from June well into September. *They add the valuable dimension of height to plantings, and, with the new hybrids now available, they provide a range of blossom forms and colors equaled by few other flowers.*

37

NEW LILIES FOR NEW GARDENS

For many years now, and particularly during the past decade, the average size of American gardens has become smaller and smaller. One old-fashioned country estate, or one fair-sized farm, provides a score or more of small home sites with sufficient room for some attractive landscaping.

Gradually, but nonetheless definitely, the character of such landscaping is improving. After the first few years of uninspired rectangular beds or long borders of garish spring bulbs, followed by mass (or mess) plantings of inharmonious annuals, one begins to see the emergence of more carefully thought-out and planned landscaping. Frequently, as in the designs of the houses themselves, there is too little individuality in these plantings; but fortunately, as time goes on, the landscaping can be altered and improved, even if the dwellings cannot.

In creating more attractive and more original home surroundings, lilies can play a most important part. There are lilies which like full sun; others which tolerate, or prefer, considerable shade. There are varieties which flower in early summer, midsummer, and autumn. There are some species and varieties that grow but eighteen inches tall; any number that go three to five feet, and many that, with good culture, will put on their impressive display up to six or seven feet above the ground, remaining in bloom for a considerable period and dominating the landscape scheme. (In the appendix the reader will find lists of varieties to help him make selections for whatever purposes he may have in mind.)

In the Mixed Border. The type of planting most frequently used in planning home grounds, especially those of moderate size, is the border of mixed perennials. Often such borders are much narrower than they might be, and are "free standing" instead of being backed by shrubs and evergreens, enhancing the display of flowers and providing protection from high winds and rainstorms.

In any mixed border, however, lilies can play a most important role in adding points of contrast and accent that will greatly enhance the general effectiveness of the planting. There are few perennials which accomplish this purpose and none to do it so effectively and over such a long period.

Modern lilies add highlights of color and interest to gardens from coast to coast: below, in the lovely Buttrick garden at Concord, Massachusetts, within a stone's throw of the bridge where was fired "the shot heard round the world"; above, in the de Graaff gardens at Gresham, Oregon.

In the average-sized hardy border a few groups of lilies, three to half a dozen bulbs of each, selected to bloom at different periods and to provide the desired heights, will add focus and dimension to the border and give it distinction.

Against Shrubbery. On many places there are boundary plantings of evergreens, shrubs, or hedges which, even though there may be no flower borders in front of them, would make perfect backgrounds for group plantings of lilies. For an artistic effect these should not be planted in a continuous row, but at irregular intervals, in groups which provide separate units of focal interest.

For color in early spring, before the first lilies come into bloom, the intervening spaces may well be planted with spring-flowering bulbs such as daffodils, tulips, hyacinths, and camassias. The dying foliage of these plants, so often a problem, makes a ground cover for the lilies.

For Formal Effects. In some types of landscaping formal design is stressed. Here, too, lilies have their place. As accent points in a formal design, where tall flowers are needed, there is nothing else that can quite equal them.

In many modern small formal gardens, color accents are maintained by growing plants in tubs or large pots. They can then be moved into place while in flower and later removed to be replaced by something else. For such use lilies are ideal, since most of them can readily be grown in pots. While not "on exhibition" they require little space or attention; and they may be carried along for two or three seasons without repotting. By making a selection of a half dozen or more varieties, they provide a succession of highlights in the garden picture over a period of two or three months.

For Shady Areas. While the majority of lilies—and especially the new hybrid varieties and strains—may be grown in full sun, there are many which prefer, or will tolerate, considerable shade. This is especially true if it is "high" shade which admits ample light, even if no direct sunshine, at the ground level.

In England many of the famous plantings of lilies are along paths in open woodlands. (See illustration, page 41.)

Unfortunately in America the opportunities for such plantings are becoming fewer and fewer, but even on small places there

Even in a woodland setting, provided there is "high" shade, permitting abundant light, lilies may be used to provide color and interest. Here plantings of Regals grace the foreground, with a group of Bellingham Hybrids in the distance.

often exist shaded, or semishaded, areas where many of the lilies will be perfectly happy. Here, illuminating the space about them, they show to the very best advantage and remain in perfect condition for a long time.

The favored few, fortunate enough to be able to keep up extensive gardens, are finding a new treasure trove of exotic form and color in hybrid lilies. The shade-loving varieties are of special value in such gardens where large, landscaped woodland areas are in need of the impressive color accents provided by lilies.

The Lily Garden. More and more, as garden lovers are discovering how successfully the newer lilies, and certain of the older ones, may be grown under ordinary conditions, they are deriving pleasure and excitement from areas devoted exclusively to lilies. This is equally true of the owners of extensive gardens and of those who do their own planning and planting.

Where such a planting is contemplated, advantage may be taken of the existing conditions. For instance, a space in part shade and

In level, open areas groups of lilies of varied heights and seasons of blooms add immeasurably to gardens such as this.

another in full sun; others with neutral or slightly alkaline soil can be devoted to the species or varieties that have marked preferences.

The fascinating hobby of growing one's own lilies from seed may be taken up with every prospect of success—a fact proved by the hundreds of amateurs now engaged in this phase of lily growing. The recent increase of the many local lily societies rapidly spreading over the United States and Canada has greatly stimulated this activity and has had much to do with the success of regional lily shows. (The reproduction of part of one of the frequently issued bulletins of the New England Lily Society, on page 225, gives an idea of the enthusiasm with which these groups are working.)

One of the advantages of making a specialty of lilies is that a collection of them will require less space than that demanded by a collection of perennials such as iris, phlox, or peonies. On the whole they require less care, particularly in the matter of dividing and replanting.

For Patio Plantings. In connection with many modern homes, especially those built on small plots or in regions where conditions make the usual types of gardening difficult, the patio offers the chief opportunity for the use of plants. Often such plantings are literally a part of the house décor, viewed through glass walls which can slide back to bring the patio garden into the living room.

Here lilies can play an important role. The patio, usually shaded from hot direct sunshine and from strong winds, provides a favorable place for the display of lilies grown in tubs or planters. These may be moved into the desired locations as the plants are coming into bloom and removed when they are through. For this purpose, kinds which are not too tall and are likely to remain in flower for a considerable period, and varieties with fragrance, are good selections.

Suitable varieties are suggested on page 319.

For Cutting. It is scarcely necessary to say that lilies are among the most decorative of all flowers for cutting. In both form and height they stand out from all others. Their colors are varied and unexcelled; they remain in good condition longer than most cut flowers, the buds continuing to open for ten days or more.

Where tall or massive arrangements are to be used, as in decorating very large rooms, churches, or a stage, lilies make possible dramatic effects such as can be achieved with no other flowers. (See Chapter 4.)

As many of the modern lilies, and a few of the species, increase quite rapidly where conditions are to their liking, the lily grower may well plan to build up a surplus stock of some of these especially for cutting.

LILIES AND COMPANION PLANTS

We are often asked to suggest suitable companion plants for lilies that are to be planted in a more or less permanent perennial border; or, conversely, to suggest lilies that can be planted with a group of long-established perennials. It should be remembered at all times that most lilies cannot and will not tolerate strong competition from large perennials, shrubs or trees feeding from the same area. Lilies themselves are gross feeders; many species and their hybrids will wander to find happier feeding grounds. Due care should be taken to give the lilies of your choice ample space.

As to specific suggestions, we should differentiate between the early-flowering plants—to accompany early-flowering lilies, such as the Mid-Century and Fiesta Hybrids—and the late-flowering types—to set off and enhance the beauty of the new colored trumpet lilies, the Auratum Hybrids and the wonderful new *L. speciosum* hybrids, such as the Potomac and Jamboree strains.

For both early- and late-flowering borders, we suggest that a thorough study be made of the available hardy plant catalogs. Far from being hard-boiled merchandising tools, most of these abound in helpful information. The nurserymen who write them have traveled far afield to find new items and tested older ones that may prove of interest to you. These people are plantsmen who have not only tried the material in their own gardens, but have actually produced it under field conditions which are often quite severe. What they suggest as "easily grown" is easy indeed and even the "difficult to establish" plants usually prove to be no problem for the average gardener.

For the early border, we suggest artemisia, heuchers, nepeta,

Lilies are ideal subjects for the creation of attention-compelling color combinations in the garden, as in this group of trumpet lilies with thalictrom (background), lupine, and phlox.

phlox, platycodon, salvia, statice, and thermopsis with a generous planting of bearded iris such as Blue Lakes, and some of the new salmon-pink or orchid varieties. Pure white phlox, now available in several varieties; improved Oriental Poppies, with their lovely foliage: delphinium: and Artemisia Silver King make good foils for lilies.

For the late-flowering border we suggest *Oenothera youngi,* with a warning to keep it within reasonable limits; *Plumbago larpentae; Thalictrum glaucum* and its improved variety Rochenbrunianum; and a good selection of asters, heleniums, and veronicas. Complete planting plans are available from several nurseries. Your local perennial grower, too, may have excellent suggestions and a good assortment of plants to show you. Do not be afraid of a "thin" planting. Perennials and lilies, fed and watered at one time, will result in an increase of both as time passes. A planting that is a little thin the first year looks just right the second year and may well be ready for division, transplanting and a little re-arranging the third year, after the flowering season is over.

Late-flowering chrysanthemums may well be used with good effect to fill in any bare spots. Annuals too are excellent in a lily border. They can be set out, once the lilies have emerged, to fill any areas that are in need of a color accent at times when the lilies do not furnish it.

CHAPTER 4. *Lilies in Flower Arrangement*

> *Go bow thy head in gentle spite,*
> *Thou lily white,*
> *For she who spies thee waving here,*
> *With thee in beauty can compare*
> *As day with night.*
>
> *Thou in thy lake dost see*
> *Thyself; so she*
> *Beholds her image in her eyes*
> *Reflected. Thus did Venus rise*
> *From out the sea.*
>
> "To a Lily"
> by JAMES MATTHEWS LEGARÉ
> (1823–1859)

Lilies have their very special niche in the art of flower arrangement. The larger, long-stemmed types are eminently suited for use as dominant material in showy, formal compositions to decorate large rooms in private homes; for hotel, club, and restaurant lobbies; for competitive classes in flower shows. Madonna Lilies, Olympic Hybrids, and other large white trumpet lilies are unsurpassed for church decorations. In floral arrangements for weddings at home or elsewhere, the colored Aurelians are most effective.

Modern strains and named varieties, brilliantly colored and less formal in habit, make excellent material for arrangements in the average home, as well as for flower show compositions. Among these are the Mid-Century and Fiesta Hybrids and such named

47

varieties as Enchantment, Destiny, Prosperity, and Harmony. One stem of any of these, with full-blown flowers and buds, combined with other garden flowers and accessory foliage, is enough to give the entire arrangement brilliance and distinction. With even a very modest lily planting, one can, therefore, occasionally afford to cut a blooming stem for beauty indoors.

All lilies combine well with other flowers and foliage. In fact, such other material is often needed to relieve the austerity of the long straight lily stems or to soften the overpowering brilliance of some of the exotic, highly colored varieties. Exceptions to this rule are recurved, outfacing varieties like Prosperity, three stems of which can be gracefully arranged alone or combined with an erect-flowered type. Some of the larger nodding, reflexed hybrids, such as Afterglow (a recent development from the Bellingham strain), make excellent cut flowers, while the smaller martagons are useful in giving height in combination with a few blooms of one of the very large-flowered, outfacing sorts like Bright Star or Fireflame.

Speciosums Red Champion and White Champion and hybrids such as Jillian Wallace, are unsurpassed for creating focal points in dramatic modern compositions. One or two blossoms, with a bud added if possible, make an eye-filling center of interest. The same holds true of some of the newer and showier Mid-Century Hybrids like Cinnabar or Firecrown, and Auratum varieties such as Red Band or Virginale, and the Golden Splendor Strain of Aurelians. With them, however, it may be necessary to remove some blooms or buds to achieve the form and lines desired.

One of the most exciting features of the recent lily hybrids is their great color range; pink, green, or yellow Aurelian Hybrids; Royal Gold Regals; the delicate creams and pale yellows of the Sunburst Aurelians, as well as those which vary from deep gold to orange.

What could be more desirable for the woman interested in competitive arrangement than such lilies as the Black Dragon, pure white inside and rich purple-brown in reverse; bowl-shaped Emerald Isle, soft yellow inside and cool green in reverse; or those of the Limelight Strain, chartreuse to apple green? The new Empress and Imperial strains of Auratum Hybrids provide even more spectacular display.

CUTTING AND CARE

Lilies for indoor decoration or arrangement classes in a flower show should be cut in the evening and permitted to "harden" all night in a cool place in deep water.

If cut when the lower blooms are just fully open and placed immediately in water, remaining buds will open in sequence. Foliage below the water line should be removed entirely.

As cutting a long stem with much foliage weakens the summer development of the bulb, it is well to cut as little of the stalk as possible. Often a false stem can be fastened to the base of the actual stem to give desired height. When this is resorted to, the base of the real stem must always be several inches below the water level, after the arrangement is made and during the hardening period as well.

Faded flowers should be removed each evening. This is easy with a home arrangement, but more difficult in competitive classes. Though the scent of many lilies is delightful when the flowers are fresh, it can become anything but sweet when they begin to fade. If a thin slice of stem is removed each time the lower, faded flowers are taken, an arrangement can be kept in good balance, though it will be slightly shorter each day, unless a false stem is added. By this method of daily care and rejuvenation, cut lilies continue in fine condition for many days.

Before beginning to work with cut blooms for an arrangement, it may be necessary to remove the anthers bearing the pollen which stains petals so badly. If the color of the pollen is desired, wrap the anthers of each bloom in soft tissue and remove only after the arrangement is completed and in its place on a table or in a niche at the flower show. (See Chapter 15, pages 212 and 214, for further details.)

Period Arrangement

For the purist in flower arrangement, it is of interest to select just the right lily for the purpose planned: Oriental species for Japanese or Chinese compositions; those already in cultivation centuries ago for early period arrangements; and for Colonial, Georgian, or Victorian bouquets, those known to have been grown in gardens of each period.

Care should be taken by arrangers planning authentic period pieces to avoid the use of modern hybrids, even though the species are less beautiful. This hurdle may be overcome in a flower show competition by stating in the schedule that an arrangement is to be *in the spirit* of a specific period, and that modern varieties of flowers are permitted.

On page 57 appear lists of species observed in ancient paintings and other works of art; and of those recorded by botanists and others as being in cultivation from the seventeenth to the twentieth centuries.

Visits to art museums and galleries, where examples of the work of Old Masters are on display, yield rich harvests to the budding period arranger. Equally valuable, because of the fact that they are always on hand for ready reference, are such works as Margaret Fairbanks Marcus's erudite work, *Period Flower Arrangement,* a history of art in its relation to the use of cut flowers from 2800 B.C. to the present, and Julia S. Berrall's *A History of Flower Arrangement.* Both of these tomes are superbly illustrated with reproductions of classic art and modern adaptations by top-flight arrangers.

Even a superficial study of the flower art of the past brings to light the fact that cut flowers in early Christian times were used as religious symbols, the lily, of course, representing the Virgin. This is also true of earlier civilizations, the lily being sacred to Aphrodite in ancient Greece, and an unidentified lilylike bloom symbolic of early Egypt.

Contemporary Arrangement

There is much latitude for the arranger in the creation of contemporary compositions employing lilies. Here is an opportunity to use all the latest hybrids in their wide variety of form and color.

Form. For tall, slender line arrangements, nodding martagons and the smaller-flowered Turk's-caps are indicated. The Fiesta, Bellingham, and Harlequin Hybrids and the variety Palomino, also nodding, bear much larger and showier blooms, gracefully reflexed.

Lilies lend themselves well to the making of horizontal table arrangements such as the tray and boat arrangements shown here. In the former (above, by Philip G. Corliss) a few Sunburst flowers are used with broad-leaved evergreen sprays.

In the simple but attractive design below (by Carl Starker) Golden Clarion is set off by araucaria twigs.

51

An arrangement of Golden Clarion with ti leaves in a low rectangular container—a substantial, long-lasting composition for home decoration.
(By Carl Starker)

Outfacing types like many of the Mid-Century Hybrids are perhaps the most generally useful, as the blooms are borne on their stems in such a way that little actual "arrangement" is necessary. Broad-petaled and richly colored, these are eye-filling when cut and displayed in a suitable container. More delicate, but equally valuable for less robust arrangements, are the Sunburst Aurelians, with *L. henryi* in their ancestry. The white, cream, pale yellow, or orange flowers, star-shaped, outfacing, are as graceful as a troupe of ballet dancers.

Such upright lilies as Enchantment, Firecrown, Destiny, and Harmony are also excellent. In some of these, the lower blooms are forced outward by those above them; and in all the buds, reaching upward, form a graceful apex. If too numerous, two or three of these can be removed to perfect the design.

The many true trumpet lilies fill another need in cut flowers. Whereas in the past these were used chiefly for church decoration, because they were white or near-white, today the new hybrids give us all their dignity of form, but are available in a wide color range, which greatly increases their usefulness.

This is also true of the Auratum Hybrids of recent introduction and of the Speciosums with graceful, recurved, wavy petals, and prominent anthers.

Color. The only color missing in new lilies is blue. From pure white through pinks to deepest red and from cream through all the glowing yellows to orange, there is little to be desired. Even newer are the lovely Patterson and Harlequin Hybrids in orchid, lavender, and mauve tints.

Among the whites are the improved strains of the ancient *L. candidum* or Madonna Lily; *L. speciosum album* White Champion; *L. formosanum wilsoni; L. auratum virginale* and Silver Sunburst.

Most of the majestic Olympic Hybrids with trumpet or bowl-shaped blooms are white or pale pink or ice-green inside with darker exteriors. Some are pure white in reverse, or self-colored like the superb Pink Perfection Strain which are fuchsia-pink on both inner and outer surfaces. The Sentinel Strain is pure white with golden throat.

Other pale trumpet and bowl-shaped lilies are Emerald Isle and Green Dragon; Heart's Desire Strain, white, cream, and yellow; Limelight; Moonlight Strain; Temple Hybrids, pink; New Era; the Pink Pearl, Pink Diamond and Pink Beauty Strains, derived from *L. japonicum* and *L. auratum.* The beautiful lilies bred and raised by Professor Palmer of Vineland, Ontario, fall into this category.

For special flower show work, where a dark color is needed to match a container or other plant material, Black Dragon, white inside and rich purple-brown in reverse, is outstanding. The Black Magic Strain, derived from Black Dragon, is less expensive and produces a variation in coloring even more desirable. The Bronzino Strain of the Fiesta type produces chocolate-brown, mahogany, and teak blooms and others of a rich amber or topaz.

If you wish to "go modern," there are lilies to suit your purpose. Here the angular stems and starfish shaped flowers of a few Silver Sunbursts harmonize with driftwood suggesting a prehistoric monster, and with the relaxed figure of a pre-Adam iron man.

There are so many yellows, golds, and oranges that it seems needless to be specific here. Selections should be made to give a variety of height, form, and hue.

Desirable reds include Paprika, a crimson *tigrinum* hybrid; Cherokee, brick with maroon dots; Sunstar, vermilion; the darker Paisley Hybrids which run from ivory to mahogany; and Mountaineer, with outfacing maroon blossoms.

Success is even being achieved today in creating pale lilac, old rose, and violet lilies, derived from orchid-lilac *L. cernuum*. It should be from these that we may look for added future colors in this same range.

We can hardly leave the subject of color without mentioning some of the improved *speciosums* and *auratum-speciosum* hybrids like the universally admired brilliant carmine-striped Jillian Wallace, with eight-inch, outfacing flowers; Red Band Hybrids and the Potomac Hybrids introduced by the United States Department of Agriculture.

Flowers which combine well with lilies include blue delphinium, Russell lupines in their wide color range, stocks, gladiolus, and snapdragons for height. Single peonies, Dutch and Japanese iris, Oriental poppies, China asters, carnations, and chrysanthemums provide large round forms. Fuchsias, freesias, montbretias, and flowering vines give delicate graceful sprays and drooping lines. Ferns, broad-leaved evergreens, and the foliage of exotic house plants, such as dracaena, croton, and large-leaved begonias, provide supplementary material.

Church Decorations

In arranging lilies for the church, a single fine stem of white lilies in each of a pair of altar vases, with supplementary foliage to relieve the bare lower stalks, is in the tradition of early Gothic religious paintings and well suited for altar decoration in a church of traditional architecture. The tips of the stems, of course, should be lower than the apex of the altar cross.

Lilies may also well be combined with aquilegias, campanulas, foxgloves, or roses, all symbolic of the Virgin. During the Renaissance anemones, cyclamen, forget-me-not, and iris were used as symbols of Christ's passion and so, combined with lilies, which represented chastity, are eminently suited for church bouquets.

Pinks and violets symbolized humility, while ripe grain, grape leaves and vines and fruits stood for the bread and wine of Christ's communion. Mixed arrangements of lilies and other flowers may, therefore, be combined appropriately for each religious season.

Easter lilies (*L. longiflorum*) and varieties, Madonnas (*L. candidum*) white and near-white trumpet lilies, new varieties of which are appearing each year, are all good selections for church decoration.

Weddings.

White trumpet lilies, the Silver Sunburst Strain of Aurelians, all ivory or pure white; Ivorine; the Reflection Strain of large, scented,

When it comes to corsages, few flowers are as graceful, as long-lasting or as easily arranged as the blooms and buds of any of the smaller lilies.

pendant white lilies; *L. regale* and *L. formosanum wilsoni* are among those which lend themselves to wedding decorations. If color is wanted, there are now many lovely pinks, icy greens, or pale yellows.

For a summer wedding, the entire color range of one of the July-blooming lily strains might well be chosen for the wedding party, each bridesmaid carrying a bouquet dominated by one variety and wearing a costume of similar or contrasting color. Possibilities here are the Mid-Century Hybrids, from pale yellow to deep orange-red; August and September blooming *auratums*, white to red; July and August, Aurelian Hybrids, from white to ivory and on through lemon and lime to gold.

LILIES FOR PERIOD ARRANGEMENTS

PERIOD OR NATIONALITY	DATES	SPECIES OR VARIETIES	SYMBOLIC OF
Egypt	2800–28 BC	*L. candidum*	Land of Egypt
Greece	28 BC–325 AD	*L. candidum*	Aphrodite
		L. chalcedonicum	Fertility
Rome	28 BC–325 AD	*L. candidum*	Venus
		L. chalcedonicum	Fertility
		L. martagon	
Byzantium	325 AD–600	*L. candidum*	The Virgin
		L. chalcedonicum	
Gothic	1200–1425	*L. candidum*	The Virgin
			Purity
		L. x *hollandicum*	Fertility
Renaissance	1400–1600	*L. candidum*	The Virgin
			Purity
		L. martagon	
		L. hollandicum	Blood of Christ
Baroque	1600–1700	*L. candidum*	
		L. canadense	
		L. martagon	
		L. x *hollandicum*	
Rococo	1715–1774	Same as Baroque	
Georgian (England)	1714–1760	*L. candidum*	
		L. canadense	
		L. martagon	
		L. pyrenaicum	
		L. hollandicum	
Neoclassic	1762–1830	Same as Georgian	
Romantic	1830–1890	*L. auratum*	
		L. bulbiferum	
		L. canadense	
		L. candidum	
		L. longiflorum	
		L. martagon	
		L. pumilum	
		L. pyrenaicum	
		L. regale	
		L. x *hollandicum*	

Art Nouveau	1890–1910	Same as Romantic
America		
Colonial	1600–1780	*L. canadense*
		L. candidum
		L. martagon
		L. philadelphicum
		L. superbum
Federal	1789–1801	Same as Colonial
Early Republic	1801–1830	*L. auratum*
		L. canadense
		L. candidum
		L. longiflorum
		L. martagon
		L. philadelphicum
		L. speciosum
		L. superbum
		L. x *hollandicum*
China	1368–1912	*L. browni*
		L. callosum
		L. concolor
		L. davidi
		L. henryi
		L. longiflorum
		L. regale
Japan	586 AD–1960	*L. auratum*
		L. concolor
		L. concolor coridion
		L. japonicum
		L. longiflorum
		L. leichtlini
		L. maculatum
		L. medeoloides
		L. nobilissimum
		L. rubellum
		L. speciosum
		L. tigrinum
		Cardiocrinum cordatum

5. Lilies Indoors

and in the Greenhouse

May I a small house and large garden have;
ABRAHAM COWLEY (1618–1667)

To most gardeners the suggestion that the tall and stately, almost majestic, hardy lilies of the garden may also provide out-of-season beauty for the sunroom or small greenhouse may come almost as a shock. The first reaction, indeed, may be that surely these denizens of mountains, woods, and meadows were never created for an indoor life.

The fact is, however, that more and more these beautiful flowers are finding a place in our homes. Not only as cut flowers, but also as growing plants, they can provide us with their surpassing beauty, often supplemented by delightful fragrance and thus prolonging by months the pleasure that they give as flowers for the garden. They can be used in numerous ways and demand no more expert care than many of the flowers usually grown to be enjoyed in other than their normal seasons.

Let me give you an example. Last fall, here in northern Oregon, I found myself with some small surplus stocks of about thirty varieties of new lilies. There were three bulbs of one variety, half a dozen of another, and so on: not enough to make a special field planting; too late to be added to our garden plantings, and yet too valuable to discard or give away.

Luckily, I had a number of large-sized flower pots, saved over the years and carefully stored away in our potting shed in the hope that some day there might be a use for them. You know how it is—only this time the use did materialize.

I also have a small greenhouse, heated only enough to keep out the frost. The lily bulbs were soon potted, placed in the greenhouse and thoroughly watered.

This past spring, by the middle of March, we had a gorgeous display of lilies—a display sufficiently striking to provide the main topic of discussion for a visiting group of commercial florists. From these lilies, so easily brought into flower, I learned several lessons.

First of all, grown under glass, they produced flowers without a spot or blemish. Secondly, grown cool as they were under glass, the advance in flowering dates—as compared to their normal seasons—did not in the least impair either size or color. In addition, having them in pots I could move them around; or, for special occasions, bring those, which were at their best, into the house. We never had conversation pieces that caused more enthusiastic comment. I found too, that, as spring advanced, I could take these pots and use them out of doors by merely "planting" them up to the rims. They thus temporarily enlivened spots about the garden which lacked color interest.

Another use we found for these pots—which bloomed in succession over a long period—was to place them on porch or patio, and even to send them to garden club meetings and flower shows. A mobile display of one's pet flowers, without having to resort to cutting them and thus damaging their growth and normal bulb development, is a great asset.

There are additional good reasons for having pot-grown lilies in flower out of season. One is that the lily grower who is interested in producing his own hybrids from seed—and a surprising number are now enjoying this fascinating aspect of lily growing—can have fresh pollen to make crosses that otherwise would not be possible. Then, too, pot culture makes it possible to plant at once bulbs which arrive too late to be put in the ground out of doors, or that are delivered before garden space is prepared for them.

Most important of all, it offers those who love lilies—and who does not?—the opportunity to extend, at both ends, the season when their beauty may be enjoyed. I can walk into my greenhouse and see a good lily show in March. One of the pleasant surprises in the experiment described at the beginning of this chapter, was the ease with which almost all the varieties involved could be flowered so early and so well. Even if one does not possess a greenhouse, a deep frame or a cold cellar may be employed to add weeks to the season of lily bloom, in giving them a very substantial start before they are brought into the house or the sunroom to complete their growth.

Highlights for Home Decoration

For reasons which have been mentioned in preceding chapters the use of lilies, formerly confined more or less to professionals and hobbyists, is rapidly becoming quite universal among home gardeners. Just the other day we received a copy of the catalog of one of the country's largest mail-order nursery and seed houses. We were surprised to find that much selling space, invariably devoted to an item with maximum popular appeal, was given over to a collection of some of our choice new hybrid lilies. Although I have long felt that, in its wonderful new forms and colors, the lily is destined to attain a place in the hearts of garden lovers not far behind that of the rose, it was, nonetheless, startling to see such concrete evidence from an unprejudiced source.

Among the many new characteristics being achieved in the lily world are some of dwarf type, such as hybrids of *L. rubellum* and *L. japonicum.* Undoubtedly among these less robust forms—which still retain all the proverbial grace and beauty of the lily tribe—there are many ideally suited to house culture, even to window boxes. In the meantime, however, one may enjoy those already available. (A list of several is given on page 319.)

Highlights in Any Display. A single lily in any collection of plants indoors, or even in the larger assortment to be found in a home greenhouse, immediately lends distinction to the whole display. Not many pots of lilies are required to provide a succession of bloom over a long period.

If one is so fortunate as to possess a greenhouse, however small, lilies for cutting, as well as for making a show in a display of growing plants, may readily be included. Until recently, the commercial growing of lilies for sale through florist's shops has been largely confined to a few white-flowered varieties similar to the old Easter lily (*L. longiflorum*). Now many new colored hybrids are rapidly gaining in popularity. With the new lilies mentioned at the beginning of this chapter, an entire new range of color and form becomes available, thus making possible original and thrilling effects, especially in flower arrangements.

The Cost Is Small. One of the great advantages of growing lilies indoors or in the home greenhouse is that, in effect, you can "eat your cake and have it too." For after you have enjoyed the flowers, you still have the bulbs which can later be planted in the flower border or naturalized in suitable locations. Even if you have cut the flowers—provided most of the foliage has been left on the stems to help nourish the bulbs so they may keep on growing—your original investment will still be intact. You have enjoyed merely the first dividend.

A most interesting historical example of this particular point is to be found in the experience of a British gardener, as described in the *Gardeners Chronicle* of February 15, 1873:

A single bulb, measuring 2 inches in diameter, was obtained early in 1865. It was potted in a 7-inch pot and placed in a cool greenhouse, where it produced three flowers on one stem. In 1866 it was repotted in a 9-inch pot and received similar treatment: the plant threw up two stems, producing altogether seventeen flowers. In 1867 it was repotted in an 11-inch pot and treated as before: the plant threw three strong flowering stems, and three smaller ones, producing altogether fifty-three flowers. In 1868 the plant was shifted into a 16-inch pot, and placed, in the month of February, in a temperature of 45° to 50°, where it remained until it flowered: the plant threw up five strong stems, and seven smaller ones, producing altogether a hundred flowers. In 1869 it was turned out of the pot and a small portion of the old soil taken away from the ball; it was then put into a 17-inch pot and treated as before up to the flowering period, when it was taken to a cool conservatory: the plant threw up thirty-nine flowering stems, ranging from 2 to 9 feet in height, from the top of the pot, and producing altogether 193 flowers, many of which measured from 11 to 12 inches in diameter. In 1870 the bulbs were left in the same pot undisturbed: they threw up forty-three stems, producing altogether 208 flowers.

In the autumn of 1870 I carefully separated the bulbs, about seventy in number, not breaking a root more than I could possibly avoid. Having ready a pot 24 inches in diameter, I commenced with the largest bulb, which measured 7 inches in circumference, placing it in the centre of the pot, and seven other bulbs each about 6 inches in circumference, around it, twenty others, averaging from 4 to 5½ inches, around these, and outside seventeen more, gradually diminishing in size to 1 inch in circumference, filling up with soil at the same time; twenty-five other bulbs (making in all seventy bulbs, the produce of one original bulb in five years), were scarcely formed, and were put elsewhere. The bulbs were on the whole more solid and compact, than I have usually seen. This done, the pot was placed in a cold pit, protected from frost, until the month of March. It was then taken to a cool greenhouse, where it remained until it flowered. The plant threw up about seventy stems, measuring from 18 inches to 9 feet 6 inches from the top of the pot, producing on the whole 225 flowers, averaging 10 inches in diameter, and was photographed on the 16th August, 1871, a copy of which was presented to the Royal Horticultural Society, South Kensington. In 1872 the plant was left undisturbed and wintered in a cold pit as before, where it remained until the stems were about 18 inches in length, but as it got too large for the place, and as I had no accommodation for it under glass at the time, I was compelled to leave it out under the shelter of a south wall during May and June; the weather being very wet and cold, the plant suffered very much; the foliage was much smaller, also the stems, and many of the flowers. There were about eighty stems on the plant, producing altogether 240 flowers, a few of which did not properly expand, which I attribute to the fact of the plant having had a severe check in the months of May and June.

The plant still remains in the same pot, and has been kept in a cool house during the past winter. It has lately had a surfacing of about an inch of the same material that I use for potting, viz., good turfy loam, two parts; peat, one ditto; cow manure, one ditto; with a little coarse leaf mould and silver sand well incorporated.

At the present time there are seventy stems showing, about the half of which seem strong enough to bear flowers.

I do not find any advantage in using liquid manure of any kind until roots are emitted from the base of the stems, which generally takes place in a healthy plant when the stems are from 6 to 18 inches in length. At that period I invariably add about an inch of the above-named compost, to encourage and strengthen the flowering stems and flowers. After the stem roots are fairly established in the soil, I apply liquid manure once or twice a week up to the time the blooms expand, and I invariably find the blooms to expand during the night, and their average duration to be about nine days.

The blooming season past, the pots are placed in an open situation, exposed to the sun, to ripen the bulbs, care being taken not to let them get saturated with water, or become too dry at any time, as I believe there are more bulbs lost through these two extremes than by any other cause.—

J. SMITH,
Quarry Bank Gardens, Allerton, Wavertree, Liverpool,
March, 1873.

Chapter 11 gives further detailed information on the culture of other lilies indoors and under glass.

PLATE 1

Modern lilies, more than any other flower, effectively highlight the garden scene.

PLATE 2

LEFT: *First "improvement" in lilies was the selection of natural variations, and the increase of these by vegetative propagation to assure uniformity, as in* L. speciosum, *variety* rubrum.
BELOW: *Not until well along in the present century was much progress made in hybridizing lilies. This is one of the Green Mountain hybrids, showing marked improvement in both substance and form.*

PLATE 3

PLATE 4

The hybrid lilies do not come true from seed. Extra choice ones, such as Destiny (above)—a Mid-Century hybrid—are therefore propagated vegetatively in order to assure uniformity.

PLATE 5

The single plant above and the garden group below are Olympic hybrids growing at Grayrock. Some of them reached a height of seven feet. BELOW: They are exceptionally vigorous and free flowering.

PLATE 6

Part Two

THE GROWING OF LILIES

ANATOMY, GROWTH CYCLE, CLASSIFICATION

> *I took a day to search for God*
> *And found Him not. But as I trod*
> > *By rocky ledge, through woods untamed,*
> > *Just where one scarlet lily flamed*
> *I saw His footprints in the sod.*
>
> BLISS CARMAN (1861–1929)

After considering the lily in so many of its phases, it is high time to pose and answer the important question: "Just what is a lily?"

Liberty Hyde Bailey, the great American horticulturist gives this definition:

A lily is a perennial, erect, leafy-stemmed herb, with an underground scaly bulb: flowers pendulous, inclined, horizontal or erect, solitary or clustered, with six separate segments which are scarcely differentiated as between petal-like and sepal-like organs, each bearing a nectar-groove or furrow at the base: stamens 6. . . .

With this general definition as a guide we can turn to a more particular study of the lily and its parts.

The Bulb. The lily, in common with many other plants—such as daffodils, tulips, and hyacinths—grows from a true bulb: i.e. a swollen underground bud in which food is stored. This food is available each season to produce stem, leaves, and flowers. Sometimes, as a special reserve, part of it is even carried over into a second year.

A tulip or daffodil bulb is made up of leaf bases (modified leaves), that form a concentric ring around an axis. Lily bulbs

67

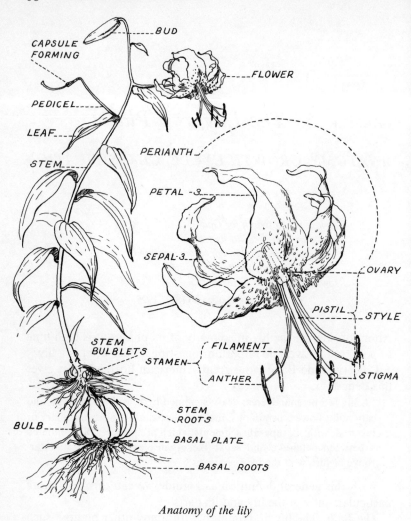

Anatomy of the lily

differ in having narrower, more fleshy leaf bases (scales) arranged in spiral fashion on an axis usually vertical, but sometimes more or less horizontal.

Concentric Type. Most lily bulbs, such as *L.* x *hollandicum, L. regale,* and *L. ochraceum,* have short, *vertical* axes or underground stems which remain always in approximately the same upright positions. Around this vertical axis, fleshy scales are arranged. In this type, young bulbs develop each year *within* the parent bulb, close against the axis, and later split off to form independent plants. They also produce strong contractile roots which pull them down into the ground each autumn as the soil becomes softer. Thus, although they grow upward each summer, they regain their optimum level below ground. Seeds of *L. regale* and others, sown half an inch deep in light soils in February, soon produce tiny bulbs at this level; but if they grow well, by late autumn the bases of these same bulbs are two to three inches below the surface!

Rhizomatous Type. The bulbs of such species as *L. superbum, L. canadense,* and other North American species grow on *horizontal* axes (see sketch, page 70) which extend themselves several inches each year, and then form new bulbs at the ends of almost naked stolons. In these stoloniferous species, the roots are not so strongly contractile, for the stolon by itself will descend almost vertically if the original bulb is too shallow. (In a shallowly placed seedling bulb of *L. superbum* three-quarters of an inch in diameter, I have seen two descending stolons produced on opposite sides, each developing a one-inch bulb at its end, and each of these fully three inches below the original bulb.)

Modifications of the two types described above are lilies like *L. humboldti, L. washingtonianum*, and *L. pardalinum* which have horizontal axes and grow sideways and (sometimes quite steeply) up and down to attain correct depths. (See sketch.) In these, new bulbs are produced within the parent rhizome to emerge later, as in the concentric type.

Bulblets. In most species small bulblets are formed in the axils of bracts on the *underground* portion of the stem above the bulb. Some species, notably *L. davidi,* have a habit of throwing out in spring underground stems which wander beneath the surface— sometimes several feet—before breaking up through the soil. (See page 75.) In such varieties, the largest bulblet on this wandering, underground stem is usually found farthest away from the parent bulb. Often it is several times larger than the bulb which produced it! Obviously, this wandering habit is a means of reaching new and better feeding grounds.

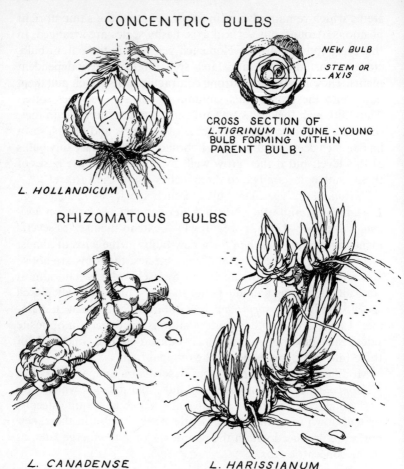

CONCENTRIC BULBS

NEW BULB

STEM OR
AXIS

CROSS SECTION OF
L. TIGRINUM IN JUNE - YOUNG
BULB FORMING WITHIN
PARENT BULB.

L. HOLLANDICUM

RHIZOMATOUS BULBS

L. CANADENSE   L. HARISSIANUM

Types of lily bulbs. Bulb of L. tigrinum, *(cut across horizontally) shows new bulb developing next to stem at center of old bulb. This will flower the following year. The outer scales have given up stored food to produce stem and flower and will now die off.* Rhizomatous *types produce new bulblets or bulbs along fleshy underground stems.*

Bulbils. Other lily species and varieties produce bulbils (tiny bulbs) in the axils of the leaves *above* ground. *L. tigrinum* and its hybrids have this desirable characteristic. In some varieties, as many as fifty bulbils may be produced on a single stalk.

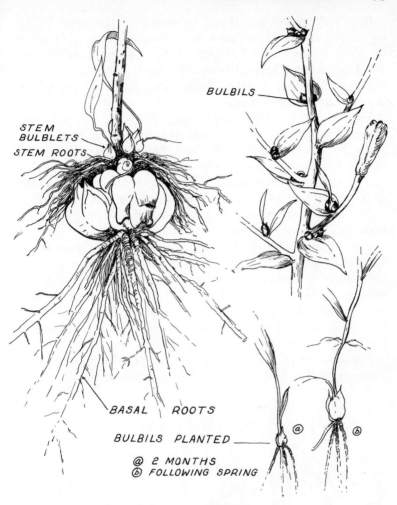

STEM
BULBLETS
STEM ROOTS

BULBILS

BASAL ROOTS

BULBILS PLANTED

ⓐ 2 MONTHS
ⓑ FOLLOWING SPRING

ⓐ ⓑ

At left: stem-rooting type of lily, producing bulblets *at base of stem. These will grow and make a clump or cluster of new bulbs where they are. At right:* bulbils *forming along stems at bases of leaves. These will drop off, to sprout where they fall; or may be removed and planted. Planted (like onion sets) in good soil, bulbils make strong contractile roots that eventually pull the developing bulbs down to their proper depth. Following season the new bulbs develop stems. Under favorable conditions some may bloom the first season.*

Both bulblets and bulbils may be used for propagation. In my experience, the bulbils are more vigorous, grow faster and mature earlier than underground bulblets of the same species or variety. Bulblets produced from scales (see Chapter 13), however, are more vigorous than stem bulblets, being comparable in strength to bulbils from the same plant.

The Axis. So far in this chapter, the word "axis" has been used to describe the short underground part of the stem bearing the scales, the whole comprising the bulb. This, however, is not technically correct. To be precise, the axis of each mature bulb elongates annually into an erect, leafy stem, bearing flowers at its apex. At the end of each growing season the above-ground or "stem" portion of the axis dies back, but the major part of the underground portion survives.

The Scales. The scales have a life of from two to three years. The outer ones give up their reserves of food to the young new stem in late spring, and then decay. Then new scales, forming near the apex of the axis, take their place. The lower part of the bulb axis, to which the older scales are attached, also decays each year. In stoloniferous types, the old stolons die off after young bulbs, formed at their tips, become independent.

The Basal Roots. Basal roots also have a life of about two years. They originate mainly in midsummer, or with autumn rains, and

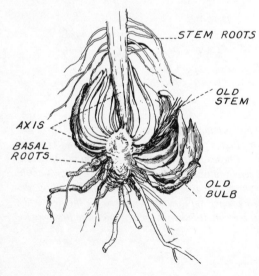

A bulb of L. speciosum *cut in half to show how axis, with scales attached, elongates to form a new central stem. The old bulb and stem (at right) will eventually die off.*

penetrate deeply into the surrounding soil. By blooming season they have ramified and permeate a large area in order to sustain the tall stem and large flower-head in times of light rainfall or drought.

The mature lily is definitely a dry land plant, sometimes almost a desert plant, in its behavior. It can withstand an extraordinary amount of drought when fully developed. This is mainly because the basal roots are very long, numerous, and well branched at their extremities, and thus are equipped to tap hidden reserves of moisture.

The Stem. The stem (clothed with leaves in pairs, or whorled below and scattered above), may grow straight up through the soil above the bulb; or (particularly in small bulbs of some species, such as *L. nepalense, L. neilgherrense,* and *L. lankongense*) may wander widely—even to two or three-and-a-half feet underground, before emerging. Just where the stem comes through the soil— in most, but not all species—a mass of stem roots is produced; some may even grow from the stem at ground level, back into the soil. The stem is always thicker and tougher just at this point, and these roots play an important part in anchoring and holding it erect, as well as contributing to the general nutrition of the plant. (A list of base rooting lilies appears on page 35.) The stem roots may appear dead or dormant during a dry summer, but grow and produce new root hairs at the first sign of rain, while the bulb itself stores food and moisture to carry on in case of unfavorable growing conditions in the future.

The Inflorescence. At the apex of the stem, and surmounting the leaves, is the inflorescence. It is basically a raceme, degenerating in some species, into an umbel or partially whorled arrangement. In breeding, the raceme is usually dominant over the umbel. It may be assumed, therefore, to be the original arrangement, the more so as this characteristic is common to other genera in Liliaceae.

The flowers may be wide open and erect, or outfacing, typical of dry climate plants; pendulous, as in the Turk's-cap type, adapted to dry or moderate climates; or drooping, long and trumpetlike, a form which completely protects the pollen from heavy rains likely to occur during the blooming season in wet climates.

Beginners who would succeed with lilies should study them constantly and carefully during their complete cycle of growth, from the planting of bulbs to the withering of stalks for the winter's rest period. The first important point to be realized is that a lily never goes completely dormant, *in the sense that a tulip or a daffodil does.*

74

In all species the anthers are versatile, i.e.: finely hinged in such a manner that they present their full length to the body of any visiting insect or bird. This is necessary because lily ovaries contain from two hundred and fifty to two thousand potential seeds and each requires a grain of pollen for its development.

Seed Pods and Seeds. The seed pods open from above in dry weather, close in the rain. The seeds are quite thin, flat, and usually winged. They are dispersed only—but then quite widely—during windy spells of dry weather after they have ripened.

Leaves. A study of the relative widths and textures of the leaves of different lily species gives a true picture of their needs as regards moisture and shade. Narrow-leafed types are adapted to strong light and drought, and the narrower the leaves, the better these conditions can be endured. The broader, thinner leaves of other species are adapted to shady, moist areas. The foliage of all true lilies is lanceolate or linear, with parallel veins.

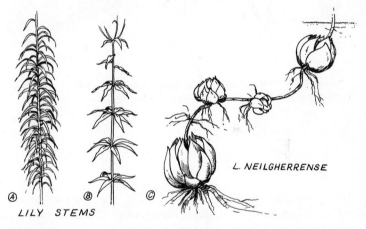

LILY STEMS

L. NEILGHERRENSE

Types of lily stems: A—leaves single or in pairs; B—leaves in whorls; C—stem wandering underground and forming new bulbs before emerging.

A similar comparison may be made between the relatively broad basal rosette-leaves of seedlings which start life under the shade of bushes or on the moist forest floor, and the narrower stem-leaves of the same plants which are thrust up through shrubs or undergrowth into the wind and bright light.

The genus now classified as *cardiocrinum* was formerly included in Lilium as *L. cathayanum, L. cordatum,* and *L. giganteum.* Leaves of these species are heart-shaped instead of linear or lanceolate and the main bulb dies after blooming, young offsets taking its place. Unlike lilies (with the exception of *L. candidum*) *cardiocrinums* are shallowly planted with the noses of the bulbs at ground level. (See page 287.)

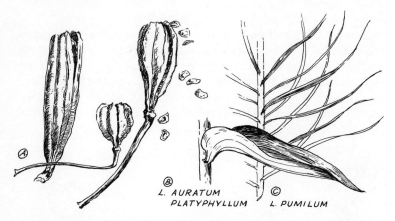

L. AURATUM
PLATYPHYLLUM   L. PUMILUM

A–seed pods and seeds; B–broad-leaf type, adapted to moist shaded areas; C–narrow leaf type adapted to dry areas and strong light.

The Life Cycle

Though the lily grows from a true bulb, *it never becomes completely dormant.* In this respect it differs from daffodils, tulips, or other bulbs having hardened dried scales as an outer covering to give protection against bruising, excess sunlight, or other injurious exposure.

In the lily, whose scales are fleshy and soft, without tough outer covering, there is no period of inactivity. The scales, with the juice of life still in them, bruise easily or break off if the bulb is dropped or packed tightly against others. For this reason quick transportation from grower to buyer, as well as prompt planting after delivery, is most important.

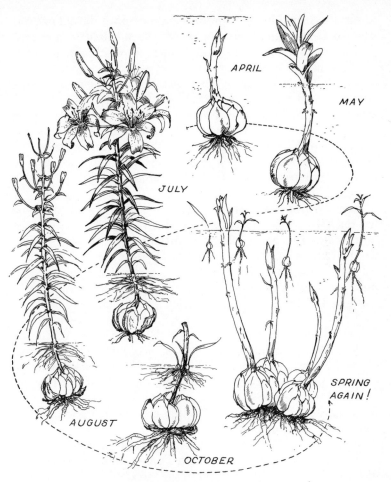

Annual growth cycle of lily plant.

Roots. When planted, the bulb immediately begins its active life cycle. First it throws out roots to gather food and moisture, to anchor the bulb and pull it to its preferred depth. As previously noted, these roots are contractile, so that, anchoring themselves deeply in the soil, they can bring the bulb down to its ideal level.

Given some initial encouragement and proper soil conditions, the roots soon develop sufficiently to exert this pull. A bulb planted too deep, on the other hand, cannot move *up*. In a strong attempt to survive, such a lily may produce a bulb above the old one, the new one being then at the proper level. Such behavior can be expected from old, established bulbs which, through inadvertence or accident, have been buried too deep.

Growth Above Ground. A newly planted bulb, however, first of all, has to make new roots. It usually exerts all its strength thereafter, during the first growing season, in the production of a stem and flowers, and so almost never succeeds in forming a new bulb above the original one. The plant, in short, takes the easier way out of its dilemma. It tries—instead of forming a new bulb—to produce flowers and set seed, thus obtaining a more certain assurance of survival.

Restoring Nutriments in the Bulb. When the newly planted bulb has made its roots, it has expended much of the substance stored in its scales. It exhausts them still further when it begins to send up the stem, develops leaves and finally forms a flower. At this stage the stored nutriment in the bulb is pretty well spent and it must renew itself from the sustenance that above-ground growth can give it. This is why the gardener should *never cut down the leafy parts of the stalks after bloom.* Leaves and stems help to feed and renew the underground bulb. On the other hand the removal of dead flowers before seed pods form, or of buds before opening, helps the newly established bulb to renew its strength without having to expend any on the forming of seeds or flowers. Removal of buds before opening is seldom actually necessary in the home garden, especially not if soil and moisture conditions are right at the time of planting.

Reproduction. The next effort on the part of the lily bulb is that of reproduction. This may be directed only toward the production of seed; or it may manifest itself in the bulb, either by an increase in size or by the production of young bulbs. It is at this time that scales, when removed from the bulb, show the greatest tendency to form bulblets. (See page 186.) It is at this stage also that plants usually sterile, when mutilated, make a supreme effort to set seed.

As the lily plant matures, the bulb prepares for the next season's flowering. Its scales begin to store up new strength, and new scales form near the apex of the axis. The oldest ones, near the basal-plate or base of the bulb, die away, together with the lowest part of the axis.

In *concentric* bulbs, the new ones are formed within the old bulbs and later split off to lead independent lives underground.

In *rhizomatous* lilies, the scales are attached to a more or less horizontal rootstock or rhizome and these may produce their new bulbs at some distance from the original location of the bulb, either along the rhizome itself, or on a stolon growing out from it. In those which are stoloniferous, the old bulbs put forth side stems or stolons and on these build new bulbs. This side stem, growing horizontally underground, is not a root, but rather a fleshy part of the bulb, for it also stores food. Each new bulb will flower, or at least throw up a stem, the following year. Then it, in turn, makes a new stolon and on this produces another new bulb.

In addition to new bulbs produced from the old bulb, very small bulbs or bulblets are sometimes formed along the underground stem above the bulb. This may occur on species whose stems grow straight up from the bulb or, more frequently, on those whose stems wander underground before emerging.

Other species and varieties, such as *L. tigrinum* and its hybrids, and *L. sargentiae* and hybrids, produce very tiny bulbs, (called bulbils) in the axils of the leaves along the above-ground stems which produce the inflorescence.

Fall and Winter Activity. With the production of new bulbs, bulbils, and bulblets, the summer work of the lily is accomplished. Its next task is to store all possible nutriment in the underground bulbs for the production of the following year's growth. During fall rains, basal and stem roots will throw out new feeding hairs to take all possible advantage of every bit of nourishment available. *This is the reason for late fall watering of lilies in sections where autumns are dry, or where rainfall at this season is inadequate.*

Lily Nomenclature

As in the case of other plants, common names for lilies differ from locality to locality and from country to country. It is preferable therefore, even necessary, to use scientific names in order to prevent confusion.

The Latin name *Lilium* is the scientific or botanical word for "lily." That is, it is the name of the whole genus (plural is genera), and is always spelled with a capital L. The second Latin name following the word *Lilium,* as *concolor, pumilum,* etc., is the species designation and indicates exactly what lily is being referred to. Usually species names are descriptive and refer to some outstanding characteristic, such as where it comes from, who discovered it, its color or growth habit. When a third Latin name appears after the species name, a specific *variety* is indicated. It may be a natural or botanical variety, such as *L. amabile var. luteum.*

Hybrids of horticultural origin, and seedlings within a species which are sufficiently different from the type to be worthy of artificial or vegetative reproduction, receive specific names, the first letters of which are capitalized. These are known as "fancy" names. L. Green Dragon is an example.

When a clone or asexually produced variety is a hybrid of known or unknown parentage, the popular or fancy name may be combined with the genus name, as *Lilium* Black Dragon or *Lilium* Destiny. The common name may also be used, as Lily Destiny. The use of Latin species and variety names to indicate such a clone is no longer permissible under the present rules of nomenclature. An example of such a name would be *Lilium davidi bulbiferum.* Growers are sometimes tempted to adopt such a descriptive and erudite fancy name, since it indicates both the type and habit of the plant; in this case a lily resembling *L. davidi,* but bearing bulbils in the axils of the leaves as does *L. tigrinum,* one of its parents. All lily growers are now co-operating in giving their introductions names in accordance with the international rules.

A group of lilies of common ancestry composed of different individuals or clones may be referred to by a fancy name followed by the word "Hybrids." The Olympic Hybrids or the Green Mountain Hybrids are cases in point. The correct name for show purposes, however, would be Olympic Lily Hybrids or Green Mountain Lily Hybrids. There is a long, carefully compiled list of fancy names, published by the Royal Horticultural Society of England, from which it may be secured.

THE CLASSIFICATION OF LILIES

As with most popular garden plants, botanists have made many attempts to arrive at a practical and useful classification of the lily family. It was not until recent years, however, that a satisfactory scheme could be worked out. While this still is open to corrections, we recommend, for the present, its adoption by all gardeners and growers.

Older classifications were based on the shape of the flower. H. J. Elwes—who wrote the fine *Monograph on Lilies* that appeared in 1877—seems to have been the first to point out the artificial nature of such a classification. A review of the work of earlier authors shows that as new lilies were discovered and the greater variation of this lovely plant became known, so also the need for further classification became more urgent.

Carolus Linnaeus, who provided the earliest attempt at botanical nomenclature, described seven species of lilies in his *Species Plantarum* of 1753. While his original work is now exceedingly rare, a beautiful facsimile edition, with an introduction by W. T. Stearn, has recently been printed for the Ray Society and is freely available. Heinrich G. L. Reichenbach, in his *Flora Germanica Excursoria* of 1830, divides the Central European Lilies into two sections. Six years later, Stephan L. Endlicher, who was the director of the Botanic Gardens in Vienna, suggests in his *Genera Plantarum* of 1836 that the family be divided into five sections. His proposal was modified in 1871 by the botanist J. G. Baker of the Royal Botanical Gardens at Kew, near London. His classified list of lilies was published by the Royal Horticultural Society in 1873. This list was again modified several times. Finally, in 1925, E. H. Wilson, in his monumental study, *Lilies of Eastern Asia,* once more reviewed these systems on the basis of actual studies in the field.

In 1949 a new classification, based this time on a combination of many characteristics and not just on the shape of the flowers, was proposed. This classification, by H. F. Comber, (with historical notes by W. T. Stearn), was published in the 1949 *Lily Yearbook* of the Royal Horticultural Society. It should be emphasized that this classification is based not on herbarium specimens only, but on actual specimens of every type and description then available in Great Britain.

The new classification of the genus Lilium, which we show here by special permission of the Royal Horticultural Society, recognizes seven sections, based on a selected number of characters, which are:

1 *a*) Germination can be *below* ground:
   In this case the first formed leaves of the plant, forming part of the embryo and the seed, remain underground. The food stored in the seed, around the embryo, is transferred to the part of the stem between the first formed leaves and the root. There a tiny bulb is formed, from the center of which emerges the first true leaf. This type of germination is called *hypogeal.*

1 *b*) Germination can be *above* ground:
   Here the first formed leaves of the plant absorb food from the seeds. They elongate rapidly, appear above ground, become green and leaflike and free themselves from the remains of the seed to take on the functions of a leaf. This is called *epigeal* germination.

2 *a*) Germination can be delayed for several months or

2 *b*) It can be immediate—that is to say, the seeds sprout within a period of from 4 to 6 weeks or so.

3 *a*) Leaf arrangement can be in a ring of leaves arising at the same level on a stem (*whorled*).

3 *b*) Or the leaves occur at random intervals (*scattered*).

4 *a*) Bulb scales can be jointed

4 *b*) or entire.

5 *a*) Seeds can be heavy

5 *b*) or light.

6 *a*) Bulb shape and habit can be erect

6 *b*) sub-rhizomatous—shape and habit is between (a) and (c)

6 *c*) rhizomatous—a creeping, underground stem, thick and swollen, rooting and sending up, successively from the apex, leafy shoots or flowering stems.

6 *d*) stoloniferous—from stolon—a branch arising from near the leaf of the parent stem, resting on the surface of the soil or growing just below it, rooting at the tip and tending to form a new plant capable of independent growth when the branch is cut or dies away between the parent and the terminal bud of the stolon.

7 *a*) Perianth segments can be covered with soft protuberances from the surface (*papillose*)

7 *b*) or smooth.

8 *a*) Nectary can be covered with soft hair (*pubescent*)

8 *b*) or hairless (*glabrous*).

9 *a*) Flower shape can be Turks-Cap

9 *b*) or trumpet.

10 *a*) Bulb color can be white

10 *b*) or purple.

11 *a*) Stem habit can be erect

11 *b*) or stoloniform.

12 *a*) The stalk of the leaves (*petiole*) can be obvious

12 *b*) or it can be obscure or absent.

13 *a*) Stigma can be large

13 *b*) or small.

14 *a*) Stemroots can be present

14 *b*) or absent.

15 *a*) Stems per bulb can be one

15 *b*) or sometimes two.

Based on these characters a diagram of the classification of the Lily family can be drawn, as follows:

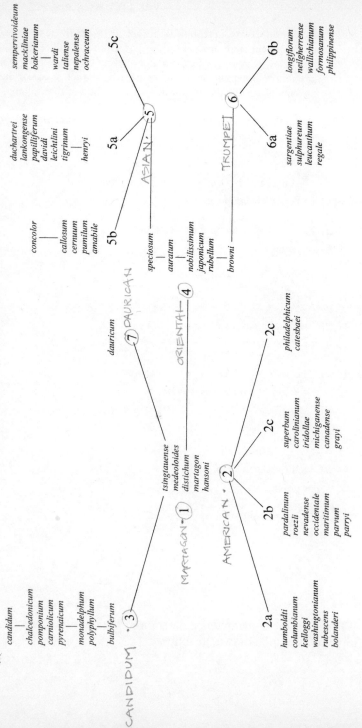

DIAGRAM OF NEW CLASSIFICATION

The diagram provides an insight into the interrelationship of the various lily species. It can thus be used by the hybridizer as a means of recognizing closely related species. It will also serve as a convenient grouping for horticultural purposes. The seven sections, possibly with convenient "fancy" names attached, might well form the basis for future show schedules. Thus section 1 might be known as the martagon group; section 2, the American group; section 3, the candidum group; section 4, the Oriental group; section 5, the Asian group; section 6, the Trumpet Lily group; and section 7, the dauricum group.

LILY LANGUAGE

A glossary of the botanical terms that are used in this book.

Alternate	Placed between other members of the same or different whorls of foliage.
Anther	The upper, pollen-bearing portion of a stamen.
Axis	The main or central line of development of the plant.
Bulbil	Aereal bulb; a bulb borne above-ground in the leaf axils.
Bulblet	A little bulb, usually formed underground, such as the underground stem bulbils of *L. tigrinum.*
Campanulate	Bell-shaped.
Capsule	Seed vessel or seed pod. When dry, it splits into three parts, each of which is filled with the thin, flat, usually winged seeds.
Clone	Asexually produced offspring of one plant. The term is also applied to any group of plants propagated by vegetative—therefore asexual—means, raised from repeated propagations from what was originally a single plant.
Concentric	Having a common center—as applied to scales.
Contractile	Having the power to contract and in so doing to pull, as applied to basal roots.
Cotyledon	The first-formed leaves of the plant, joining part of the embryo in the seed.
Embryo	The rudimentary plant within the seed.
Endosperm	Food stored in seeds outside the embryo but formed inside the embryo-sac.
Epigeal	Having the cotyledons raised above the ground level on germination of the seed.

Filament	Stalk of the stamen which bears the anther at its tip.
Genus (plural *Genera*)	The entire group of *Lilium* which is one division of the family Liliaceae.
Hybrid	A plant resulting from crosses between two or more parents that are more or less unlike.
Hypocotyl	The part of the stem between the first-formed leaves and the root.
Hypogeal	Seeds germinating slowly—the cotyledon remains below ground; a tiny bulb is formed which, in turn, produces the first true leaf to appear above ground.
Inflorescence	Flower-bearing parts of the lily.
Nectar-furrow (or *groove*)	The nectar-producing depression or furrow found at the base of each lily petal or perianth segment.
Ovary	The ovule-bearing part of the pistil.
Ovules	The bodies in the ovary which, after fertilization, become the seed.
Pedicel	The slender piece of stem between the base of a flower and main stem of plant.
Perianth	The six petal-like segments, actually perianth-segments or tepals, which form the flower.
Pistil	The central female part of the flower made up of ovary containing ovules, style and stigma.
Pollen	Spores or grains borne by the anther, containing the male element.
Raceme	A simple, elongated cluster of stalked flowers.
Reflexed	Sharply recurved, bent backwards.
Rhizomatous	Forming underground rootstocks or stems.
Scale	Modified leaf of fleshy substance forming part of the bulb and varying in size, color and form with each species.
Segment	One of the parts of a petal, perianth or leaf, that is divided but not truly compound. As applied to the lily flower, one of the six perianth parts.
Species	The wild lilies as found in nature. Each is designated first by its genus name *Lilium* and second by its specific or *species* name, as *Lilium concolor,* concolor being the species name.
Stamen	The male organ of the flower of which the upper part or anther, bears the pollen.

Stigma	The upper part of the pistil which receives the pollen.
Stolon	The underground sideshoots or branches in some lily bulbs, which produce new bulbs.
Stoloniferous	Producing stolons, as *L. canadense.*
Style	The lower, slender part of the pistil which bears the stigma at its upper end.
Tepal	One segment of a perianth.
Umbel	A cluster of flowers arising from a common point at the top of the stem, and about equal in length; radiating like the framework of an umbrella.
Undulate	Wavy.
Variety	The designation, *under a species* designation, which denotes a recognizable difference or individuality in one member of that species. May be applied to a hybrid clone developed by man; to a naturally produced variant in any species, whether local, regional or widespread in its distribution.
Whorl	Ring of leaves arising at the same level on stem.

CHAPTER *7. Selecting the Location:*

FAVORABLE AND UNFAVORABLE FACTORS

> *By cool Siloam's shady rill*
> *How sweet the lily grows!*
> REGINALD HEBER (1783–1826)

Preceding chapters have emphasized the fact that while the natural species of lilies have marked preferences as to soil, climate, moisture, and light, *most of the modern hybrids are not nearly so selective* and will grow satisfactorily under average garden conditions. Nevertheless, as with any other species of flower, there are some lilies with definite likes, dislikes, and tolerances which must be taken into consideration if they are to thrive satisfactorily and grow lustily.

Not every place can provide conditions ideal for the growing of lilies—nor, for that matter, any other plant species. In most gardens, even those quite limited in size, there exist areas where lilies will find conditions more to their liking than in others. The first step should be to determine, as accurately as possible, where these areas are. In some cases it may be only by a period of "trial and error" testing that these locations can be found.

In general, however, success can be made more certain, and much time saved, if the gardener is guided by what others have learned concerning the preferences of most lilies, and then applies this information to his own particular situation. Following that, on his own place he can either select the positions and soil conditions which seem best to meet the requirements of lilies; or—if none such exist—take steps to provide them, keeping in mind, of course, that it is always better and easier to make any such changes *before* planting than after.

Lilies will thrive under a wide variety of conditions. Most of those with delicate coloring hold their color better if provided with moderate shade, especially during the bright midday hours—just as is the case with roses. In this Oregon garden a wide variety of lilies is grown in full sun.

Selecting the Location

Drainage. The one condition that all lilies, without exception, insist upon is thorough drainage. The wild or species lilies grow, as we have seen, in many parts of the world, where climates, soils, elevations, rainfall, length of growing season, and other factors affecting growth vary widely. The one condition they do have in common is good drainage.

As would be expected, a growth characteristic so universally held continues to apply when the wild lilies are brought into cultivation, and is passed on to the progeny when they are crossed with each other.

Exhaustive experiments carried out by the Royal Horticultural Society of England in which lilies of many species—including our native swamp lilies, *L. superbum* and *L. pardalinum*—were planted at varying depths above water level, proved that all perished when placed deep enough to be constantly in wet soil. Most of those just above wet soil did poorly. All planted several inches above water level succeeded and produced normal growth.

Unfavorable and favorable conditions for growth; Left: poor drainage, competition from other tall plants, deep shade. Right: good drainage; low groundcover over roots; abundant sunlight; protection from high winds.

Good drainage, then, should be the first consideration in selecting the site, or sites, for lily plantings. Lack of it is probably the most universal of all the causes of failure. Methods of providing adequate drainage are discussed in Chapter 8. The one frequently employed, and still sometimes advocated—that of putting sand in the bottom of the planting hole—is *not* the one to use.

Sun or Shade? In much that has been written in the past concerning lily culture, considerable emphasis has been given to the

In this semishaded border, which receives full sun for part of the day, lilies thrive with other flowers. Their roots are well protected by undergrowth of perennials and shrubs.

amount of shade that should be provided. In general, this factor, in our opinion, has been overemphasized. In any event, whatever importance this question of sun versus shade may have had in connection with establishing wild species in gardens, it is a matter of minor concern with the modern hybrids, and apparently becomes less and less so the farther these new varieties are removed from the original species.

There is, however, one factor connected with shade that should not be overlooked. With few exceptions lilies, including the modern types, grow best where they can have what the old-time horticultural writers termed a "cool root-run." Overhead shade helps to provide such a condition. The same result, however, may be obtained with adequate mulching; or, in the case of tall-growing varieties, with suitable low plants to shade the soil about the lily roots, while the flower-bearing stems grow up through them to the light. Such an overplanting also provides support to help hold the lily stalks erect—a matter of considerable importance in wind-swept exposures.

Another point to be considered is that some lilies hold their normal color much better if they can have a moderate degree of overhead shade. This should be only semishade, and it should also be "high" shade, such as is provided by fairly tall trees with bare trunks. No lilies, even among the wild species, succeed in dense shade.

Lists of lilies which seem to prefer some shade, and of those which will tolerate moderate shade, are given in Chapter 18, together with a list of sun-loving varieties.

Wind Protection. Most lilies in nature establish themselves where they are provided with protection from high winds. Even the several species of what may be termed "field" lilies are sheltered by neighboring grasses or low shrubs, though the flowers at the tops of their stems are exposed to boisterous breezes.

In selecting locations for one's plantings of lilies, this should be kept in mind. As lilies are self-sufficient and need not be planted in beds or borders, as are most annuals and perennials, it is usually possible to find for them places more or less protected from high winds. Where no such protection exists, it often may be provided by sheltering shrubs or low-growing evergreens, or even by a rustic fence.

The lilies planted in this heavily shaded border at Grayrock received only a few hours of direct sunshine in the morning. While they grew and flowered satisfactorily, their distinct leaning out toward the light indicated that they would have liked more of it.

As a last resort, tall-growing varieties may be staked. The most satisfactory and least expensive stakes are of bamboo, with one-quarter inch holes drilled through them at the desired heights. Through these holes soft cord or raffia is passed to secure the stems. (See page 126.)

Air Drainage. While excessive exposure to wind is to be avoided, the opposite extreme of planting in a location so sheltered that the free circulation of air may be prevented, is just as undesirable. Stagnant air favors the development of that most prevalent of lily diseases, botrytis, which is encouraged by excessive humidity and wet foliage.

Any location, in the nature of a hollow or a pocket, where air circulation is poor is also likely to be a "frost trap" in spring, and an oven in midsummer. The former may result in the loss of a season's flowers, the latter in short-lived or imperfect blooms.

A slope, if one is available or can be formed artificially, is ideal for lily plantings. It provides water drainage below ground and air drainage above ground. Furthermore, it shows off the lilies to good advantage, as the flower stalks do not hide one another. On level ground they are apt to do so, unless great care is exercised to arrange the planting so that the shorter varieties are at the front and the taller in the rear—a difficult thing to do, especially for the beginner.

Lilies in the Landscape Plan

In selecting the location, or locations, where lilies are to be planted the gardener has other things to consider. Before deciding to grow lilies in the first place, he will have had an idea of just what he wishes them to do for him, and these objectives will be a factor in his decisions as to where they should be planted. In some cases this factor will, *for him,* be more important than growing the most perfect flowers. Of course, if he wishes to grow lilies for show purposes—and it is surprising how rapidly the number of lily shows is increasing throughout the country—he will select the site which offers the most perfect conditions for producing prize-winning blooms (See Chapter 15).

In all landscape planning, one of the most important considerations in selecting materials is height. Among annuals and perennials, there are but few of sufficient height to stand out among their neighbors and provide this important dimension in any mixed planting. Here lilies have two distinct advantages. Not only do they tower above their surrounding neighbors, but the flower forms are so distinct that they immediately attract attention, conspicuous as dominant centers of interest either in the mixed border or against shrubs or other background plantings.

For Naturalizing. For some reason not easy to explain, no other flowers seem quite so at home, when "naturalized" or used in completely informal surroundings, as do lilies. Perhaps it is because in most people's minds they are still associated with half-remembered glimpses of groups, or even individual specimens, in meadows or by stream sides, or in the semishaded vistas of a woodland walk.

When many lilies for cutting are wanted, it is best to grow them in garden rows, so that flower borders need not be robbed. For a long season of bloom however, several different types should be grown. (See list on page 318.)

Whatever the reason, the fact remains that no other cultivated flower looks quite so natural, under such conditions, as a group of lilies. The effect, of course, is more or less—or perhaps one should say completely—spoiled if several varieties are planted close together. Also many of the newer, more exotic-looking hybrid varieties are less suited to naturalizing than the species or their descendants which still retain the original characteristics. (For varieties especially desirable for naturalizing, see page 317.)

For Rock Gardens. While most lilies are too tall to be good subjects for use in a rock garden—unless it covers a large area and is fairly well sheltered—there are a few which may be used to excellent advantage. They offer an interesting contrast to the general type of rock-garden plants, and if good judgment is used in their placement, will look thoroughly at home and add much to the over-all effect. Species and varieties suited to this purpose will be found in the list on page 319.

For Cutting. In any garden where more than a few lilies are grown, it is likely that some of them will be wanted as cut flowers for decoration indoors.

Under such circumstances it is advisable, where possible, to provide a separate area, if even a small one, to accommodate plants to be used for this purpose. To cut flowers from a planting in the mixed border, or one made for a specific landscape effect, will definitely injure the garden picture.

Furthermore, cutting with even moderately long stems—essential to get the best effect indoors—robs the plant of much of its mechanism for producing food to enlarge the old bulbs or develop new ones. This is much less serious in a cutting bed, where smaller bulbs may be used and where they may all be allowed to recover during the following season, than it is where a maximum display is wanted year after year.

When possible it is desirable to have *two* areas for cutting, one located where it will get an early spring warm-up and produce early flowers; the other in a northern or a somewhat shaded situation, resulting in later flowering. Especially is such a "double exposure" system of planting important where flowers are wanted for show competition, as even a few days' difference in flowering may mean the difference between winning coveted prizes or losing them.

Another wise precaution to assure health and long life for the bulbs themselves is to cut blooms every other year only, thus giving each plant time to recover completely from removal of part of the stem and foliage when the bloom is taken. This may best be accomplished by cutting the blooms in *every other* row or group, and marking these with the year when the cutting was done.

CHAPTER *8. Lily Soils*
and Their Improvement

> *The noisome weeds, that without profit suck*
> *The soil's fertility from wholesome flowers.*
> WILLIAM SHAKESPEARE (1564–1616)

SOILS AND THEIR IMPROVEMENT

He who would grow lilies well should know something of the character of soils, and how—where necessary—they can be modified or altered to suit the needs of plants that are to be grown in them. Usually such modification is not nearly so difficult as it is supposed to be. The soil and its character is a fascinating subject.

Soils are originally derived from four classes of rocks; namely, igneous, shale, sandstone, and limestone. After long periods in humid regions the soils are subjected to the solvent and leaching action of water containing acids and various salts in solution, and as a result become so modified that they may bear little resemblance to the original rocks. In fact, under similar conditions of temperature and moisture, there is a tendency for a rather uniform soil to evolve, regardless of what the original rock may have been.

To the average gardener this is of only academic interest. More important are the three features of any soil: physical—whether the soil is light or heavy, well or poorly drained, high or low in organic matter; mineral—amounts of available elements of the kinds needed for plant growth and health; biological—the population of microorganisms needed to convert raw material to plant food; and also the possible presence of harmful organisms in the soil.

98

Soil Bacteria.

Soil must be considered as a living, breathing substance, swarming with myriad forms of microscopic life, in themselves as necessary to higher plants as light, air, and water. Without this living component of our soils, organic material could not decay and raw minerals would remain locked up in forms that plants could not use. The result would be a lifeless desert.

It is obvious that if we provide a favorable environment for the microorganisms in our soils, they can do their full part toward providing the nitrate and mineral requirements of plants. To this end, we need to have a good supply of organic material, plus nitrogen, phosphorus, potash, and other minerals in small amounts. If the soil bacteria have a good supply of nitrogen, they will consume raw organic material—such as fallen leaves and stems, straw, etc.—and convert it into humus. In the process, minerals and nitrogen contained in the original organic material are made available to plants and, incidentally, some waste products of this process may break down and release other natural nutritive minerals in the soil.

Humus. The need for *organic material* is obvious, since it is the basic food of the microorganisms. Since, however, at times most of the available nitrogen may be in use by the soil bacteria during the most active part of the breakdown cycle, it is advisable to *add the organic material several months in advance* of planting time. Good aeration of the soil and warm moist conditions greatly speed the breakdown.

Drainage. Good drainage is of paramount importance in lily culture. The location and physical properties of many soils are such that they are naturally well drained, and any gardener who is fortunate enough to have such a location can well be thankful. Even if the soil is not well drained, one can do much to help it.

Deep trenching is a good practice where a hardpan interferes with the downward passage of surface water. Some people put in a layer of gravel, cinders, or other porous material at the bottom of the deep trench, but unless the adjacent layers drain well, this is a waste of material and energy.

If the location has sufficient slope to remove surface and surplus sub-surface water by gravity, then proper grading of the
surface will prevent water from standing. If sub-surface water
is a problem, a line of good *clay tile drains,* perhaps 30″ to 36″
deep and strategically placed, should solve the problem.

If nothing else works, then *raised beds* are the answer and the
worse your drainage problem, the higher you should raise them.
Raised beds are excellent for lilies, even if you feel that your
drainage is adequate. In cold climates, it is well to give extra
attention to mulching raised beds, so that they are not left exposed
during winter.

Soil Acidity

Another important factor is soil acidity. While it is true that
lilies grow best under slightly acid conditions, it is also a fact that
lime is needed to release the other plant foods in the soil. In many
places rain water carries acid into the soil and the decay of
organic matter produces more acids, resulting in a reduction of
the lime content. Moisture-retaining soils selected for lily plantings are, therefore, usually acid in character; sometimes even too
much so for lilies. If so, such a condition may readily be corrected.

Soil acidity is measured in pH units. At the pH of 7, a soil is
neutral, that is, the acid and the alkaline materials "balance," or
neutralize each other. For lilies a pH value of 5½ to 6½ is to be
preferred. A few lilies, especially *L. candidum* and *L. martagon,*
are tolerant of lime and grow well in soils with a pH value up to
7 or even 7½. *L. davidi* and *L. amabile, L. cernuum* and *L. henryi,*
as well as *L. centifolium,* are also rather tolerant of lime. We
must not overlook, however, the fact that these lilies are stem-
rooting and under normal garden conditions are likely to be
mulched with leafmold or compost which is usually acid.

These notes on soil acidity may look somewhat forbidding to
the amateur gardener to whom lilies are just one of many kinds
of flowers he wishes to grow. Most of our American gardens,
especially those with thoroughly drained, porous, well-aerated soils,
and sufficiently high humus content, will be found well suited to
lilies. If you want to make sure, send a soil sample (about a cup-
ful) to the nearest state college or experiment station and have the

soil analyzed. You will be told what to do to make it right. An application of hydrated lime or ground limestone (used according to these instructions) will soon bring the soil to the desired pH for lilies. If the soil is too alkaline—with a pH of 7 or higher—a light application of sulphur or aluminum sulfate will make it more acid.

Fertilizers

The fertilizer requirements of lilies are simple enough for the average experienced gardener to understand, since they are not much different from those of other flower and vegetable plants ordinarily grown. Of course, it is impossible to give any formula which will be perfect for your particular garden, since there is such a wide variation in soils. Soil testing to show the chemical analysis has some value, but few gardeners have the knowledge and experience to evaluate such a test.

Any standard complete fertilizer, used according to directions, will furnish the minimum nitrogen, phosphorus, and potash needs of lilies, but a little experimentation will enable you to grow better than average flowers. Remember that additional nitrogen, applied during the early stages of growth, makes larger plants and flowers, but will also make the lily foliage softer and more subject to botrytis fungus. It may also make them more attractive to certain insect pests.

Complete fertilizers may be mixed with soil before planting, or worked into the surface around the plants during early stages of growth. Application of fertilizer after flowering time, except for potash, is largely a waste of material for that season. Many people are in doubt as to how much complete fertilizer to use. Where directions are not available, an easy and generally safe method is to add a zero to the nitrogen percentage figure of the fertilizer, then use the resulting figure as the number of square feet one pound of the mixture should cover. Most fertilizer packages have the analysis printed on the container; in many states this is required by law. Sometimes the analysis is stated as 5–10–10, 6–8–12, or some other similar figure. The first number always represents the percentage of nitrogen, the second the percentage of phosphorus, and the third the percentage of potash in the mixture.

If we apply our formula to the 6–8–12 mixture, we find that one pound should cover 60 square feet of surface.

In applying fertilizer of this type, care should be taken to avoid direct contact with either bulb or foliage, and distribution should be as even as possible. Liquid fertilizers must always be diluted, and then applied carefully according to manufacturers' directions.

On the west coast of the United States and Canada liquid fertilizers, derived entirely, or in part, from fish and whale solubles, have become very popular. The straight fish or whale solubles are of generally rather low analysis. The ingredients are all organic, very safe and easy to use. The fortified types usually have been enriched by the addition of urea and phosphoric acid, bringing the analysis to an excellent level, but requiring a little more care in their use. Both types are usually deodorized and are easy to handle.

Besides being a good source of the major elements, these materials are also among the best sources of the minor, or so-called trace, elements. It is now generally recognized that these minor elements are needed by plants. In addition to nitrogen, phosphorus, and potassium, other essentials are copper, iron, zinc, manganese, molybdenum, chlorine, boron, sulphur, aluminum, silicon, calcium, and magnesium. It is also possible that plants may need traces of cobalt, vanadium, and sodium. There may, as well, be a need for certain hormones and vitamins from the soil.

Actually, no one need worry about the minor elements, since traces of most of them are found in average garden soil. The gardener who wants to do a superior job can use either some organic fertilizer, such as fish oil or dried blood, as a natural source of most of the minor elements; or else some commercial fertilizer with added trace elements. This is insurance against any nutritional deficiency.

In general, it is better for the inexperienced grower to be careful in the use of high nitrogen fertilizers. The veteran gardener will enjoy learning the knack of growing flowers of exhibition size and quality by providing near optimum soil conditions. See also Chapter 10, page 122.

Mulches

Since mulches modify soil conditions and sometimes become part of the soil itself, they must be considered under the general heading of soils.

Mulches, used as winter cover, help to protect bulbs from freezing in cold climates and serve to keep down winter weeds in mild areas. In cold areas, mulch should be applied after first

While soils should be thoroughly improved and prepared before lily bulbs are planted, lightly digging under a half-decayed mulch each spring or fall will improve still further. In this garden, a heavy sawdust mulch is applied annually. (Photo taken in the garden of Professor George Slate, Geneva, N.Y.) The great value of adequate mulching lies in the fact that it helps keep the soil moist and cool.

freeze. Coarse "strawy" materials, such as twigs, sawdust, etc., are commonly used. Materials that do not readily pack down are to be preferred. Such mulches act as an insulating medium and protect against alternate freezing and thawing which may do damage by causing the soil to heave.

If a mulch is applied in the spring, at time of emergence of the plants or afterward, it is most important that it be wetted down thoroughly. If this is not done, the mulch may act as an insulating medium and, when a frost occurs, prevent the radiation of heat from the soil. Frost injury to the top growth could be a greater hazard in this case.

Summer mulches serve to keep down weeds, conserve moisture and keep soil temperatures low. This is particularly helpful in areas where summers are hot. Shallow-rotted ground covers also serve these purposes and make the garden scene attractive.

Since the soil in spring serves as a reservoir of heat to help protect early emerging plants from frost, we can use this knowledge to advantage. In areas where spring frosts are a problem, cover of some sort, such as a lath screen, serves to reflect this radiant heat back down to the plants and affords an amazing amount of protection. Nearby trees and shrubs may also serve as reflectors. (See also Chapter 10, page 124.)

Enemies in the Soil

The soil can be the home of enemies as well as friends. These may be symphilids, nematodes, insects or fungus diseases. Nematodes (microscopic worms) are of two general types as far as lilies are concerned. First, there are the root-lesion nematodes, which may use many types of plants as hosts and, incidentally, attack the roots of the lilies. Symptoms are usually a rotting of part of the root system and a consequent yellowing of the foliage. The bulb itself usually does not rot, but makes little or no growth. These same symptoms may also occur where nematodes are not present, due perhaps to poor drainage or some other cause. Positive diagnosis can be made only by an expert.

The second type of nematodes usually works in the bulb tissues and, carried upward by growth of the plant, continues to work on the leaves. These types are highly specialized and may be considered as a specific lily pest. The result may be dwarfing, browning of the foliage resembling frost injury, and general debility of the plant. Positive diagnosis can be made only by an expert, but if a lily plant in your garden shows these symptoms every year, it would be well to destroy it.

It is unlikely that the average gardener will encounter the nematode problem, but if he does, some sanitation measures are in order. The area should be cleared of all plant growth and treated in order to destroy the pest. Several nematocides are available, but the most commonly used is ethylene dibromide. Directions must be followed with utmost care. Materials available in capsule or dry powder form are easier to handle than liquids.

If harmful insects are present in the soil, they may usually be eliminated by some of the newer insecticides such as aldrin, heptaclor, or chlordane. Again, it is important to follow directions exactly.

Most harmful fungi in the soil may be controlled by general sanitation, rotation of crops and/or treatment with materials such as Terraclor. Used as a bulb treatment Terraclor gives considerable protection, even when the bulb is planted in soil where harmful fungi are present. Commercial growers now use a combination dip of Terraclor and Ferbam. The usual concentration is 4 pounds of Terraclor and 2 pounds of Ferbam per 100 gallons of water. Since these materials are wettable powders, they do not go into solution and must be kept agitated or they will sink rapidly to the bottom of the treating tank. The addition of a wetting agent, such as Du Pont spreader-sticker or some similar material, increases the effectiveness of the treatment. Bulbs should be left in for ten or fifteen minutes, or until thoroughly wet, and planted soon after treatment.

Summary

Most soils can be made fit for lily culture with a moderate amount of preparation. Listed in the order of their importance, the following four rules should be observed:

1.) Be sure drainage is adequate. Lilies do not like "wet feet." *This point is more important than all the others combined.*

2.) If possible, prepare planting site several weeks in advance by incorporating organic materials and mineral elements essential to plant growth. If this is done, only light supplemental feeding will be needed during the growing season.

3.) Protect with a winter mulch in cold areas; a summer mulch or ground cover in hot areas.

4.) If harmful parasites are present, treat soil to eliminate them.

Optimum Conditions

For the most part, lilies prefer a neutral to slightly acid soil that is friable, reasonably fertile and well drained. A heavy and clay-like soil retains too much moisture and is not sufficiently aerated to produce good growth, while too sandy a soil dries out and contains little available plant food. As a general rule, any soil that will grow good potatoes will grow good lilies.

On our farms we maintain one field that is devoted to experimental plantings and hybridizing work. It is a field that slopes gently toward the south. At its lower end there is a dammed-up creek which makes an attractive little lake. During the summer this provides an ample water supply for irrigation, though this is not often needed. The soil, a heavy "shot" loam that bakes in the sun and has a tendency to become rather solid unless it is worked at just the right time, is often trampled between the rows of lilies to a concrete-like hardness by the feet of our visitors and workers. This field is where we grow our choicest stocks, both the wild lilies and the hybrids, in full sun and with a minimum of irrigation or cultivation. Under these conditions the lilies actually thrive.

Here, in this one field, are scores of varieties of *L.* x *hollandicum* and the new hybrids between them and the Tiger Lily. Here stand the hybrids of *L. henryi* in their full glory, on stems that sometimes reach up eight feet into the sky and carry from thirty to forty blossoms. Here also is *L. centifolium* and its hybrid relations in serried ranks, on stiff stems six feet or more in height, loaded with flowers and yet not breaking or bending in the wind. The Harlequin Strain of *L. cernuum* Hybrids grows in the same field, with seedlings of *L. davidi* and the Fiesta Hybrids, *L. amabile* and *L. amabile luteum, L. auratum, L. speciosum,* and many other lilies from our country, from Europe and Asia, species and hybrids too numerous to mention.

In such a field there is no question of special preparation of the soil for this species or that. There are no pockets with sand or humus, no locations where soil is especially dry or damp. There is no shade of any kind. The entire field is treated in our routine manner of farming.

Why, then, do our lilies grow so well? It is partly because we build up the soil. For two years we plant cover crops of oats and vetch. We then alternate with bulbs for the next two years. Green crops are plowed under early in the year and from then until fall the land is summer-fallowed. Each year part of the field is planted, and by rotating our crops we can keep the most interesting lilies, our "laboratory and workshop collection," close at hand.

Like all our land, this field is perfectly drained. Yet, even though our summers are dry, there is always moisture present, for the rains of winter and spring are retained by the large amounts of humus. The lilies grow well, too, because we start with healthy bulbs, planted at the correct time and in a very porous soil. Even though it is trampled down between the rows of lilies, the ground immediately around the bulbs is loose, and we purposely keep it so.

You may say that under these conditions and in the ideal climate of the Pacific Coast region success with lilies is inevitable. Let me tell you, however, about another planting on the other side of the continent, the garden of the late William N. Craig of Weymouth, Massachusetts. I first met Mr. Craig many years ago and until his death we met every year at the various flower shows.

I visited his charming home, his gardens and greenhouses, and I had the privilege of his wise counsel and advice. Here on a couple of city lots, in an extremely heavy soil considered by "expert" gardeners to be good for little, Mr. Craig grew over a hundred varieties and species of lilies, many of them in commercial quantities. His success with lilies, the many medals that his perfect blooms won at local and national flower shows, are still being talked about among lily enthusiasts. The secret was a soil, that, though heavy, was well-drained, that retained moisture, yet was never waterlogged. In addition to this good soil, his stock consisted of healthy bulbs selected from the far corners of the world. Success was inevitable.

I could cite many other instances, gardens in northern Canada and gardens in the Deep South. Wherever lilies are well grown, we find the same conditions—perfect drainage, a porous yet moisture-retaining soil, and healthy bulbs for the initial plantings.

9. *Planting*

> *... such gardens are not made*
> *By singing:—"Oh, how beautiful!"*
> *and sitting in the shade.*
>
> RUDYARD KIPLING (1865–1936)

PLANTING

A lily is a living plant. Unlike the usual spring and summer-flowering bulbs such as tulips, daffodils, and gladiolus, the lily never sleeps. In that respect we must look upon the lily as a shrub or a perennial. No true gardener would let a newly purchased rhododendron sit around and dry out until he felt like planting it, or leave a flat of annuals in the garage until he came back from a business trip or a vacation. The same holds true for lilies. If treated as though they were completely dormant bulbs, failure is inevitable. This mistake—the failure to understand the true nature of the lily—is one of the main reasons for lack of success. It is a mistake that is made by some nurserymen as well.

It is important, first of all, that we know something about the bulbs; second, that we understand their methods of increase and the way the root systems take up food supplies. In a daffodil, the scales which form the bulb are overlapping and cling tightly to one another—so firmly that one can hardly pry them loose. Such a bulb also has an outer covering composed of a layer of hardened, dried scales which serve as a protective cover against bruising, drying, excess sunlight or other injurious exposure. In a lily the scales are fleshy, soft, and unprotected by any such covering. The outer scales, those we see when we handle the bulb, are usually larger, and possibly a little tougher, than the inner scales close to the heart of the bulb. However, all of them bruise easily, and in many varieties, if the bulb is dropped or packed tightly against others, will break off.

When the Bulbs Arrive. From both the gardener's and the dealer's viewpoint a lily should be handled like a living plant: kept growing, moist and cool, even in transit and storage, as its root system is necessary to its very life. One should therefore always try to get bulbs with their roots intact and do nothing to interfere with their growth. With these roots the newly planted bulb grips the soil. They anchor the bulb and keep it from heaving when frost disturbs the top layer of garden soil. The roots pull the bulb down to the level it prefers under the conditions given it.

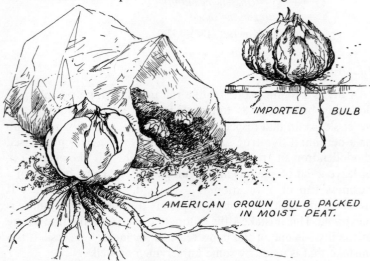

Good and poor lily bulbs. Right: freshly dug, plump bulb, with fleshy roots attached, packed in moist peatmoss. Left: partly shriveled bulb; roots cut off or withered.

Imported stock with its roots cut off, dried-out bulbs that have been displayed on store counters, pinched and bruised by inquiring fingers, cannot grow well. Such bulbs will often flower once, for hurt as they are, they try to perpetuate themselves by means of one more seed crop before they die. This may seem like a rather dramatic picture, but it is, nevertheless, an entirely true one.

A lily bulb should be out of the ground for as short a period as possible. It can, of course, be stored for spring planting, but this must be done with expert care and under ideal conditions. For that reason, it is always best to order lily bulbs very early. The seedsman or nurseryman will then reserve them with the grower, who digs and ships at the right time. In the meantime, the gardener can pick the best spot for planting and prepare it well—as described in the two preceding chapters.

Of course, the bulbs cannot be kept growing actively while they are in transit. It is to be expected that they will dry out somewhat on the trip. When the package is opened, in some instances the scales may be a little soft or wrinkled. In such a case, the bulbs should be put in moist sand or peatmoss in a cool place, and, within a few days, the scales will again be firm and new roots begin to form. The bulb can then be planted and should establish itself well in the spot chosen for it. If set out in the garden at once upon arrival, it will do as well only if the soil is cool and moist and remains so for several weeks.

Grades and Prices. Finally, the size of the root system and the number of roots vary with each type of lily. They even vary as individual bulbs. The size of a bulb is not necessarily an indication of its value. Lily bulbs differ greatly in size, according to the species or the parentage of hybrids. For instance, *L. formosanum* flowers well from bulbs not more than three inches in circumference, while *L. pumilum, L. cernuum,* and several others never produce large bulbs. *L. regale, L. centifolium,* and many others, on the contrary, make large bulbs even when young. In lilies, more than in any other family of bulbous plants, price can usually be depended upon to express quality. All seed stores and mail-order houses use practically the same system of pricing and maintain the same modest profit margins. Hence, it can safely be assumed that bargain offers of lilies are based upon cheap imported stocks which have been exposed to virus diseases; upon surplus lots— usually kept in storage awaiting a market, long beyond their proper planting season; or on stocks of unknown or doubtful value, or not true to name.

Good lily bulbs must necessarily be more expensive than tulip or daffodil bulbs. Since they are growing plants, they cannot be handled as easily as many other bulbs. They must be graded and counted by hand and then packed carefully to prevent bruising of the fleshy and often brittle outer scales. Yet no other garden plant can be so rewarding and represent such a sound investment in gardening pleasure, if the finest bulbs are purchased. They must, however, be of top quality. Poor or disease-ridden stock brings only trouble and disappointment.

Within any one species or variety, it is safe to say that large-sized bulbs produce better stalks, more heavily laden with flowers. Large bulbs divide naturally into large splits, each one of which will produce a flowering stalk in one or two years. Thus, for exhibition or maximum effect, purchase the largest bulbs possible—bulbs that have not yet "split." For general garden use, however, the more moderate-sized are fully satisfactory.

Having selected the best available location (see Chapter 7) and prepared the soil as suggested in Chapter 8, the gardener is now ready to plant his lilies.

Drainage. There are a few simple rules to follow. Don't forget that lilies like drainage both beneath and above ground. No water should ever stand around the roots, for lilies are not bog or water plants. Air drainage too, is important, for stagnant air is a breeding place for fungus troubles.

Give Lilies Room to Grow. Don't expect lilies to thrive well in strong competition from shallow-rooted trees such as maples, elms, beeches, or other plants that are heavy feeders and vigorous growers. They must have a good breathing space around them, so that the sun and wind can reach them freely. This is especially important not only in humid climates, but elsewhere, too, for only then will lilies grow with straight stems. On the other hand, lilies appreciate a low-growing ground cover to keep the soil around them cool. (See Chapter 10.)

Time to Plant. Lilies should be planted just as soon as possible after they are received. This practice is advisable because the longer the period given them before winter sets in, the better they will do. This is another reason why American-grown bulbs give superior results. Since they do not have to travel so far, they reach the purchaser fresher and in better condition, ready to grow more vigorously than bulbs shipped from a great distance.

Lily bulbs can be planted until the ground freezes, if necessary;

even later, if the ground is mulched heavily to keep it from freezing. In this case be sure that a mulch is applied at once *after* planting to prevent the soil freezing so quickly that the roots may not get a good start. If well mulched during cold weather, roots will develop even when the tops are not growing. Often lilies can be planted even under the snow if the soil has not frozen too hard.

If it is impossible to plant the bulbs in the fall, pot them up in a light, friable garden loam and store them until spring in a cold, but not freezing, cellar; or in a cold frame under a heavy mulch. They can then be moved to their permanent quarters without disturbance to the root systems.

By the same token, if one receives bulbs in the spring and a place to plant them cannot be got ready for several weeks or months, pot them up and plunge the pots outside in a sheltered place in the garden until they may be planted permanently. A wooden box filled with damp peatmoss serves as a good place in which to sink such bulbs temporarily. They will, however, inevitably start growing, and it may be difficult to transplant them to the garden without damage to the new roots.

Spring planting of lilies, however, is possible. We have done it on a commercial scale and with very fair results. Nevertheless, better results have invariably been obtained from fall planting. Even though a number of English and Dutch growers—and a few in certain sections of this country—seem to favor spring planting, we must not forget that their climate is unlike ours. In spring planting there is always danger of injury to the bulbs and their roots, for they do not have as much time to become re-established before they must begin to support above-ground growth. The long storage period will inevitably weaken the bulbs.

The Madonna Lily, *L candidum,* is the one lily that demands a different treatment. The bulbs ripen and are dug in summer and should be planted during August or September, the earlier the better. They start growing at once, throw out roots and produce rosettes of leaves which remain green all winter.

Depth to Plant. Much has been written about the depth at which the various lilies should—or even must—be planted. In our case bitter experience has taught us to discount this advice. First of all, no two soils are alike. In light sandy soils the bulbs should be planted comparatively deeply. In heavier soils they should be planted more shallowly. Although a column of depths to plant is included in the chart in Chapter 18, it is not advised that this be followed slavishly. Rather, it should serve as a general guide.

To determine the best depths for planting, separate lilies into two types; the base-rooters, which produce roots only from the bases of the bulbs; and the stem-rooters, which also throw out some roots from the stem above the bulb. The stem-rooters should obviously be planted a little deeper than the base-rooters, so that the stem roots may find some good solid soil in which to take hold.

The Madonna Lily, however, is again an exception to this rule. It should be planted very shallow, with the top of the bulb either at the surface of the soil or, at most, not more than an inch beneath it. The reason is that this lily is actually a dry-weather plant, at home in hot, dry regions. It needs sunlight and heat to do well in the garden. It is also the one lily bulb that needs warm and dry conditions during storage. Actually, it comes nearer to reaching complete dormancy, for a brief time, than any other lily.

As might be surmised, the stem roots give the stem and flower additional strength and substance. They allow the plant to flower and set seed, even if the bulb underneath is removed. This has been tried with *L. speciosum* and *L. auratum* and, given the right soil and weather, seed has been produced. It is also the reason why bulbs from imported stocks often give a fine performance the first season after planting and then never appear again! The untimely digging, the long trip, and the subsequent planting at an unseasonable date—usually after months of storage under poor conditions—are all factors fatal to any but the strongest bulbs. Under such conditions the bulb fails to make basal roots and consequently the entire plant is fed only by the stem roots. It will flower and try to set seed, but it does not build up the bulb for another season's flowering. From being a perennial it has been forced to become an annual.

On our farms it would obviously be impossible to set every lily variety, and every one of its bulb sizes, at different depths. In the garden you need only remember that small lily bulbs are planted with about two to three inches of good soil over the tops. Large bulbs should have four to five inches of soil over them at planting time—in very cold regions even somewhat more. Medium-sized bulbs are in between in this respect.

How to Plant. Over the many years that we have been growing lilies, a great many tricks have been advocated, such as setting the lily bulbs on top of large rocks or over inverted empty flower pots to insure drainage and prevent basal rot; or laying the bulbs on their sides, to keep water out of the crowns. With the proper attention to selection of a location, planting time and healthy stock, such practices are unnecessary. With diseased, bargain-counter stock all the tricks in the world are of no avail. Just the same, it is the shrewd observations of green-thumb gardeners that have given us many good ideas and hints and we have always listened to them with respect and attention.

Here are some definite suggestions to follow: Dig a large hole six to twelve inches deeper than you plan to set the bulb and fill in the bottom with a loose, friable garden loam such as has already been described. Then put in the bulb and carefully spread out the roots. Fill in the remainder of the hole, firm the soil and mark the location.

A hole one foot in diameter is not too generous for a moderate-sized bulb and is downright "stingy" for a large bulb. It is much better to dig a hole large enough to accommodate the entire group of bulbs and set them according to their proper distances apart. (See chart in Chapter 18.) Work the prepared soil firmly in around each bulb to eliminate all air spaces. This gives the roots immediate nourishment.

If many lilies are being planted, it is well to prepare an entire bed and simply dig the planting holes large enough to accommodate all the roots comfortably and at the proper depths. In other words, the entire bed is fertilized and spaded before planting is begun.

It is sometimes suggested that each bulb should be surrounded with sand to insure drainage and discourage mice, slugs, wire-worms, and diseases. Some writers have gone so far as to recommend filling the planting hole with sand right to the surface of the soil to make it easier for the stem to push through. A pocket of sand in a heavier soil—particularly when it extends to the surface —obviously acts as a cistern and accumulates water around the bulb. In all our years of growing lilies, other conditions being favorable, have we ever noticed any that had trouble pushing up through the ground.

If in transit or handling, the bulbs or roots have been damaged, remove all injured portions. Just as a bruised apple will rot, so will an injured lily bulb. Dusting with one of the newer disinfectants, such as Arasan, is of material benefit. This treatment can be recommended for all lily bulbs prior to planting. Put a teaspoonful of the powder with the bulb in a paper bag and shake it for a few seconds. An Arasan dip is equally effective.

Mulches, Summer and Winter. After the bulbs are planted, it is decidedly beneficial to cover the soil with a two- or three-inch layer of some mulching material to conserve moisture, keep it cool, discourage weeds, and eliminate the need for cultivation. A mulch also helps to prevent too early growth in the spring and lessens the danger of injury from late frosts. This is especially important with newly planted bulbs, where root systems are not yet firmly anchored in the soil. (For further details concerning mulches, see pages 103 and 124.)

Name Stakes and Markers. Although strong lilies, grown where they receive sufficient light, rarely need staking even in exceptionally windy situations, it may be necessary to resort to this practice to identify varieties. In such cases, use sturdy three-quarter to one-inch stakes, preferably painted green, and before planting, set them in the ground to a depth of two feet. By doing this before planting all danger of damaging the bulb or roots is avoided. Be sure the stakes are treated with a wood preservative to give them longer life. They are available in a green color that is unobtrusive in the garden picture.

Even in the best-regulated garden, it is often difficult to recall the exact location of certain plants. With lilies it is doubly important to have them plainly marked, if one wants to avoid accidental injury to the bulbs before they start their spring growth. Use a permanent type of marker of metal or treated wood and of sufficient size so that it will not be lost in the periodic clean ups. A very inexpensive marker can be made by fashioning a ring out of a metal clothes hanger, such as those returned by the cleaner. Don't depend upon the small wooden plant labels that are excellent for temporary use, but attach a label of weatherproof plastic or metal, marked in black India ink. (See also Chapter 10, page 121.)

Another little trick is the use of small spring-flowering bulbs in the lily bed. They will not identify the lilies, but do serve to mark their locations and thus save them from damage before they come up in the spring. Except with the very smallest of the lilies, minor bulbs offer no serious competition and are an attractive addition to the spring garden.

CHAPTER *10. Culture*

Let us cultivate our garden.
VOLTAIRE (1694–1778)

I bring fresh showers for the thirsting flowers,
From the seas and the streams.

"The Cloud"
PERCY BYSSHE SHELLEY
(1792–1822)

Like all other plants, lilies are subject to the inexorable law of nature, namely, that too much or too little of any of the factors that influence the life of a plant is adverse to its growth. For instance, if a lily receives no water, it dies. If however, it receives too much, it cannot live, since the oxygen supply to its roots is cut off. Temperature, light, and many other factors, such as the composition of the soil, also influence the growth of lilies. If the water and light supply are just right, but the temperature too low or too high, the plant will die, just as surely as if it had too much or too little water or light. These are but a few examples. There are others that influence the lily to a greater or lesser extent.

Fortunately, lilies have considerable ability to withstand adverse conditions. They also show a marked variation in this respect. Some species are rugged and perfectly at home in what might be considered unfavorable surroundings, whereas, under identical circumstances, others will succumb.

To understand the reasons for such behavior, to know just why one lily does well and another does not, is to have the key to successful lily culture. We grow more than seventy-five acres of lilies,

118

both the wild ones and the new hybrids, so these problems have been uppermost in our minds for a number of years.

As a result of study, experiment and systematic scientific tests, many interesting facts have become evident. Some surprising flaws in previously held theories have also come to light. These findings are of importance to the home gardener who wants to grow just a few lilies, as well as to the commercial grower.

Some Erroneous Ideas

After many trials we have found that, despite what lily growers used to believe, it is *not* necessary to provide every wild lily with exactly the conditions of its native habitat. For instance, the climate in the home garden is rarely like that of a valley in China or a mountain crag in Jerusalem. Again, filled as our soil is with the debris of civilization, the decayed foliage of plants and the remnants of fertilizers and sprays, it cannot be like such virgin soils as those of the Siberian wastelands, to mention but one region where lilies are found.

Even if one could duplicate these soils and reproduce the climates of the places where wild lilies grow, what is one to do when two or more species must be grown in one nursery, or side by side in the garden? Obviously, if on our seventy-five acres of lilies—which include many species and hundreds of varieties—we tried to re-create the conditions under which they grow in their native habitats, our nursery would look like the set for some fantastic movie with mountain crags, alpine valleys bordering the ocean, fresh water lakes, pockets of coral sand, bogs and swamps and desert stretches of every kind and description. Impossible, you say. And obviously it is!

It would not even be desirable to attempt such a project since instead of growing from choice in such wild areas, the lilies may be there because these were the only spots left for them. They may be growing in such places not because of, but in spite of, the conditions of their environment. Grazing cattle, or the encroachment of man cultivating his fields, may well have pushed some of our lilies to the hedgerows. Plant them in the open, give them half a chance, and see how they will thrive.

The depth of planting, so carefully noted by our botanists when they find lilies in the wild, is again not a sure indication of the lily's true preference. It may grow in spite of deep planting, but it might do better if planted less deeply. The proper depth of planting varies with each soil type, with each climate and, it is true, with each type of lily. Grown in the wild, erosion, earthquakes, or

Cross section of planting hole for individual bulb. Large hole, dug out and filled in with properly prepared soil to correct planting depth—better when several bulbs of one variety are to be planted, or for a lily border.

just the accretion of leaves falling and decaying into compost over a long period of years may bury the lily bulb to a considerable depth. If vigorous, it will grow in spite of its heavy covering. Who knows if it might be happier with less? In order to grow good lilies, we must not follow blindly the theories of earlier growers, but profit from the constantly accumulating evidence provided by current experience.

Location and Soil. In the preceding chapters we have stressed the facts that a sunny, well-drained location, a porous yet moisture-retentive soil that is neutral or slightly acid, are the essentials to success with lilies.

Soil Acidity. This last factor, that of relative soil acidity, is a most important one. (For details, see Chapter 8, page 100.)

The reaction of the lily to ideal surroundings and soil conditions is made evident by strong, healthy top-growth, by good flowers of fine color and heavy substance. It is also demonstrated by a better-than-average growth of the bulb, its root system and rate of increase. Whether one grows lilies for pleasure or profit, it is very important that the bulbs increase in number and size. Large bulbs throw good spikes, stems laden with flowers, and divide naturally into large splits, forming what bulb growers call more "noses." Each one of the larger splits produces a flowering stalk in one or two years.

General Culture

As Chapter 9 covers all the details of correct planting, we are now ready to consider the other phases of general culture.

Early Spring Growth. Assuming that the newly planted lily bulbs have been mulched immediately, as advised on page 116, and carefully marked with *permanent* labels, the gardener has done all he can until growth appears in spring. Since some lilies do not come up in the exact spot where they were planted, the ground around them should be closely watched so that the tender young shoots, often very brittle, are not broken off or damaged during the usual spring clean-up of borders and the subsequent weeding.

Species and hybrids which produce new bulbs from stolons or along rhizomes may come up at some distance from where the original bulb was planted. *L. davidi* and *L. nepalense,* for instance, throw out stems that wander as much as two feet under the surface before coming up. Indeed, such lilies create so much of a problem that growers are trying to develop similar lilies of hybrid origin that will stay in one place! This habit of wandering underground is also sometimes caused by the search for food, sun, and warmth; and occasionally simply by the effort to get out of a wet spot in the garden.

Weeding and Cultivation. As soon as spring growth appears above ground, all weeds should be carefully removed. If the lilies are not mulched, a light cultivation should be given to remove weed seedlings. We cannot emphasize too strongly, however, that deep hoeing is dangerous. If you do any more than loosen the surface, you are apt to destroy many of the stem roots which grow very close to the ground level. Unmulched lily beds should be lightly cultivated at regular intervals during the growing season. This is necessary to keep weeds down and break up any crust which may form if the soil bakes under the hot summer sun after a hard rain.

The weeding of mulched beds is a much simpler problem. Any weed seed which manages to germinate is easily removed, roots and all, by hand or by gentle hoeing, since the mulch forms a soft friable medium in which the roots cannot get a strong hold.

Fertilizing. Since the lily bulb never sleeps, it is always hungry and ready to be fed. In fact, in spite of its delicate appearance, it is a voracious feeder. In addition to constant moisture it needs a well-balanced meal of nitrogen, potash, and phosphates, plus all the minor elements about which we hear so much these days. (See also Chapter 8, page 101.)

Many ways of feeding lilies have been tried. The first and best method is to give them a choice location in field or garden, a spot strong in humus content with a top layer of decaying and decayed leaf-mold. This can be reinforced by the use of old, well-rotted *cow manure.* Hard as this may be to obtain, its use is one that is most rewarding. It can be used as a summer mulch with excellent effect. It may also be mixed with leafmold and incorporated into the soil or applied in extract form as liquid manure when watering. At all times it has been our experience that such natural manures give better and quicker results than chemicals, partly due to a natural balance of major and minor elements that seem to suit lilies. Animal hormones either benefit the plants directly or influence the soil structure and soil bacteria to the ultimate advantage of the lilies.

Wood ashes also are good. They should be applied at the rate of one pound per 20 square feet. A tablespoonful for every clump of lilies is just about right.

When cow manure is not obtainable in sufficient quantity, various *commercial fertilizers* may be substituted. We have found a 5–10–10 formula quite satisfactory. In commercial practice the lilies are planted in fields that have had at least one, and preferably two, heavy *cover crops* of vetch and oats incorporated in the topsoil. The porous quality of soil so enriched, and the thorough aeration that the decomposing particles of straw and stems give the top layer, suit lilies extremely well. In a sense this method is that advocated by Faulkner in his book *Plowman's Folly*. The "organic" method of gardening benefits lilies.

In fact, any method of soil management that puts emphasis upon a well-rounded program of fertilization and maintenance of good soil structure is right for lilies. Where manure cannot be obtained, the use of commercial fertilizers is permissible, as noted above. Here again our preference is for the organic type, with *dried animal manures* first, and *cottonseed meal* or *tankage* next, on the list. If chemical fertilizers must be used, they should be supplemented by the incorporation in the soil of such humus as is provided by a cover crop, or by peatmoss or other humus applied in the form of a mulch.

When advising large groups of amateur gardeners with widely varying soils, we often recommend a good *potato fertilizer* (which has a 5–10–10 analysis) to be used at the rate of two or three ounces per square yard, to be worked into the soil before the lilies come up in spring, and again a few months later. The liberal use of *bone meal* in the soil is also beneficial, but excessive stimulation of foliage caused by heavy doses of nitrogen is sure to give added susceptibility to disease.

Fresh manure, or an overdose of strong fertilizer of any kind, is, of course, injurious, as it would be to any plant. The facts are that the common troubles of lilies do not usually stem from balanced overfeeding, but rather from diseases inherent in the bulbs.

To summarize:

1. The lily bed before planting should be enriched as described in Chapter 8.
2. A mulch of well-rotted cow manure (if available) may be applied as a permanent mulch immediately after planting, and added to from time to time as needed. If this cannot be obtained, a rich compost may be substituted.
3. Where other mulches are used, such as those described on page 104 and 124, two pounds of cottonseed meal or five pounds of tankage per 100 square feet should be added to provide enough, *but not too much,* nitrogen.
4. A 5–10–10, or other similar complete fertilizer, should be applied in spring at the rate of one pound per 100 square feet of bed. In small

plantings, a trowelful or a handful may be scattered over an area of 20 square feet. Repeat two or three times during the growing season.

5. If soil or water is alkaline, scatter a pinch or two of agricultural sulphur over the soil around each clump of lilies two or three times during the growing season.

6. In spring apply wood ashes, if available, at the rate of one pound per 20 square feet.

Mulches. Since lilies thrive best when their roots are shaded and kept cool and moist, permanent mulches are usually applied. As stated above, *well-rotted* manure is the preferred material for this purpose, with rich compost the next best substitute.

If neither of these materials is available, many others may be used: peatmoss, buckwheat hulls, ground corncobs, bagasse, dried hardwood leaves, pine needles or hardwood sawdust. When one of these is employed, more fertilizer may be required to keep up the needed fertility.

Special treatment is needed when hardwood sawdust is used as a mulch. It has many advantages, in that it keeps the soil cool during hot weather, conserves moisture and prevents weeds from germinating. During the time it is decomposing into humus, however, the bacteria engaged in breaking down the organic matter tie up the nitrogen present in the soil, in a form unavailable to plant roots. This creates a temporary nitrogen deficiency, soon evidenced by the lily foliage turning a lighter green than is normal. To make up for this deficiency, sulphate of ammonia may be used—at the rate of one tablespoon per gallon or one cup per sixteen gallons of water—to be watered in around the base of the plants.

With established plantings, an additional inch or two of sawdust may be added each spring. One of the chief advantages of a sawdust mulch is that it may be left indefinitely undisturbed, without hoeing or other cultivation.

Ground covers. By the proper use of shallow-rooted ground covers, the roots of lilies in a home planting may be kept shaded and cool where a mulch is undesirable. Like a mulch, they too help to keep weeds in check. Naturally such overplantings must not offer root competition to the lily bulbs or rob them of their food or moisture.

Among plants recommended for the purpose are *Vinca minor, Phlox subulata,* iberis, creeping veronicas, forget-me-nots, and violas. Primulas are especially attractive. Early in spring they offer gay flowers, at the same time protecting the young lily shoots as they emerge. During the summer the tall lily stems provide needed shade for the primula foliage. Thus they complement each other in an ideal way.

It has often been stated that the association of lilies with other plants is of great importance. The detailed information given by plant explorers as to the exact flora of a location where new lilies have been discovered has led many gardeners to attempt to duplicate it in their own gardens. It is unnecessary, however, to grow bamboos, alpine heathers, or other such shrubs in order to have lilies. The role of these plants in nature should be correctly evaluated. If a plant associated with a lily in the wild gives it shade, we can do so by other means. A native American fern, for instance, will give protection and, for tall, shade-loving lilies which prefer a cool, moist but well-drained soil, makes an ideal underplanting.

Watering. Lily bulbs require constant moisture, as well as excellent drainage, and thus, artificial watering should be resorted to whenever necessary. Wet the ground thoroughly to a depth of from four to six inches, using a water wand or hose with nozzle removed to produce a very slow stream. *Wetting the foliage may spread disease,* so avoid the use of sprinklers or rain machines. Such a thorough soaking should last from ten days to two weeks, even in dry weather, and is much more effective than frequent light applications.

Though most gardeners are on the alert for dry spells during the growing season, many amateurs fail to realize that equal damage may be done by insufficient moisture at other times of the year. *Never let your lily bulbs go into the winter dry.* If you live in a section where autumn rainfall is light, before the ground freezes, give one deep thorough soaking. Remember, the lily bulb is never dormant and so needs constant moisture.

Spraying and Dusting. It is easier to prevent plant troubles than to cure them. Lilies treated with an occasional all-purpose dust or spray, such as that used for roses, are not likely to be attacked by aphids or fungus diseases. (In case of the threat of serious trouble, see Chapter 12.) Never wait until the entire planting is affected, but *at the first sign* of any pest or disease, discover its cause and promptly apply the advised treatment.

Staking and Tying. A few very tall lilies with heavy heads of bloom, and some species with weak stems which grow in natural habitats where they are supported by surrounding growth of some kind, may need staking. Where possible, it is best to set the stake at planting time, thus preventing the chance of injuring roots or bulbs by driving it in during the growing season.

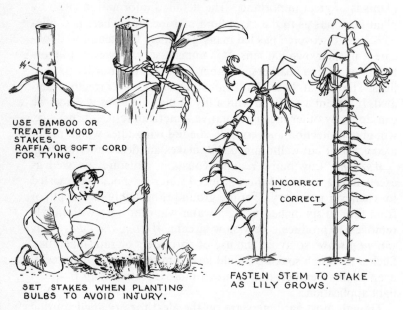

USE BAMBOO OR TREATED WOOD STAKES. RAFFIA OR SOFT CORD FOR TYING.

SET STAKES WHEN PLANTING BULBS TO AVOID INJURY.

INCORRECT

CORRECT

FASTEN STEM TO STAKE AS LILY GROWS.

Details of staking and tying lilies.

It is best to select strong three-quarter or one-inch stakes treated with green cuprinol to preserve the wood and also to make the stake inconspicuous. These are sunk at least eighteen inches underground or even up to two feet, if the plant to be supported is very tall. If not sunk deep enough, stakes will heave and fall, and the job will have to be done all over again.

There is quite a trick, too, to tying the stem correctly to the stake, so that it will be supported but not bruised or broken. Use a very soft cotton cord or raffia. Tie a loose loop around the stem with a firm knot which cannot slip; carry the double cord back to the stake and tie it firmly again, leaving enough between the two knots so that the stem will be supported, but not bent backward against the stake. (See also Chapter 9, page 116.)

Buds and Flowers. Because we are more familiar with it, we are apt to look upon the above-ground activity of lilies as the more important part of their life. Actually, just as much life is going on underground. The newly planted bulb starts making its roots, sending them down after food and water. In so doing it spends the substance of its scales and exhausts them still further when it begins to send up the stem, leaves, and finally the flower. At that stage its strength is exhausted and it must renew itself from the substance its above- and below-ground growth can give it.

It is also imbued with a strong instinct to survive. Its efforts have gone into a good root system and top growth. Finally, to live on in spite of what nature or man may do, there is the instinctive urge to reproduce itself. This effort may be directed toward seed production or toward the increase of the bulbs underground. It is at this stage that scales taken from a bulb show the greatest tendency to form bulblets.

Disbudding. Commercial growers usually pinch off the lily buds in order to prevent flowers and permit the strength to go back into the bulb. The principle is the same as removing the first strawberries or refraining from harvesting the stalks in a young asparagus bed.

This is pretty hard practice for the amateur who may have stretched his budget to buy the lily bulbs and is waiting breathlessly to see the first bloom. For home plantings disbudding is not necessary and is not often advocated, but there is no doubt that it is good for the newly planted bulb.

Cutting. The thing to remember in cutting is to refrain from taking too much of the stem. For indoor decoration it is best to cut stalks just as soon as the first blooms open, as that gives a longer period for enjoyment before they fade. Spent blossoms may be removed one by one as they begin to wither. As the pollen creates a stain on clothing or elsewhere, commercial florists often remove the anthers from cut lilies.

Removal of Dead Flowering Heads. Where flowers are left in the garden for outdoor color, it is well to remove the inflorescence as soon as color fades. If left on the plant, some of the strength must

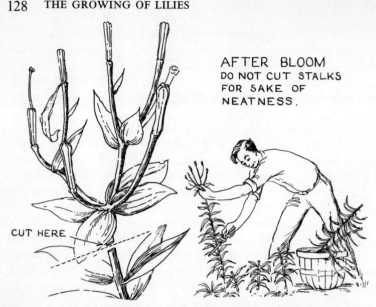

AFTER BLOOM
DO NOT CUT STALKS
FOR SAKE OF
NEATNESS.

CUT HERE

How to cut lilies: most of stalk should be left to help in development of strong new bulb for following year.

go into an effort to form seed and this means that less will be left to help the bulb create fine blooms the following year.

Do not cut stalks. This does not mean, however, that the flowering stems themselves should be cut down after bloom for the sake of neatness. Just as is the case with spring-flowering bulbs, which soon die out or deteriorate if foliage is removed before ripening, so lilies need all their foliage to manufacture food for next year's growth and bloom.

Transplanting. To leave lilies alone is the best advice we can give the gardener who can afford new stocks to round out his collections. If lilies have increased a great deal, then moving them may be necessary. What should be done when you want to move the stock in the garden or make additional plantings?

Lilies can be transplanted at almost any time of the year and stocks can then be divided. We have moved some of them when in full flower and have moved growing plants in our gardens both in fall and spring with good results. *L. candidum* is again an exception to this rule. It should be moved as soon as it is through flowering. Late fall-planted Madonna Lilies have flowered for us,

PLATE 7

In lily breeding today the emphasis is on enchanting new colors such as those shown above; (left, Moonlight strain and right, Pink Perfection strain). BELOW: *The colors of earlier hybrids were more like those of the wild or species lilies. Many of the hybrids are also exceptionally vigorous.*

PLATE 8

PLATE 9

One great advantage of lilies is their versatility for decorative purposes. Grown in containers such as planting cans, either out of doors or in the greenhouse, they may readily be moved, as they come into bloom, to any location where a dramatic effect is desired. The varieties shown here (left to right) are: Harmony (orange); Tabasco (tall red) and Enchantment in the background. In the foreground, three reds: Fireflame (outfacing); Cinnabar (upright); and (extreme right) the lower growing Sunstar.

Many of the modern lilies, like these pink trumpets, tower well above the usual "tall" flowers of the hardy border, thus adding both distinction and charm to the picture.

PLATE 10

PLATE 11

PLATE 11

Lilies alone, without other flowers or foliage, provide material for dramatic, quickly achieved decorative designs.

PLATE 12

Mid-Century hybrids arrange themselves.

PLATE 13

An arrangement of L. auratum platyphyllum, *by Carl Starker.*

PLATE 14   PLATE 15

Burgundy strain, grown from plants selected for uniformity of color and habit. Plants in a "strain" are not all precisely alike, but sufficiently so to form a distinct group. In a clone, such as the lovely lilies below, all plants are exactly alike, as they have been produced from a single parent bulb, of which they are actually living parts, just as are roses grown from cuttings of one original bush. The lily here shown (above at right) *is Clone P-11, a new broad-petaled Aurelian hybrid.* BELOW: *Lilies are displayed to the very best advantage when placed in front of evergreen shrubs. Here four named varieties (clones) selected from the Mid-Century hybrids, flower against a background of Mountain Laurel. They are* (left to right) *Harmony, Fireflame (deep red) Prosperity (yellow) and Enchantment, one of the most popular of today's lilies.*

PLATE 16

but invariably with some loss in size and vigor. Whenever you move lilies, remember to do so with the least possible disturbance of the bulb and its roots.

Going through the normal cycle of its life, a healthy lily is always active. When this cycle is suddenly interrupted, when the lily bulb is exposed to unnatural conditions, such as long storage or moving, it may be thrown into confusion. Such bulbs may put out some roots, perhaps even some top growth, but not finding the climate or soil conditions to their liking, may then suspend all effort to grow until the full cycle of seasons has gone by. This is not like the true dormancy which occurs in tulips and other bulbs, but is rather a metabolic shock causing suspended animation. It is a condition which is not beneficial to the bulb and its future health. Not only may the bulb dry out too much, and remain exposed to danger from rodents or upheaval from gardening operations, but also, lacking the top growth that announces its location, it may easily be destroyed by being cut with a hoe or spade.

When planting a lily bulb which during digging or at some other time has had its basal roots damaged, first moisten the base and then dip it in one of the root-growth-inducing hormones, such as Rootone or Hormodin #1. This treatment will encourage a flow of root-making materials from the scales to the basal plate and thus stimulate immediate growth.

When it is necessary to dig up bulbs to divide them, transfer them to a new location to provide new sources of plant food. If that is impossible, be sure to dig out the old soil in the root area and replace it with new prepared soil. Among the lilies most likely to need such handling are: *L. bulbiferum, L. concolor, L. hansoni, L. henryi, L. pardalinum,* and *L. tigrinum.*

The Winter Mulch. Just before hard freeze, after the late fall watering which may be necessary if the ground is dry, *but not while the soil is still soft,* the winter mulch is applied.

If a permanent mulch is used on the lily bed, this need not be removed. Simply add to it by putting on two to three inches of well-rotted cow manure, if it can be obtained. If not, combine one part dried cow manure with three parts peat moss, and apply to a depth of two or three inches on top of the old mulch. Or add a few inches of whatever mulch you may have selected for your lily bed and leave the fertilization until early spring.

Who loves a garden loves a greenhouse too.
WILLIAM COWPER
(1731–1800)

One characteristic of lilies, which makes them of such great value to the gardener, is the fact that they may be had in bloom out of season. Commercial growers, with proper facilities for storing the bulbs and controlled temperatures for growing the plants, provide cut lilies throughout the year. Any home owner, with no more elaborate equipment than a cool cellar and a warm sunny window, may enjoy them through late winter and all spring.

While commercial growers usually force only lilies of the Easter type (Croft and Estate Lilies for example) which are universally sold by florists, the lily enthusiast may enjoy a wide range of forms and colors, either as cut flowers or growing plants. Not all species lend themselves to such out-of-season flowering, but a great many of the new hybrids force readily and very successfully.

Anyone who grows flowers or plants indoors, or in a small home greenhouse, can easily visualize what a great addition a few lilies in pots would be to the decorative effects possible. Lilies are so distinctly different from other flowering plants that even two or three in a collection on a window sill or sun porch will add much in the way of character and distinction to any group, just as they do in an outdoor garden.

The same holds true where cut flowers are desired. It is not difficult, where space is available, to grow a few lilies for cutting, even without a greenhouse. In fact, their culture is less demand-ing than that of many other plants frequently grown indoors. When one does have a greenhouse, they should by all means be grown, es-pecially as one is not restricted to the type usually forced for the florist trade.

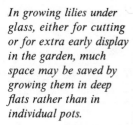

In growing lilies under glass, either for cutting or for extra early display in the garden, much space may be saved by growing them in deep flats rather than in individual pots.

Varieties for Forcing

On page 319 a list will be found of species and varieties of lilies which can be forced most successfully.

As mentioned in a previous chapter, extensive trials, both in greenhouse and sunroom, have shown that some lilies, particularly the newer sorts, lend themselves well to pot culture. The Mid-Century Hybrids are ideal for large bowls and containers. Three to five bulbs in a 12-inch pottery bowl, at least 8 inches deep, make a magnificent display. Great care should be taken, however, to

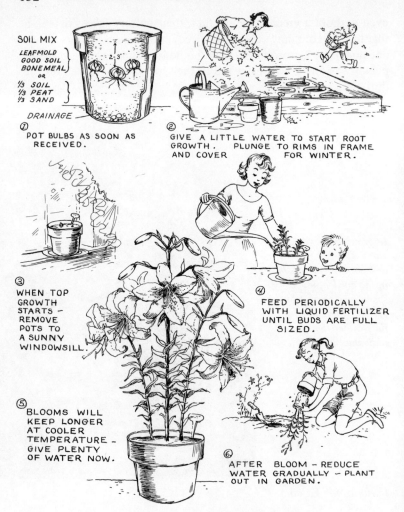

SOIL MIX

LEAFMOLD
GOOD SOIL
BONEMEAL

OR

⅓ SOIL
⅓ PEAT
⅓ SAND

DRAINAGE

① POT BULBS AS SOON AS
RECEIVED.

② GIVE A LITTLE WATER TO START ROOT
GROWTH. PLUNGE TO RIMS IN FRAME
AND COVER FOR WINTER.

③ WHEN TOP
GROWTH
STARTS –
REMOVE
POTS TO
A SUNNY
WINDOWSILL.

④ FEED PERIODICALLY
WITH LIQUID FERTILIZER
UNTIL BUDS ARE FULL
SIZED.

⑤ BLOOMS WILL
KEEP LONGER
AT COOLER
TEMPERATURE –
GIVE PLENTY
OF WATER NOW.

⑥ AFTER BLOOM – REDUCE
WATER GRADUALLY – PLANT
OUT IN GARDEN.

Details of pot culture for the amateur lily grower.

provide perfect drainage and to check it at regular intervals. On no account should bowls or pots without drainage holes be tried.

The Golden Chalice and Rainbow Hybrids also force successfully. These new hybrid strains of lilies are not uniform in flowering time, but this is no drawback to the home gardener; in fact, a slight difference in period of bloom prolongs the pleasure to be derived from three to five bulbs planted in a pot or pan. *L. marta-gon album* also makes a very fine showing, as do the Fiesta Hybrids. Henryi Hybrids, such as the Sunburst Strain, are really magnificent when grown in deep pots.

The new *auratums, L. speciosum* and its varieties and *L. form-osanum,* especially the late, tall strain, also make fine pot plants. When in bud they can be moved to desirable locations on the terrace or in the garden, so that they may be fully enjoyed by all visitors. Their delicate perfume and glorious flowers create an un-forgettable impression.

From among the hardy lilies one might add *L. browni, bulbi-ferum, hansoni, maculatum,* and the dainty *pumilum.* These, although not new, are less well known as lilies that can be grown in pots.

Add to these lilies a display of the varieties of *L. longiflorum,* the Croft and Estate Lilies. The latter are particularly noted for their size and vigor and both are a decided improvement over the older imported sorts. They are now being grown in the Pacific Northwest, and, consequently, reach the home gardener in much fresher condition, and also are much more likely to be disease-free.

Much has been written about the role of the lily in the garden and little about its use in the house. This is curious, for it is as a pot plant that the lily has found one of its widest uses in our country. *L. longiflorum,* especially the Croft variety, is probably the most widely grown lily in America. It is the one we take home the day before Easter in its gaily crepe paper and ribbon-decor-ated pot. Many who have planted their Easter Lilies in the garden, after they were through blooming, have been surprised by a second flower in the fall of the same year and by still another the following June.

Although the Easter Lily may have given many a gardener the first hint that lilies are hardy and will grow well in the garden, by no stretch of the imagination can it be called a good, or even fair, garden lily. For one thing, when grown outdoors, the stem is too short; for another, the flower is so white, so formal in character and so long that it does not give a well-balanced effect. Further-more, it is not entirely hardy in all sections of the country. Forced, it grows on a much taller stem and lends itself much better to arrangements.

Pot Culture for Amateurs

Lilies in pots, lilies grown out of season, lilies that can be moved from sunroom to living room, are very cheerful plants to have in the house. Their perfume, rich coloring and ease of growth make them ideal plants for indoors, sunroom, or terrace. Little or nothing is lost by planting lilies in pots. The bulbs do not suffer greatly from the confinement and the effect of shelter and tempered light on the flowers is good, for they will be spotless and of a soft delicate coloring.

Potting. Especially for the Southern states, where the hot sun may easily bleach their color, planting in pots is to be recommended. If lilies are moved indoors or to a sheltered location, when the buds begin to swell, they will then open in their full beauty. One of our friends grows a large collection of lilies in this manner and puts them around his patio and along the approach walks to his house, constantly replacing the earlier kinds as they fade and the season changes with those that flower later.

Lilies make a strong root growth, which is obviously at its smallest diameter where it is attached to the bulb. From there it widens out to take in as much territory as it can reach. The ordinary flower pots that taper sharply toward the bottom are not ideal for lilies, and therefore large "pans" or pots with straighter sides are preferable. We have, however, successfully forced a number of different lilies in regular six- and eight-inch pots. Since lilies delight in a porous and rich, well-drained soil, we can give them ideal conditions by preparing a mixture of leafmold and good garden soil. Some charcoal or pebbles should be placed in the bottom of the pot to assure good drainage, and some bone meal mixed with the soil. Plant the bulbs as soon as they are received.

Bulbs should be planted according to their type; stem-rooters two to three inches deep, the others more shallowly. *L. candidum* and *L. testaceum* are planted near the surface with the soil barely covering the bulb. After potting, the pots can be set (preferably plunged up to the top of their rims to help prevent frost breakage, as well as to retard drying out) in any sheltered location, such as a small frame made out of 1 x 8 inch boards. Fill this frame with light soil or leafmold, or simply cover it with leaves and twigs from the garden. In cold climates some additional protection may be advisable—such as leaves or evergreen boughs—but, as a rule, where there is enough winter snow, it will do a better job than any covering the gardener can provide. As soon as the lilies begin to make top growth, the pots may be removed to the greenhouse, the sunroom or to any sunny room that can be kept at a temperature of around 60 degrees Fahrenheit. They will then start to grow and flower much earlier than in the garden, thus considerably lengthening the lily season.

Soil Mixture. Results of work done at Cornell University by the Plant Pathology Department indicate that the control of root rot is primarily a matter of soil mixture. Lily bulbs grown in a well-drained soil were far superior to those grown in straight soil with no additional drainage added.

Where Croft Lily bulbs were planted in straight soil with no drainage material added to the bottom of the pot, the total growth in inches of the 24 plants checked was 86 inches. In the ⅓ soil, ⅓ sand, and ⅓ peat-moss mixture the Croft Lilies had a total growth of 158 inches, almost double that of the straight soil, no drainage treatments.

Another very obvious difference in the two types of soil was that in the sand–soil–peat-moss mix, the plants were relatively uniform, while in the straight soil there was a wide difference in the height of the lilies.

Although the test is not yet complete, the results thus far are very promising and seem to indicate that all that is necessary for relatively good lilies free of root rot is that they be planted in a soil containing ⅓ soil, ⅓ sand, and ⅓ peat moss with adequate drainage in the bottom of the pot.

Fertilizing. Do not overwater the plants, but be sure to give liquid manure periodically until the buds are full-sized. Once the flowers have opened, lower the temperature again, or remove the pots to a cool room in the house. At this lower temperature most of the lilies will keep for several weeks.

The secret of growing fine lilies in pots, both for the garden or the greenhouse, is in providing perfect drainage, watering judiciously and feeding the plants a good liquid fertilizer. A sack filled with cow manure and hung in a barrel of rain water has for years been our favorite standby. The liquid seems to give the plants just what they need to offset the unnatural conditions to which we expose them. If manure is hard to obtain, then a commercial dried manure will serve the purpose. A balanced liquid fertilizer may be made by using the standard formula of 5–10–5 at the rate of a level tablespoonful dissolved in a gallon of water. Give every plant about a third of a pint of this mixture every week.

Watering. Care should be taken in watering potted lilies. When the bulb is first planted, they should be watered very little, barely enough to allow for root growth to start. Later, when the plant is above ground, give a little more water, increasing the amount as the buds begin to develop. At the flowering stage the lily needs a great deal of water, but as soon as the flowering is over, the supply should again be diminished to let the plants "ripen off" slowly.

Aftercare. Upon examination of the potted bulbs, when the tops are dying down, it will be found that most of them have made a good growth, even though they have been confined to the comparatively small area of the pots. They can be kept in the same pots for another year, if the soil around and above them is removed without disturbing the new roots and new soil is filled in. Or, they can be knocked out of the pots and set in the garden, again disturbing the roots as little as possible. Even a pot-grown lily with its top growth wilted and dried up *is not dormant.* Knock any of them out of the pot and you will note plenty of new, fleshy, white roots, already at work for the next year's growth.

COMMERCIAL CULTURE

Lilies have been of great importance to commercial florists. For many they are now a significant part of the year's turnover. Various types of *L. longiflorum,* the so-called Easter Lillies, are being forced in enormous quantities, not just for the Easter holidays, but also year-around for weddings, funerals, graduations, and other occasions. The experience of these florists, and of the experiment stations and colleges which have studied various phases of the industry, has taught us a great deal about the growing and timing of lilies under glass.

While at the present time the Easter Lilies are still of paramount importance as a florist's crop, other varieties are now also grown under glass for cut-flower purposes. *L. auratum, L. speciosum rubrum,* and the new Mid-Century Hybrids are used in appreciable quantities. Several other new hybrids have shown great promise as greenhouse lilies and may soon be used in quantity.

The varieties of strains of *L. longiflorum* most commonly grown commercially are *eximium*—generally known in the trade as *harrisi—giganteum,* and *multiflorum;* with the more recently originated clones Croft, Ace, and Estate becoming more and more important. For years most of these lilies were imported from Japan, Formosa, or Bermuda, but, unfortunately, much of the stock was diseased. Better and healthier stocks are now coming from the extensive Pacific Coast plantings, and from Georgia, Louisiana, and Florida. Even so, *L. longiflorum* is still quite susceptible to virus diseases, and all plantings from year to year must be rigorously selected, if the quality of the stock is to be maintained.

In commercial greenhouses the forcing procedure is roughly this:

Lily bulbs should be stored at 40 to 45 degrees Fahrenheit from the time they are received until they are planted. Do not store them in a place such as the boiler room, where the temperatures will be extremely high, since this high temperature will make useless the precooling treatments previously given the bulbs and cause a delay in flowering, or possible blindness of the plant.

The soil for Easter Lilies should be carefully prepared. Select a loam soil that is low to moderate in fertility and add some organic matter, preferably peat. The amount to add will depend on the original soil, but one-quarter to one-third by volume should be satisfactory. The soil should be only slightly acid, or neutral, pH 6.5 to 7.0. If the soil is more acid than this, ground limestone can be added to decrease the acidity to at least a pH 6.5. Soil sterilization is necessary in order to eliminate a possible source of root rot infection.

The potting of lilies for the next Easter should be done approximately 15 weeks before they are needed. They are potted in 5½ or 6 inch pots, usually placing them midway in the pot so they have an inch or so of soil over the tip of the bulb. For larger-sized plants, two bulbs are grown in a 7 to 7½ inch pot. Drainage material must be put in the bottom of each pot to insure that water will not collect, but drain away readily. A handful of fine gravel, screened cinders, or similar material is satisfactory.

Lilies should be grown at 60 degrees F. (see p. 142) for their entire forcing period. At this temperature they should begin to show above ground in 10 to 14 days. Some growers prefer to start their bulbs at a cooler temperature of 50 to 55 degrees and then to raise it when the plant shows through the soil. When this is done, at least two to three weeks longer are required for forcing, which means they are potted November 25–30.

Fertilization is begun when the new growth is 2 to 3 inches tall. This would be approximately January 5–10. Use a complete fertilizer low in phosphorus, or only a nitrogen fertilizer such as sodium nitrate or calcium nitrate, at the rate of 2½ lbs. to 100 gallons of water. This fertilizer application is repeated every two weeks.

Avoid Crowding. When bulbs are first potted, they may be placed pot to pot. When, however, they begin to grow, they must be spaced to prevent crowding and a loss of lower leaves due to shading. At eight weeks before Easter the plant should be 12 to 15 inches tall. At a temperature of 60 degrees growth should continue so the buds begin to show in the center of the leaves by six weeks before Easter. Flower growth is rapid after the buds are visible.

If plants are slow in developing, the temperature should be raised to 62 to 65, or even 70 degrees. Raise only sufficiently to get the necessary speed-up in growth, since continued high temperatures cause a tall, soft spindly type of growth.

Approximately three weeks before Easter, the largest buds on each plant should be 2 to 3 inches in length and beginning to bend over. By two weeks before Easter, buds should be 3 to 4 inches long. A week before, they should show whitish color.

Retarding Growth. Plants which have developed rapidly, ahead of schedule, should be placed in a cool greenhouse, 50 to 55 degrees, to retard growth. It is possible to place plants in the dark, if the temperature is 40 to 45 degrees. Plants which have the buds swollen when they are placed in this cool temperature will open rapidly when brought out again into a warmer temperature.

Lilies are watered regularly and the soil kept wet. Later, as they become larger, they may be kept on the slightly dry side.

Death of the lower foliage is due to crowding, a lack of nitrogen, or a lack of phosphorus. The imbalance of nitrogen and phosphorus, or a lack of available calcium, is the likely cause of leaf scorch.

Insect Pests. Insect pests—except for aphids—are generally not a trouble in lilies. Injury from aphids can be serious. They may cause a twisting or curling of the leaves, and splitting of the flower buds. The presence of only a few insects, dead or alive on the plant, detracts from its appearance. Control is essential. Malathion, parathion, or lindane are effective.

Croft Lilies grown at 60 degrees, fertilized and watered regularly and not crowded, will produce high-quality plants.

Commercial lily culture has been outlined as follows by Frederick H. Nelson, assistant Hartford (Connecticut) agricultural agent, and Jay S. Koths of the Connecticut Extension Service.

I. TROUBLES

Common lily troubles and some possible causes:

a. *Bud-blasting:* One or more of the following culprits could give this trouble: insufficient water, root injury, lack of sufficient light, extremely high forcing temperature, and calcium deficiency.

b. *Bud-splitting:* Usually caused by aphids, sudden lack of water, or fluctuations in temperature.

c. Loss of lower foliage: Low nitrogen, crowding plants, lack of water, root trouble.

d. *Aphids:* Control with malathion, parathion, lindane, or systox. (Use of nicotine spray or dust may cause leaf tip burn.)

e. *Root rot:* As far as possible, buy good clean bulbs; use new, well-drained soil (try a little gravel or traprock in the bottom of the pot); be careful in your fertilizing and watering practices. Root rot and leaf scorch have been decreased in some cases by dipping the bulbs before planting in the formula given below. In the event of severe damage to roots, usually occurring 3–6 weeks before flowering, new roots may be encouraged by the application of oxyquinoline sulfate (3 oz./100 gals. or 4 tsp./10 gals.) for up to five applications at 5-day intervals.

University of Wisconsin Formula:

4 oz. 15 per cent W.P.
    Parathion
2½ oz. Ferbam
2½ oz. Terraclor

In 10 gals. water.
Soak 30 min.

Use for 3 or 4 batches, then discard.

    f. Streaked or specked leaves: Caused by viruses which are spread by aphids. These bulbs are diseased before you receive them. You can do nothing for them.

    g. Croft tip burn: Death of tips of leaves commonly starting as semicircular spot near end of leaf. Conditions alleviated by maintaining a pH of over 6.5, a calcium level over 150 and nitrates over 15 (Spurway). Avoid high phosphate levels.

    h. Inspect plants weekly for signs of insects or root rots.

II. BULB STORAGE

    a. If your bulbs arrive early, store immediately at 32 to 34 degrees, never over 45 degrees, until potting time.

    b. Inspect for excessive wilting or damage. Cut a bulb or two through the center from top to bottom to inspect interior.

    c. Pot as soon as possible, for good bud count.

III. POTTING

    a. Soil should be well drained and of moderate fertility with a pH of above 6.5. Have this soil tested well in advance of potting.

      1. Incorporate up to 10 lbs. agricultural limestone per yard of soil. If this amount does not raise the pH to 6.5, apply ½ teaspoon per pot in late January as a dry feed.

      2. Place ½ in. crushed stone in bottom of pot to insure adequate drainage.

      3. Leaf scorch is more severe in acid soil and at low nitrate levels.

      4. High fertility or soluble salts at planting time injures developing roots, dwarfs subsequent growth, and reduces bud count.

      5. Pasteurized soil is generally recommended, although if a disease organism contaminates the soil, the crop damage may be more severe. Be sure to use the root rot dip when planting in pasteurized soil.

b. Lilies are commonly potted in 5 inch, 5½ inch or 6 inch standard pots depending upon bulb size—below 8's in 5-inch pots, 8–9's and 9–10's in 5½-inch pots and 10's and up in 6-inch pots.

c. Bulb tips should be 2 inches below soil surface.

d. Bulbs may be started at temperatures as low as 50 degrees, or up to 60 degrees. Low starting temperatures may mean a higher bud count and taller, grassier plants. If bulbs are planted 115 days before Easter they may be started at 60 degrees. If started earlier, the temperature may later be increased to 60 degrees.

e. Water all benches with Captan-Terraclor mixture (1 lb. each/100 gal./500 sq. ft.) before placing pots on benches.

IV. FERTILIZATION

a. Fertilization should commence when the shoots are between ½ inch and 1½ inch high.

b. Complete fertilizer, or just nitrogen alone, will maintain a good green color, if applied regularly (every one to two weeks) until buds are ½ inch long. To avoid lowering the pH, sodium or preferably calcium nitrate may be alternated with any complete fertilizer low in phosphates.

c. A weekly feed of calcium nitrate at 1 lb./40 gal., replaced with an occasional complete soluble fertilizer low in phosphates, should fit most soils.

d. Fertilization does not increase height.

V. WATERING

a. Water thoroughly upon potting.

b. Keep moist throughout the growing season, but do *not* over-water.

1. If the soil is carried on the dry side before the plants are 6–8 inches high, roots are not stimulated, the bud count is reduced and foliage is often injured. A light reduction in water after this height is reached will reduce excessive stretching.

2. If overwatered, or if the soil is too "heavy," certain root rots are encouraged through lack of oxygen in the soil.

VI. TEMPERATURE**

    a. A 60-degree night temperature is recommended for forcing Croft Lilies. Sixty-two degrees is usually used for Ace. Buds should be just visible in leaf cluster six weeks before Easter.

    b. Advanced lilies should be placed in cooler (55 degrees) locations. If a very cold (40–45 degrees) night is followed by a warm sunny day, severe wilting followed by blasting may occur even though plants are wet.

    c. Plants started early and grown at 50–55 degrees F. will be taller than those grown at 60 degrees.

    d. To force slow plants raise night temperature to 70–75 degrees. However, if held too long at this temperature, Croft Lilies will become softer and taller.

    e. Usually some sections of a greenhouse are warmer or cooler than others. By shifting pots in the house according to growth rate, starting the second week of January, the crop may be kept relatively even without involving other houses.

VII. LIGHT

    a. Shade from any source, i.e., dirty glass and, particularly, crowding, will cause stretching of the stems and decreased bud count.

    b. Artificial light, in addition to natural light, increases the rate of growth, if grown below 65 degrees F. If grown at 65 degrees F. or above, artificial light does not hasten flowering.

VIII. STORING MATURE PLANTS

If plants are maturing too early, they may be held in good condition for about two weeks in a dark cold storage at 40–50 degrees.

1. Plants should have at least one bud in the "white puffy" stage, or at least one day from opening.

2. Water plants thoroughly prior to storing.

** *TEMPERATURE EQUIVALENTS (approximate)*

FAHRENHEIT	CENTIGRADE
70°	$21\frac{1}{2}$°
60°	16°
50°	10°
40°	5°
32°	0°

IX. VARIETIES

The principal varieties are Croft and Ace. Choice is a matter of personal preference and type of market. Ace Lilies are characterized by smaller, darker green leaves and smaller, tougher flowers. Bud count is higher, a 7–8 Ace being somewhat equivalent to an 8–9 Croft. Being smaller leaved, more Ace plants may be grown in a given area (up to 30 per cent more). The smaller, harder flowers may be better adapted to shipping. Since Ace Lilies sometimes start less uniformly than Croft, more labor may be necessary to produce a uniform crop.

EASTER SCHEDULES FOR LILIES—1962 *

DATE	NUMBER OF DAYS TO EASTER	SUGGESTED STATUS OF DEVELOPMENT
Dec. 27–31	119	Pot your bulbs—start at 60° F. Be sure your soil is well supplied with Calcium with a pH of 7.0.
Jan. 14	99	Breaking the soil
Jan. 25	88	New growth showing
Jan. 31	81	New growth 1–3 inches
Feb. 7	74	New growth 4–6 inches
Feb. 14	67	New growth 6–7 inches
Feb. 21	61	New growth 10 inches
Feb. 28	54	New growth 12–15 inches
Mar. 6	47	You can feel the buds
Mar. 10	43	Buds just showing
Mar. 14	39	Buds ½ inch long
Mar. 20	33	Buds ¾–1 inch, few bending down
Mar. 25	28	Buds 1½–2½ inches
Apr. 1	21	Buds 3–4 inches long
Apr. 8	14	Buds fully developed being held
Apr. 13	8	Whitish-fully developed being held
Apr. 21	1	Sold out
Apr. 22	0	Easter

* Adapted by the authors, from information prepared by Dr. W. R. Jenkins, Department of Entomology, Rutgers University, New Brunswick, New Jersey, published in *The Florists Exchange & Horticultural Trade World* magazine and used by permission.

Diseases and Pests

. . . we have . . . worms in our gardens,
and spiders and flies in the palaces
of the greatest Kings.

JEREMY TAYLOR (1613–1667)

DISEASES

The problem of diseases in plants, while in many respects different from that in man, bears enough resemblance to it to make a comparison possible. That healthy plants—like healthy people, living or growing well in a medium and in surroundings that suit them—are strongly resistant to disease is a fact that all observant gardeners have noted. It is this natural resistance to disease that is so important to the lily.

Diseases, such as those caused by specific bacterial or virus infection, manifest themselves in man in two forms. One is the acquired, specific immunity which develops as the result of exposure to a specific microorganism. This may be a natural exposure, as when we catch a cold or a specific bacterial or virus infection. Or it can be artificial, as when, through vaccination, dead or attenuated organisms are introduced into the system. In both cases the body develops antibodies, substances that provide immunity against the specific disease-producing organisms. The length of this immunity varies from a few weeks to a lifetime.

There is in man another type of immunity, that is not the result of exposure to a specific disease-producing organism. This is a general immunity which gives resistance to diseases caused by virus or bacteria as well as to all other diseases. This immunity, which we might call natural, is, without doubt, in lilies controlled

145

by one or more genetic factors. It is strongly inherent in some lilies, while in others it seems totally absent.

That temperature is a factor influencing this immunity seems certain. It is also extremely likely that the degree of acidity or alkalinity in the soil may have a strong effect. The studies of the late Dr. Louis Pillemer of Western Reserve University in Cleveland, Ohio, suggest that a protein substance plays a significant role in maintaining the human body's natural resistance to disease. It is quite possible that such a substance will be found in lilies as well, and that by supplying the required amounts in some way their resistance to disease can be increased. It is more likely, however, that the road to healthy lilies will be found through the combination of genetic factors with new, improved methods of production and the practice of sanitation and good culture.

Botrytis

Like the diseases of all living organisms, those of the lily are of various types. First of all, there are a number of fungus diseases, of which botrytis blight is the most common. This can be controlled and prevented by the use of a mild Bordeaux spray. Some growers have recently used another copper product, called "Micronized Copper Dust." In our extensive trials we have yet to see that it shows any advantage over the dependable Bordeaux spray with which almost every gardener is familiar. This spray is also a good preventive or control for other fungus diseases and it does not harm the lilies in any way.

The ingredients can be bought at any seed store and a fresh mixture should be made up for each application.

1. Using a nonmetallic container, in a gallon of water dissolve five level tablespoonfuls of copper sulfate.
2. In another nonmetallic container dissolve in two gallons of water eight level tablespoonfuls of hydrated lime.
3. Pour the copper sulfate solution into the lime solution, stirring constantly, and *use at once.* A wooden bucket and a small stirrup pump, equipped with a spray nozzle, will handle the job, unless your lily plantings are very extensive.

In that case, a small power sprayer might be used to advantage.

On our nurseries we maintain a regular spray program and cover all of the fields at least once every ten days or two weeks. In the garden such frequent sprayings may not be necessary. As always in disease-control programs, an ounce of prevention is better than a pound of cure. We recommend that if botrytis is present, or that if conditions of moisture and possibly some slight frost damage to the foliage make it likely that some botrytis may develop, spraying is resorted to before damage is done.

Botrytis blight shows different types of symptoms, all of which need careful watching. When first emerging and when the young shoots are from five to seven inches tall, the entire growing point can be destroyed. Such plants make no further growth during the current season. If the diseased parts are removed it is quite likely that the plants will grow again the next spring.

A less serious blight is the botrytis leaf spot. This is directly correlated with the degree of susceptibility of the plant and with local weather conditions. Flower blight or bud blight would occur later. It results from unchecked spreading of the leaf spots and can destroy both buds and flowers. Control by means of thorough spraying with Bordeaux has proved to be effective in all but the most serious cases.

Virus (Mosaic)

The other main lily disease is called virus or mosaic infection. It is prevalent in many cultivated lilies. Especially the stocks imported from abroad have shown very heavy infestations of this disease, which manifests itself by a curious mottling of the leaves and a stunted growth of the entire plant. At present no cure for this disease is known. One can prevent its spread in several ways and minimize the risk of infection by planting stock of uncertain provenance in isolation until its health is proved. The virus diseases are spread from affected to healthy plants by aphids. Moving from one plant to another they carry the virus with them. Virus diseases can be transmitted from tulips to lilies. Possibly a great many other plants may harbor virus diseases harmful to lilies.

No other group of diseases has come into prominence in such a short period. It is quite possible that virus may be spread through the pollution of the water used to irrigate our plants. Scientists have not been able, as yet, to develop techniques for isolating and identifying virus in dilute solutions, although it is known that it often is there. The effects of pesticides, insecticides, and detergents, and their relation to virus are, as yet, little understood. Their removal from water sources is practically impossible. Black as the picture is, it is definitely possible to control the spread of virus diseases in lilies. This can be done by using one of the many fungicides, new types of which are being introduced almost yearly. Some of these substances leave an unpleasant odor in the garden. Others seem to affect the flavor of fruit and nearby vegetables. Still others are extremely dangerous to use and the tolerance of lilies to these chemicals is still a matter of conjecture. None of them should be used without checking with local experts and without full realization of the risk involved.

While at the present time it is impossible to cure virus disease once it is present in a lily, it seems quite likely that in the near future effective chemical weapons against the disease will be found. Recent findings of the British Medical Research Council's London laboratories and of scientists working at Johns Hopkins University in Baltimore, Maryland, suggest that in the living cells a substance is being produced naturally, in response to a primary virus infection. The substance extracted from the fluid surrounding the infected cells is capable of protecting others against infection.

Because it was possible to interfere with virus infection, the substance has been called "interferon." It is quite possible that from further studies a single drug may be developed for both the prevention and treatment, as well as possibly a cure, for the entire range of virus diseases—at least in plants.

Virus Symptoms. The most obvious virus symptoms, shown by a large number of species and hybrids, are a mottling of the leaves with lighter colored streaks or spots and a distortion of the stem, leaves, and flower. The mottling is seen in practically all *L. tigrinum* in our gardens and in all stocks of L. *x testaceum*. The flower distortion is quite evident in *L. formosanum,* where it causes the flower to split. In *L. auratum* varieties we find infection, during the current growing season, showing up immediately. Here the tip of the plant bends downward, the leaves turn dark purple and may drop, leaving a bare stem. Late season infection may not show the same year, but will be quite evident the next season, when mottled leaves and distorted flowers will be produced. Since *L. formosanum* is extremely sensitive to current season infection and shows the symptoms quite clearly, it has been used by us as an indicator—to reveal the presence of lily or related virus in the garden.

In diagnosing virus great care should be taken not to confuse the symptoms with those of *chlorosis*. This is a deficiency disease, a condition produced by many causes in which the normal green of the leaf is replaced by pale green or yellow, or patches of pale green or yellow. In our experience this condition arises when too much free lime is in the soil, or too high a pH condition exists rendering the iron necessary to the plant unavailable to it. We have successfully used iron chelates, available from most of the garden stores.

There is a great deal of variation, both in the susceptibility of lilies to virus and their tolerance to it. The ability to grow, in spite of virus infections, is quite noticeable in many of the newer hybrids.

In our extensive trials and field plantings we have observed that four broad groups of lilies can be listed. Some lilies seem to be completely immune to virus or are so highly resistant that virus presents no problem in their cultivation. This group includes *L. hansoni, L. pardalinum,* and *L. davidi*. The second group does have virus, but is not affected to the point that it shows marked mottling or spotting of the leaves, nor does it show a lowering of vitality, size, or substance qualities. This group would include the Mid-Century Hybrids; selected clones of *L. tigrinum, L. candidum,* and also hybrids such as L. x T. A. Havemeyer. The third group, which includes the Aurelian Hybrids, the Olympics, the Preston, and Bellingham Hybrids, and several others, will acquire virus but survive for many years. Finally, the fourth group, including *L. auratum, formosanum, japonicum,* and several American species, is extremely susceptible. Recent hybrids of these species have already demonstrated a far greater ability either to live with virus or resist it strongly. They can be classed with group 3 or even group 2.

It is important to remember that, planted in suitable locations in well-prepared soils, healthy lilies will show a remarkable resistance to all pests and diseases and need not be sprayed at all. Furthermore, raised from seed, healthy lilies are and remain healthy until exposed to virus. The following quotation from the Royal Horticultural Society's Journal by E. H. M. Cox, a well-known British authority, is of interest.

CLEAN GROUND AND L. auratum

We are absolutely certain that the older and the longer cultivated the garden, the more essential it is to plant all lilies in clean ground, which has not known a lily bulb for years. On several occasions we have planted lilies in the same ground after a lapse of two or three years only to find them disappear in a year or two with virus. As between the wars we used to plant batches of the notoriously infected *L. auratum platyphyllum* from Japan, it is not surprising that much of our soil is suspect.

Four years ago Mr. de Graaff sent us six bulbs of virus-free *L. auratum platyphyllum* and we decided to give them a fair chance of survival. We made a new bed in age-old turf right in the open in full exposure and at the edge of a frost pocket. The bulbs have never been shifted. This year the left-hand group of three carried 166 individual flowers on ten stems, the right-hand group 177 individual flowers on eleven stems.

Other lily diseases, mentioned in literature, such as lily rosette, necrotic fleck, and black scale do not occur in this country or, if they do, would present so obvious a picture of strongly diseased or dying plants that any gardener would remove them without delay. Lily rust, often reported, has never been a problem in our gardens. We suspect that often slight frost damage is mistaken for evidence of "rust." Obviously such damaged foliage is extremely susceptible to fungus attacks. If frost damage is noticed or signs of infection, that look like "rust" or "leaf spots," are noticed, an immediate application of Bordeaux spray is indicated. This and a change in the weather—a few, dry sunny days—will usually give complete control.

The last lily disease to discuss is fusarium basal rot. This rot attacks the bulb usually at the basal plate and spreads into the scales so that the whole bulb falls apart. In our opinion there is a definite correlation between basal rot and virus. Obviously, too, mechanical or insect damage to the bulbs and especially to the root plate will give a ready entry to basal rot organisms. It is amazing, however, how bulbs that are even seriously infected will often grow and recover. Once the new roots are becoming established, the plant will form new scales and grow. There is little doubt that the organism causing the rot remains in the soil for years. When lilies fail to grow and basal rot, not just mice or rodents, is suspected as the cause, then other lilies should not be planted in the same spot.

While there is no cure known for the rot, it can often be carefully cut out of the bulb (or affected scales removed with any diseased part of the basal plate). A dip in a dilute solution of formalin (40 per cent formaldehyde, commercial grade), of one part formalin to fifty parts of water, will clean up surface contamination and the utensil (knife or even hands) used—thus preventing further spread of the disease. Infected soil can be cleaned by drenching with the same formalin solution. Plant not less than one week after soil treatment.

Related rots are tip rots and storage rots—in most cases caused by mechanical injury. Bulbs so damaged usually will grow normally, and under good conditions of soil, climate, and drainage the plant will soon outgrow such symptoms.

A last condition which should be mentioned here is called fasciation. This is a condition where the stem of a lily flattens out and seems to be composed of several stems grown together. The number of flowers is generally very much increased and may be as high as several times the normal crop.

Such abnormal stems are called *fasciated,* and *fasciation* is something that occurs quite often in lilies. The cause of this condition is not known. It may be due to unusually strong bulb growth which normally would lead to a division of the bulb in several parts, each one of which would flower. If such a division is interrupted, due to unusual climatic or soil conditions, the stems will grow just the same, but will not have separated. The following year the plants will usually produce normal stems and no more than a normal number of flowers. Since fasciated lily stems are abnormal and ugly, they should be beheaded before the flowers come out.

In recent years we have noted that the tendency to form fasciated stems may be a genetic factor. The tendency is inherited to a greater than normal extent and the incidence of fasciation in certain strains of hybrid origin is becoming quite noticeable. Obviously the use of fasciated plants in hybridizing should be avoided.

Frost Injury

In some sections of our country and in many areas abroad late spring frost can severely injure lilies just emerging. Damage from frost can look very much like virus or nematode injuries and care should be taken to make the correct diagnosis. Since damaged foliage affords an opportunity for *botrytis* to attack, it may be worthwhile to cut the infected sections. Using a very sharp knife or small scissors, many plants not severely injured can be made to look quite respectable.

Certain lily species and their hybrids, notably *L. regale* and *L. hansoni,* and related varieties, emerge very early. If frequent frost damage can be expected, care should be taken to select late-emerging types and fit the variety selection to the climate. Air drainage is of paramount importance in frost control and protection. Plant on a slope or in locations where air is not stagnant—never in low places where cold air will settle.

We have used our sprinkling system with good effect to protect lily plantings against frost. While the temperature cannot be raised much in this manner, the water has a tempering influence and the ice, formed on the surface of the leaves, protects the tender foliage. It is only when the foliage itself freezes and the cells are ruptured that damage occurs. Smoke pots, bales of hay, saturated with oil and set afire, and even large fans have been used by us to protect particularly valuable hybrid lilies, planted inadvertently in low or exposed places. Water seems to have given us the best protection and, at least, using it gave us the satisfaction that we had tried to the best of our ability to protect our lilies.

PESTS

Ants. In our experience ants do not directly harm the lilies. They do, however, occur together with aphis and may carry them from plant to plant. They can be easily controlled with chlordane.

Aphids. As discussed under the virus heading in our disease section, aphids are a primary factor, if not the only one, in the spread of virus diseases. Control and, if possible, complete eradication of all aphids feeding on lilies is therefore of great importance. Both Malathion and Lindane have been used by us with excellent results. The newer systemic poisons, such as Thimet, which are absorbed and translocated in the plants, show great promise. Systox is another proprietary pest control that has proved itself. These materials, similar to parathion, are formulated as an emulsifiable concentrate. These systemic poisons are extremely dangerous. They should not be used in the garden without taking all the precautions suggested on page 157.

Bulb Mites. The loose structure of lily bulbs renders them susceptible to infestations of the lily or bulb mite. The resulting damage opens the way to various bacteria, causing rots, and to fungus diseases. Clean bulbs planted on well-prepared, well-drained soils will not be affected.

Lily Thrips. Lily thrips may cause considerable damage, before their presence is known. They can be controlled with D.D.T. and, if present between the bulb scales, a light fumigation with methyl bromide may have to be resorted to.

Nematodes. Nematodes, microscopic worms that can do untold damage to crops, already cost the American farmer a tenth of all he grows. Damaging the roots and basal plates of lilies, they afford entry to fusarium, fungus, and rots. Their relationship with these disease-causing organisms and of these again with virus has by no means been fully studied. Water from many rivers carries nematodes. They breed in sewage-disposal plants, among other places, and escape into streams. These nematodes carry disease-causing bacteria and viruses. Chlorination does not kill them.

Before discussing specific control measures for nematodes, it might first be better to outline the types of injury caused by nematodes and how they may be spotted.

General symptoms of nematode injury, regardless of crop or culture conditions, are similar to those caused by many other agents. Stunt of top growth, little leaves, and reduced flower production and size are symptoms caused by any of the root feeding nematodes. Chlorosis, resembling iron deficiency or a deficiency for other nutrients, is quite often apparent. An increased susceptibility to other diseases often accompanies heavy nematode infections.

It should be pointed out that a crop parasitized by nematodes is seldom uniformly affected. Rather, a single area or several areas, in the garden will exhibit these symptoms. All parts of a planting will not necessarily show symptoms of injury even though cultural practices have been identical throughout. The reasons why nematodes will build up in one spot and not in another are not known, but a number of research workers are attempting to shed some light on this problem. It should also be pointed out that often a high population of nematodes can exist without causing any apparent injury in one case while causing heavy losses in another.

Of the specific diseases caused by nematodes, the best known is the root-knot disease. Symptoms of this disease are galled and swollen roots. These galls are caused by the feeding of the nematodes within root tissue. It is thought that an esophageal secretion initiates this swelling. Root-knot nematodes invade roots while worm-shaped larvae feed and undergo a series of molts during which they swell to nearly round females or become very long, slender males. The females may lay several thousand eggs but probably average 500–600. Each egg is capable of developing into an egg-laying female. With new generations occurring constantly because of favorable growing conditions, this nematode can be an especially severe problem in greenhouses.

Another group of nematodes causes lesions and death of root tissue. These nematodes include the meadow or lesion nematodes, spiral nematodes, ring nematodes, and lance nematodes. Others may, from time to time, cause this type of injury also. Among these, the meadow nematodes, Pratylenchus spp., are probably the most common. They penetrate root tissues, killing cells as they go. They then move up and down inside the root, feeding, laying eggs, and destroying additional cells. These nematodes do not become swollen but retain their wormlike shape. Spiral, lance, and ring nematodes do not usually enter the root but may partly penetrate several cells deep. All of these forms remain worm-shaped during their life cycle.

Devitalization of Roots. Ectoparasites, or those nematodes which remain entirely outside the root and feed strictly from outside, include the dagger, stunt, stubby-root, and pin nematodes. These nematodes generally cause a devitalization of roots resulting in stunted tips and reduced root systems. Frequently no symptom of root injury is evident although the nematode is causing severe stunting and reduced vigor in the plant. One of the dagger nematodes, Xiphinema diversicaudatum, causes galls similar to root-knot galls.

Other nematodes may be found associated with plant injury. The same plant disease symptoms would be caused by them as those described above so that a discussion of them at this point is unnecessary. However, the foliar nematodes deserve mention. These nematodes live in the soil but when a suitable host is present, they move up the stem in a film of water, invade stems, leaves, and flowers and completely destroy these plant parts. The most common of these is the chrysanthemum foliar nematode but there are also species which will attack begonias, cyclamen, African violet, ferns, and lilies. Control of foliar nematodes is best accomplished by keeping foliage dry and not providing the water film necessary for nematode movement. Parathion has also been effective in keeping these pests in check.

Control of Root Attacks. Control of root-attacking nematodes is best accomplished through the use of sterilized soil, nematode-free planting stock and sanitation. Soil may be adequately sterilized with steam, methyl bromide, chloropicrin, Vapam, or Mylone. Any of these methods will give satisfactory nematode control.

The material marketed as Nemagon by the Shell Chemical Company and as Fumagone by the Dow Chemical Company may be applied as a soil drench and then watered in with about two inches of water.

A new material which has shown a great deal of promise may be available in another year or two. This material is under development by the American Cyanamid Company. It is an organophosphate which is applied to the soil in granular formulation, or as a drench. It has also shown a high degree of insecticidal activity.

Sanitation is an important control in that nematode-diseased plants and soil from infested areas should not be placed on any other. This procedure merely serves to disseminate nematodes throughout a garden. Tools used in infested soil should not be used in other soil unless they are thoroughly washed. Nematodes are small and are easily carried about in soil adhering to garden tools.

Rodents. We have found that *benzene hexachloride* keeps the rodents away. One good spraying of a field of lilies was sufficient to make all the moles leave and no sign of them, or of field mice, has been seen in this field for several months.

In the smaller gardens mice can be controlled with poison grain, placed in their runs or in the mole runs they use. Moles should be trapped. Gophers, that can do great damage to lily plantings, have been successfully controlled and eradicated by us with methyl bromide. This material is now available in small cans and the gas can be injected in the runs and burrows. Extreme care should be taken with methyl bromide as it is extremely poisonous, has cumulate effects and no odor. Empty cans should be discarded and put out of reach.

Symphilids. These very small insects are extremely difficult to eradicate. The number can be reduced by spraying with lindane or benzene hexachloride.

It cannot be repeated often enough that healthy plants, growing in well-drained, rich, and porous soils, will need very little if any care and attention. The lilies themselves, both the foliage and bulb, contain a juice that is poisonous and has shown great promise as an insecticide. While it is, apparently, ineffective against aphids, it does show a slow, but considerable, insecticidal effect against such insects as the Colorado potato beetle larvae and cockroaches.

Fully aware of the great danger inherent in the modern insecticides, the hybridizers are working toward more and better virus-immune and virus-resistant lilies. Similarly, all breeding effort is directed toward raising plants more strongly resistant to bulb rots, leaf diseases, and toward the encouragement of greater vigor. Starting with good garden lilies, obtained from dependable sources, planted under good conditions, no spraying, dusting or special disease- and pest-control measures will be necessary. Already lilies have shown themselves to be fully as easy to grow as any other cultivated garden plants. The new hybrids are showing the way toward even better performance.

Safety precautions when handling all insecticides can be summed up as follows:

1) Do not swallow or get in eyes, on skin or on clothing.
2) Do not breathe dust or spray mist.
3) Wear clean rubber gloves and clean protective clothing; replace gloves frequently and destroy used gloves.
4) When recommended by the manufacturer, wear a face mask or respirator approved for insecticide protection.
5) Wash thoroughly with soap and water after handling and before eating and smoking.
6) Observe the directions on the label at all times.
7) Consult your physician about obtaining an adequate supply of $\frac{1}{100}$ grain atropine tablets for emergency use. Atropine is the emergency antidote for first-aid treatment of insecticides of the phosdrin-type poisoning.
8) In all cases of suspected poisoning, call a physician at once.
9) Lock all insecticides before and after use. Make the supply completely inaccessible to children and all unauthorized personnel.

Extreme as all these precautions may seem, it is a fact that annually many children die from insecticide poisoning and that harm done by even minute quantities inhaled or absorbed through the skin, because of their cumulative effect, may be considerable.

We have, in most instances, abstained from giving exact directions as to dosage and frequency of application. It is our belief that the gardener, who feels he must use a variety of dangerous pesticides, will do much better to study, each time, the manufacturer's recommendations as they appear on the containers he purchases. Dosage and methods change all the time. They should never be memorized. Check each time you use any of the new garden products and make sure that it cannot get into the hands of others, not fully acquainted with the inherent danger.

A list of insecticides and fungicides follows. We must repeat most emphatically that, while we have used these with excellent results, we cannot guarantee in any way that they will be equally effective under different conditions. The manufacturer's recommendations should be most carefully followed to insure effectiveness of the product and safety to the user.

FUNGICIDES AND INSECTICIDES

Aldrin   Insecticide effective in control of insects in the soil.

Arasan   A disinfectant dust effective for use on injured bulbs.

BHC   (benzene hexachloride). Wettable powder preparations have been used in nurseries for the control of weevils, leaf miners, thrips, certain aphids, chrysanthemum gall midge, earwigs, and other soil pests. These preparations should be used as indicated on the containers.

Bordeaux Mixture   A fungicide of great value in controlling plant diseases. The powder form that is sometimes available ready to be mixed with water at the time of spraying is not recommended.

Captan   A general fungicide which prevents rots, damping off, etc., but not rusts.

*Chlordane   The most outstanding use of Chlordane has been in its remarkable control of ants and earwigs. Also effective against weevils, leaf miners and thrips.

*DDT   (dichloro-diphenyl trichloroethane) has been used rather extensively by nurserymen, especially for the control of caterpillars such as the omnivorous looper, azalea leaf miner, oak moth; weevils; thrips, leafhoppers, plant bugs, earwigs and the crawlers of certain scale insects such as the oystershell scale.

Ferbam   A fungicide sold under trade names such as Fermate, Carbamate and Kerbam Black. It is especially effective against rusts.

Heptachlor   an insecticide effective in control of insects in the soil.

Lindane   An insecticide effective against aphids.

Malathion   General insecticide for aphids, scales, mites and many others. Less toxic to warm blooded animals than DDT and others.

†Parathion   is one of the most promising materials developed for the nurseryman, but is not available to amateur gardeners because it

*Toxic to man
†Highly toxic to man

is so poisonous. Effective against mealybugs, scales, white flies, aphids, thrips, catepillars, red spider, and cyclamen mite as well as many others.

†*Systox*   an insecticide effective against aphids.

†*Terrachlor*   a material for the control of soilborne diseases.

  VAPAM or VPM   a nematodicide used to treat the soil two weeks before planting. Also destroys disease-producing fungi and most weed seeds.

†*Zineb*   a dithiocarbamate fungicide sold under such trade names as Parzate, Dithane z-78 and Du Pont Fungicide. A. Excellent for leaf spots and leaf blights.

  All of these materials should be used with great care, and exactly as directed by the manufacturers thereof. Your local county agent, extension agent, your local garden shop or nursery handling a good line of insecticides and disease-control materials will always be found ready to assist you.

I ask not for a larger garden,
But for finer seeds.
RUSSELL HERMAN CONWELL
(1843–1925)

PROPAGATION BY SEED

Of all methods of propagating lilies, growing from seed offers the most immediate advantages. One seed pod will contain 200 or more good seeds, of which 75 per cent may be expected to grow. Since one lily bulb will produce several seed pods, it is evident that this is a higher rate of increase than is possible from the twenty or so scales one bulb will produce, even if each scale multiplies fourfold.

So far there has been no evidence of transfer of virus from parent to seedlings. That means that even if nothing but virus diseased parents are available, they can be used to raise seed and the seedlings will be free from virus disease. One can thus have a fresh start and rejuvenate a stock. This cannot be done by any of the methods of vegetative propagation.

There is a variation in seedlings of a species, allowing for selection of better parents and the consequent improvement of stock over a period of years. Different species or varieties may be crossed with one another and the best members of the first generations crossed among themselves, giving a wonderful range of new forms from which to choose still better forms.

All sorts of new virtues may be infused into a group of lilies; characteristics such as enhanced height, color, shape, hardiness, vigor, and resistance to various diseases. None of these is obtainable in any other way. The only disadvantage is that the mother plant is not reproduced *exactly* in all its details, and if it were a very beautiful new variety, its progeny might not all attain the same high standard. However, this works both ways. There is and always will be room for improvement. Some of the new lilies will undoubtedly be superior to the parents.

POLLINATING

It therefore becomes evident that one may get the best results from seed sowing by selecting the best parents and crossing them. In fact, since most lilies are self-sterile—that is to say, the pollen taken from one individual will not pollinate a stigma on the same plant—it is always better to use a selected male parent for the pollen than to rely on the chance ministrations of insects and hummingbirds. This is best done by opening up a bud, removing the anthers and covering the stigma generously with dry pollen from the selected male parent. If the stigma is then covered with aluminum foil, no strange pollen has reached it and none will. It is wise, however, to save unopened anthers one day, dry them under protection from insects for another day, for use on the third, since it is obvious that a hummingbird may transfer pollen from one anther to another of a different plant, in addition to leaving some on a stigma. One might in all innocence thus pick mixed pollen.

Pollen Storage. Pollen can be held over for weeks and even months. Dr. Norma E. Pfeiffer of the Boyce Thompson Institute for Plant Research, Inc. at Yonkers, New York, has established the longevity of lily pollen at various temperatures, relative humidities, and air pressures. Her finding is that lily pollen can be kept for almost seven months, if held at a temperature of 50 degrees Fahrenheit and in a relative humidity of around 50 per cent.

The pollen can be kept dry by putting it in small medicine bottles, with a little calcium chloride covered with cotton and a little sheet of blotting paper at the bottom. Putting the dry anthers, with pollen, on the blotting paper and keeping the little bottles closed with corks, will preserve dry pollen in good condition.

We have found it advisable to dry the pollen well for several days in a warm and shaded room, with good air circulation, before putting it in the medicine bottles. A temperature of 50 degrees Fahrenheit is found in any household refrigerator.

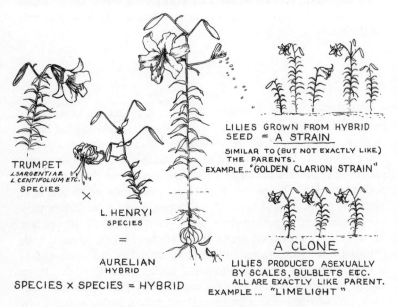

LILIES GROWN FROM HYBRID SEED = _A STRAIN_
SIMILAR TO (BUT NOT EXACTLY LIKE) THE PARENTS.
EXAMPLE..."GOLDEN CLARION STRAIN"

TRUMPET
L.SARGENTIAE
L. CENTIFOLIUM ETC.
SPECIES

×

L. HENRYI
SPECIES

=

AURELIAN
HYBRID

SPECIES × SPECIES = HYBRID

A CLONE
LILIES PRODUCED ASEXUALLY BY SCALES, BULBLETS ETC.
ALL ARE EXACTLY LIKE PARENT.
EXAMPLE ... "LIMELIGHT"

How lily hybrids, strains and clones are developed.

If in doubt about the quality of pollen stored for some time, then a simple test will reveal if it is still alive and in good condition. Take some of the stigmatic fluid from the same lily species or hybrid that produced the pollen and place it on a glass slide or piece of polyethylene film. Put some of the pollen on the sticky fluid and, if alive, it will germinate in a short time. Examination through a magnifying glass, small hand lens or a low-powered microscope will reveal if the pollen is alive.

Labeling of Crosses. All crosses should be labeled immediately, thus: name of seed parent x name of pollen parent. If this order is adhered to, the "x" always means "pollinated by," which may be valuable information later on, especially in cases of partial sterility. Further, the label is complete and may be detached with

Hybridizing. *The art of hybridizing lilies is not difficult. Pollen from the anthers of one flower is applied to the stigma of another, from which the pollen sacs have been removed. Each flower stem is carefully labeled, and placed in a cellophane bag to prevent any other pollen from reaching it. In a few weeks, if the cross has been successful, the seed pods will have formed, and bags may be removed. (For more details, see text.)*

the seed, giving all necessary information without additional writing. When the flower parts become wilted and detachable, remove them, for the decaying remains are most susceptible to botrytis and may transfer this fungus disease to the new pod. Spraying with Bordeaux mixture, or some other approved fungicide, is most desirable.

The first indication of probable success in pollination is that the pedicel bends upward and the seed pod becomes vertical and dark green. Continued swelling of the pod with its walls parallel—not tapering at the base—is the next good omen; but success is only certain after harvesting, when one can separate the heavier seeds with full endosperm and embryos from the chaff. In compatible kinds, all seeds may obviously be good, but where they are not compatible, lots of chaff and few heavy seeds appear. These few heavy seeds may be the rare new forms being sought, and should be treated as carefully as possible.

A good lily seed consists of endosperm—a store of food material—enclosing an embryo visible as a thick line all or part of the way across the seed. In some hybrids, the fertilization process in the ovule is never completed and the endosperm develops without an embryo to use it. Conversely, the embryo may develop without the endosperm. In neither case can the young plant develop under normal conditions; but where such cases have been found, the cross has been repeated, the embryos have been cut out of the half-grown green seeds and implanted into agar cultures. Here, under similar conditions to those in which orchid seedlings are nurtured, these embryos grow until they are transplantable into ordinary soil.

Harvesting the Seed

Harvesting the seed crop calls for care. If the pods have been sprayed frequently, or if the weather is dry, they should be left on till just ready to split. By this time, the seeds are brown and nearly ripe. Then is the best time to pick and dry off in a warm room. If left longer, the pods open and the unprotected seeds are exposed to damp and botrytis infection. If picked sooner, the green seeds may dry too rapidly and be difficult to germinate.

By the time any fungus is visible on the outside of the pod, the

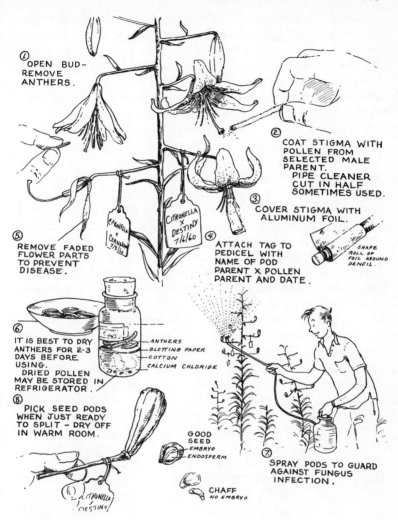

① OPEN BUD – REMOVE ANTHERS.

② COAT STIGMA WITH POLLEN FROM SELECTED MALE PARENT.
PIPE CLEANER CUT IN HALF SOMETIMES USED.

③ COVER STIGMA WITH ALUMINUM FOIL.

SHAPE. ROLL OF FOIL AROUND PENCIL.

④ ATTACH TAG TO PEDICEL WITH NAME OF POD PARENT X POLLEN PARENT AND DATE.

⑤ REMOVE FADED FLOWER PARTS TO PREVENT DISEASE.

CITRONELLA X GERANIUM 7/3/60

CITRONELLA X DESTINY 7/6/60

⑥ IT IS BEST TO DRY ANTHERS FOR 2-3 DAYS BEFORE USING.
DRIED POLLEN MAY BE STORED IN REFRIGERATOR.

ANTHERS
BLOTTING PAPER
COTTON
CALCIUM CHLORIDE

⑧ PICK SEED PODS WHEN JUST READY TO SPLIT – DRY OFF IN WARM ROOM.

GOOD SEED
EMBRYO
ENDOSPERM

CHAFF
NO EMBRYO

⑦ SPRAY PODS TO GUARD AGAINST FUNGUS INFECTION.

CITRONELLA X DESTINY

Developing new lilies: the details of pollinating.

seeds also are infected and *useless*. Seeds sticking together indicate the presence of fungus. Separating them and drying is no cure. It appears that the collection of fungus threads—the botrytis mycelium—invests the seed coat and ceases active growth as the seed dries. When sown, it quickly resumes activity, permeates the endosperm and makes a rounded black sclerotium—a hard resting body—which sooner or later produces spores to infect the foliage of healthy plants. Sometimes—and this has been frequently observed—germination takes place successfully, if somewhat weakly, before the embryo is destroyed. Then the tip of the cotyledon, the last part to emerge from the endosperm, is infected and like a smoldering candlewick, consumes itself and a cloud of spores is liberated to poison the surrounding seedlings.

This attack is so minute, so quick, so insidious, and so little recognized, that only careful and regular inspections and the prompt removal of any weak or laggard seedlings, together with protective sprayings of Captan or Parzate, can save the bulk of the crop. Since even these mild sprays harden and check the expansion of the growing cotyledons, it is best, if possible, to avoid their use. It is therefore advisable to grow only clean seed in the first place, and to delay spraying until the first infection is seen.

No spray can stop the progress of botrytis, once it is in the tissues, so diseased leaves should be removed, but a coating of spray can kill or inhibit germination of spores. A dry atmosphere and bright sun will also prevent germination of the spores. These grow only when some moisture is present and they greatly slow down the growth in the leaves. Once botrytis has attacked a juicy stem or seed pod, it rarely can be halted.

Seed which is unusually light, or appears to have an exceptional amount of chaff mixed with it, should be examined to see whether or not embryos are present and the seed is viable. This is easily done by placing the seed on a heavy piece of paper or frosted glass, with a strong light coming from below. Spread the seed out and if there are embryos, they will show up prominently as dark lines running lengthwise in the middle of the seed. Seed which does not exhibit these dark lines, or embryos, will not germinate and should be discarded. If proper precautions in hand pollinating the flowers have been taken, most varieties and species of garden lilies yield heavy plump seed with large, dark embryos embedded in the endosperm.

After the pods have ripened, seed is gathered and stored. Some types may be sown at once, in an outdoor frame, and will germinate in a few weeks. Plants shown here were photographed September 22, four months after sowing. Seeds were held over winter in a refrigerator.

Seed Sowing

Before any attempt is made to raise lily seeds, the grower should ascertain to which class the seeds belong. The commonest lilies germinate within three to six weeks; but others may take as long as eighteen months before appearing and may long since have been thrown away as failures. Since some of the most beautiful lilies belong to this latter class, such a mishap must be avoided.

In the following paragraphs we will discuss the classes to which the seeds belong. As stated in Chapter 6, pages 81–85:

Germination can be *below* ground: In this case the first formed leaves of the plant, forming part of the embryo and the seed, remain underground. The food stored in the seed, around the embryo, is transferred to the part of the stem between the first formed leaves and the root. There a tiny bulb is formed, from the center of which emerges the first true leaf. This type of germination is called *hypogeal.*

Germination can be *above* ground: Here the first formed leaves of the plant absorb food from the seeds. They elongate rapidly, appear above ground, become green and leaflike and free themselves from the remains of the seed to take on the functions of a leaf. This is called *epigeal* germination.

Germination can be delayed for several months or it can be immediate—that is to say, the seeds sprout within a period of from four to six weeks or so.

In most quickly germinating lilies the embryo first pushes out of the seed a rooting tip, which goes on down into the ground; then an almost indiscernible node, the future bulb, which follows it; and then, all in the same piece, a long, flat, doubled-up strap-shaped cotyledon, which elongates rapidly upward above the soil, becomes green and finally straightens itself and leaves the exhausted endosperm and seed coat behind. As soon as it turns green, it helps in the nourishment of the new plant. Next, true basal leaves are produced and the plant rapidly begins to grow.

In the more slowly germinating seeds, germination follows a rather different pattern. Not always, but usually after a definite period at a high temperature, about 70 degrees or so, the *root* end

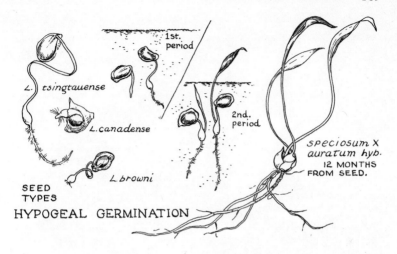

1st. period

L. tsingtauense

L. canadense

2nd. period

L. browni

speciosum X *auratum hyb.* 12 MONTHS FROM SEED.

SEED TYPES

HYPOGEAL GERMINATION

Details of germination of Hypogeal (slow) and Epigeal (quick) germinating types of lilies.

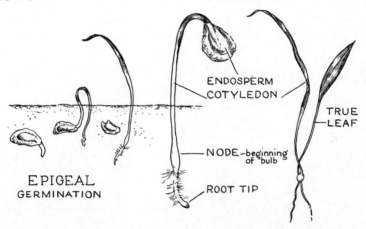

ENDOSPERM COTYLEDON

TRUE LEAF

NODE-beginning of bulb

ROOT TIP

EPIGEAL GERMINATION

of the embryo emerges from the seed below the soil, turns down and swells out into a small bulb. During the process the root tip at its end is activated and grows on down into the soil. Then, after a resting period, from inside this tiny bulb a broad-bladed true leaf is formed and sent up into the open air, to expand and

Slower growing types may be sown in pots or flats and treated according to the requirements of the types of lilies involved. Seedlings differ widely in time required for emergence, and in appearance.

manufacture carbohydrate foods for the complete nourishment of the new plant. The cotyledon in this case remains short, underground, white, and acts only as a link to transmit the food of the endosperm to the bulb. Like most plant tissues, however, when exposed to light, it can turn green and sometimes in some species, is longer than one would expect.

At this stage, these under-ground germinators are divided into two classes, "Immediate" and "Delayed." Some species, such as *browni australe, parryi,* and *speciosum,* do not rest, but continue growth and, in general, are reasonably prolific in the number of leaves produced in the first season. They may be treated with the above-ground germination group, but take two or three weeks longer to show up.

The majority of lilies which germinate under ground go into a resting stage after the high temperature start and wait—with roots in the soil and a plump store of food—till after the arrival of cold weather. Then they push up a broad-bladed leaf, gambling all their scanty reserves on it. If this leaf attains a certain size, another larger one will be sent up; but if not, that is all the above-ground growth made for the season. If this first leaf remains sound throughout the season, the young bulb will attain the size of a pea, or perhaps that of a hazel nut, and be large enough to grow an aerial leafy stem the next year. If not, a sparse succession of larger basal leaves may feed the young bulb to an equal size.

One rarely gets a full germination of seeds of this class. This may be a wise provision of nature. It is a common occurrence in our nursery to dig a seed bed three and a half years after sowing in June and find seeds just forming tiny bulbs. Obviously some are held in reserve in case of failure. The seed germination is divided as follows:

Types of Seeds

Epigeal	Immediate	1.
Epigeal	Delayed	2.
Hypogeal	Immediate	3.
Hypogeal	Delayed	4.

GERMINATION TABLE I.

Epigeal—Immediate—which includes the following species:

amabile	nobilissimum
Aurelian Hybrids	nepalense
bakerianum	papilliferum
callosum	philadelphicum
cernuum	philippinense
concolor	primulinum
davidi	pumilum
delavayi	regale
duchartrei	sargentiae*
formosanum	speciosum v. gloriosoides
lankongense	sulphureum
leichtlini	taliense
leucanthum*	tigrinum
longiflorum	wallichianum
Mid-Century Hybrids	wardi
neilgherrense	wilsoni

* Slow and irregular. See also Table 2.

TABLE 2

Epigeal—Delayed—including the following:

Aurelian Hybrids	leucanthum
candidum	pyrenaicum
carniolicum	pomponium
chalcedonicum	sargentiae
henryi	

TABLE 3

Hypogeal—Immediate

browni v. australe	parryi
Golden Chalice Hybrids	speciosum

TABLE 4

Hypogeal—Delayed—including: 1

auratum	monadelphum
bolanderi	nevadense
browni	nobilissimum
bulbiferum	occidentale
canadense	pardalinum
columbianum	parvum
distichum	philadelphicum
grayi	polyphyllum
hansoni	rubellum
humboldti	rubescens
japonicum	speciosum
kelloggi	superbum
maritimum	tsingtauense
martagon	washingtonianum
michiganense	

When sowing seeds, one must have a clear idea of the results desired, particularly whether one wishes maximum size, full germination, maximum number per square inch in the facilities available and the ultimate aim in numbers and sizes of mature bulbs. Commercially, one must consider expense against possible results.

Sowing Methods for Tables 1 and 3

Full germination of most "immediate" kinds is undoubtedly best obtained by sowing as soon as ripe. Lily seeds are usually plentiful and ripen in October and November, just at a time when it is difficult and expensive to maintain the warmth and conditions in a greenhouse most conducive to their success. A major concern is the specter of botrytis in the seed beds, always a threat during the dull months; as well as the slowing down of growth during winter. Therefore, unless one has a very small quantity of doubtful seed, or desires the quickest possible growth regardless of expense, it is recommended that lily seeds of the "Immediate Germination" type be sown in February. Given sound clean seed, most lilies of

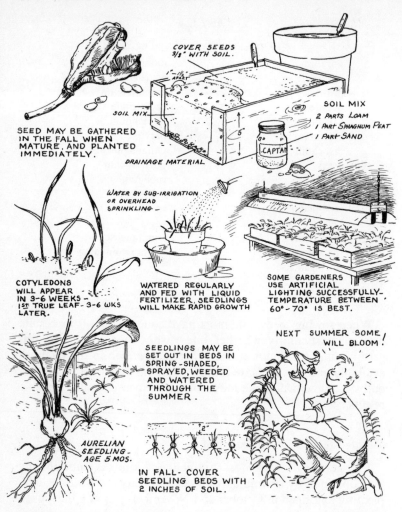

COVER SEEDS 3/8" WITH SOIL.

SEED MAY BE GATHERED IN THE FALL WHEN MATURE, AND PLANTED IMMEDIATELY.

SOIL MIX

DRAINAGE MATERIAL

SOIL MIX
2 PARTS LOAM
1 PART SPHAGNUM PEAT
1 PART SAND

CAPTAN

WATER BY SUB-IRRIGATION OR OVERHEAD SPRINKLING -

COTYLEDONS WILL APPEAR IN 3-6 WEEKS - 1ST TRUE LEAF- 3-6 WKS LATER.

WATERED REGULARLY AND FED WITH LIQUID FERTILIZER, SEEDLINGS WILL MAKE RAPID GROWTH

SOME GARDENERS USE ARTIFICIAL LIGHTING SUCCESSFULLY- TEMPERATURE BETWEEN 60°-70° IS BEST.

SEEDLINGS MAY BE SET OUT IN BEDS IN SPRING-SHADED, SPRAYED, WEEDED AND WATERED THROUGH THE SUMMER.

NEXT SUMMER SOME WILL BLOOM!

AURELIAN SEEDLING- AGE 5 MOS.

IN FALL- COVER SEEDLING BEDS WITH 2 INCHES OF SOIL.

Growing lilies from seed: how to start the Epigeal or quick-germinating types indoors.

this type will do well in special flats 5 inches deep. Seeds should be dusted with Captan before sowing.

The soil should be a fairly porous mixture of two parts loam, one part sphagnum peat, one part sand; and it should have a nearly neutral reaction. If flats are to be fed with light doses of an appropriate liquid fertilizer, none need be added to the soil mixture.

In flats, the seeds may be sown at the rate of one to the square inch, or one to two square inches, (i.e., one and a half inches apart each way) and covered with about ⅜ inches of soil. The soil must be level in the flats and the flats level on the bench, so that, when applied, water will soak in evenly. The flats should remain undisturbed until the leaves begin to turn yellow in late October (white bulbs) or November (purple bulbs). The tiny bulbs may be taken up and, if conditions are suitable, set out in beds. If not, they may either be stored dry in the flats or removed and stored in dry peat, in polyethylene bags, at 35 to 40 degrees until February or March (white bulbs) or March and April (purple bulbs). If well grown, they should average medium walnut size and be large enough for fifty per cent to flower. At the wider distance, i.e., 1½ inches apart, all should be large enough to flower.

Alternatively, lily seeds may be sown in deep beds, 8 to 11 inches deep; and here again, the deeper the bed within these limits, the better the growth. Adequate drainage and aeration of the soil in the bed is necessary and a layer of gravel in the bottom helps greatly. Six inches apart seems to be the most satisfactory distance for the rows, though eight inches would undoubtedly produce larger, but fewer, bulbs. The percentage of seed which may be expected to germinate *promptly* in any special variety—a point at which even the specialist often has to guess—determines how thickly the seed should be sown. (Late germinating seeds are at a great disadvantage and never grow as well.) The furrow in which seeds are sown may be 2 inches wide. An average germination of three or four seeds to the inch along the row is desirable for the maximum number of bulbs which will hold their own when planted out in the field. Thinning to 2 inches apart will, however, give nearly the maximum growth for each bulb, most of which will flower freely and be sizable at the end of the second year.

The seed, as when sown in flats, should be dusted with Captan and, when sown, covered not more than ⅜ of an inch. Sowing in rows allows one to cultivate lightly between them and break up moss which often tries to overtake slow-growing lily seedlings.

In the Greenhouse. Night temperature of 60 degrees is advisable, with regular dampening of the floors to avoid excessive drying of

In commercial production, seeds are often sown directly in greenhouse benches. Those shown above are Pink Perfection Strain seedlings, five months after sowing. For the smaller grower, either professional or amateur, the ordinary flat serves equally well.

the soil in flats. In beds the prompt watering of dry edges and corners, together with gentle overhead spraying on hot days, is necessary to maintain the soil in suitable moist condition, neither too dry nor too wet. Germination will be slower in the dry areas and quite quick in the moist ones; but with too much moisture in the soil, growth will be much poorer.

Subsequent care consists of regular inspection for botrytis and aphids and prompt spraying when either is found. Malathion is the best insecticide and Parzate a very satisfactory fungicide. Captan is good, but often scorches a few young leaves. Bordeaux mixture is undoubtedly an efficient fungicide, but also hardens and slows growth of young tissues under glass, as well as being very messy on glass and blocking off light from the leaves.

Shading. Since one already has to keep an adequate shade on the greenhouse roof to protect the youngest leaves, the most susceptible parts of the plant, any heavy deposit on the older tougher leaves is a distinct disadvantage to the growth of the bulb, because it cuts out light and hinders photosynthesis.

Watering. With adequate care, watering till June or July is easy; but after that, the leaf cover is so heavy that the usual overhead watering mats the leaves together so that they do not dry out. Sprays cannot get between them and botrytis can spread very rapidly. Here some form of subirrigation is valuable, if already installed, and a trickle irrigation system is most useful, for adequate water may be given without wetting the leaves.

In general, leaf growth continues at a rapid pace till mid-August; then the numerous leaves feed the bulb. In Oregon, we remove the shade early in September and gradually reduce the water supply until by November no more is required. Too late watering after a drier period may start undesirable new stem growth from the bulbs. In fact, *L. pumilum* and *L. concolor,* and some Mid-Century types, white bulbs which mature earlier, frequently put up a stem and flower in November, nine months after sowing!

Sowing Out of Doors. Sowing of the "Immediate Germination" lilies out of doors is relatively simple and easy, but naturally results are not so quick. Seeds may be sown as soon as the soil is workable and a month earlier than the latest estimated frost of, for instance, 22 degrees Fahrenheit. It takes about a month for the seed to come up and ten degrees of frost will kill seedlings of

Seeds sown in the open are usually planted on slightly raised beds to afford more perfect drainage. Such beds may be covered with lath sash, as below, to provide shade and wind protection.

many kinds. It is good practice to sow on a gentle south-facing slope, in beds 3 feet wide, separated by 18-inch paths. After treating with Captan, the seed is scattered thinly, one inch apart, over the level, well-raked bed, and soil from the paths spread over it to a depth of about half an inch. This is then raked well back and forth with a light wooden rake until a few of the seeds show on the surface. Such raking has always been of great benefit, but it is uncertain whether this is due to a general settling of the surface or to slight lifting of the seeds in the soil, or perhaps because they become better bedded in. If they have a constant supply of moisture and plenty of minerals and fertilizer, there will be no check in the growth, even during the hottest part of the summer. Bulbs dug in the fall should provide a crop, most of which, in the common varieties, will be salable at the end of the third growing season. The seed bed must be kept evenly watered to prevent its drying out, checking the young growth.

Naturally, weeding must be carried out while weeds are small. Usually the first crop can be burned off with a flame gun just when the few earliest seedling lilies appear. The loss of one or two per cent is offset by the greater number of weeds killed; but again, like the raking, the burning must be done with skill, knowledge, and caution. Spraying with Bordeaux mixture is routine and Malathion is added to kill aphids and leaf hoppers which may bring in virus diseases.

Feeding is best done through the irrigation system, whether that be a water can or large-scale motor and pump. Seasons and soils vary, and, since sowing is done on virgin land as much as possible and virgin land differs, results are not always the same from year to year.

Young lilies like company, and a sowing of one inch apart each way is about right for a usual 50 per cent germination. It is too thick for a good germinating type or one of large growth. In general, *regale* types germinate easily and fully and *sargentiae, centifolium,* and *sulphureum* much less regularly, but their various hybrids, on an average, may give a 30 to 50 per cent germination, with individual lots ranging from 15 to 100 per cent.

Maximum size at the end of two years is obtained by leaving the young bulbs untouched, provided they have enough room and are regularly watered, fed, and sprayed throughout that period.

The greatest size for three years' growth is obtained by lifting at the end of the first year—provided that the season, soil, and treatment have been favorable—grading out the larger bulbs and planting them down for two years. Of the smaller bulbs—usually about half—many are too small to transplant well and never make salable size, even after two years. The greatest size of the greatest number of bulbs is obtained by leaving the seed bed alone for two years and then replanting for two years. Some bulbs may even be too large for a special market, but in a stock required for selection, this age and maturity are desirable. It corresponds roughly to the greenhouse-grown stock planted out at one year old and left in for two years.

At the end of the first year, well-grown seedlings may have roots long and strong enough to pull themselves deeper into the ground, but the smaller ones remain near the surface, vulnerable to frost, which in many sections of the country has considerable lifting power.

To avoid such damage it is sound practice in late autumn to remove any remaining leaves and to cover the seed beds with two inches of soil, which can be taken from the pathways between the beds.

During the second year, an appreciable number of bulbs will flower in the seed beds, but unless they are unknown hybrids which one simply must see in order to evaluate them, *all buds should be removed* as soon as they form. They should then be burned, as dead flower parts dropping into a seed bed can encourage botrytis.

Although this schedule calls for four years, two years in the seed bed and then two years in the nursery rows, with some varieties such as *L. auratum, japonicum,* and *rubellum,* it will be found that good flowering plants will not show up until about the fifth year. Small lots of these same varieties may be handled in a similar manner without field planting. Incubate and germinate the seeds indoors, as described above, and as soon as the bulbs are formed, plant them out in flats. After the flats have been planted, stack them out of doors or in a cool basement and leave them from four to six weeks. This is to reproduce the effect of their natural winter. At the end of the six weeks bring them back into the house, or into heat 55–60 degrees, and the true leaves should

In a field of hundreds of thousands of seedlings there may be the one plant with some special characteristic that will make it worth selecting as the beginning of a line that may be carried on to become a new variety or a new clone.

emerge within four to six weeks. If the plants make sufficient growth the first year to form sizable bulbs, they can be picked out of the flat at the end of the first year and given more space either in other flats or planted out of doors in nursery rows or beds. This method does not gain any time over the other one, but it is much more practical for handling small quantities of these varieties.

Sowing Methods for Table 2

Delayed above-ground germination occurs in a few species and it is probable that experimentation could show that some of these require definite temperatures and conditions of moisture before responding. Few of them are commercial plants and detailed experience is lacking. Individual recommendations are listed below.

candidum } Germination is very irregular, some immediate, some in June and some in September. One may sow a lot of seed and take just the first crop; or, on a small scale, prick out the seedlings as they show up.

carniolicum
chalcedonicum
pomponium
pyrenaicum
henryi } Sow as soon as ripe in deep flats or pots, place in a cold frame, and examine for germination in early spring and from September to December. Bring into a greenhouse when growing.

Aurelian Hybrids
leucanthum
sargentiae } Some batches of seed are quick and regular, others require treatment as for candidum (See above).

Sowing Methods for Table 4

Seeds of the delayed under-ground type need altogether different treatment. Most species of this type require about three months at a temperature of 70 degrees to stimulate bulb growth, and then a cold period of six weeks at 35 to 45 degrees to stimulate leaf growth. After this the plants must look after themselves.

Before sowing, one must decide during what period of the year young, tender, shade-loving foliage will have the best chance for development and survival and time seed sowing accordingly, allowing about five months from sowing to the production of

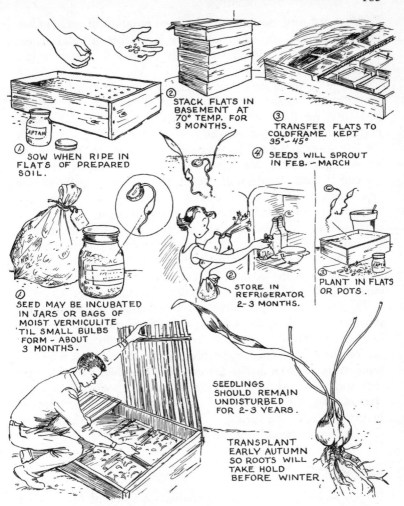

① SOW WHEN RIPE IN FLATS OF PREPARED SOIL.

② STACK FLATS IN BASEMENT AT 70° TEMP. FOR 3 MONTHS.

③ TRANSFER FLATS TO COLDFRAME KEPT 35°-45°

④ SEEDS WILL SPROUT IN FEB. - MARCH

① SEED MAY BE INCUBATED IN JARS OR BAGS OF MOIST VERMICULITE 'TIL SMALL BULBS FORM - ABOUT 3 MONTHS.

② STORE IN REFRIGERATOR 2-3 MONTHS.

③ PLANT IN FLATS OR POTS.

SEEDLINGS SHOULD REMAIN UNDISTURBED FOR 2-3 YEARS.

TRANSPLANT EARLY AUTUMN SO ROOTS WILL TAKE HOLD BEFORE WINTER.

Growing lilies from seed: two methods of starting the Hypogeal or slow-germinating type indoors.

young foliage above-ground. Seed planted the first of October, for instance, may be placed in a greenhouse at 70 degrees for three months, until the end of December, and then transferred to a frame where the temperature can be kept between 35 and 45 degrees from January first until the middle of February. In the

Pacific Northwest, normal growth above ground will begin in late February. In the Northeast, seed sown November first and treated in a similar manner, would normally begin leaf growth in late March or early April.

George L. Slate, author of *Lilies for American Gardens,* a lily specialist and breeder whose home is in Geneva, New York, suggests that for those who do not have a greenhouse, the seeds planted in flats may be stacked in the cellar of the residence for the first three months. This, of course, is practicable only for the amateur germinating a comparatively small number of seeds. At the end of three months in the cellar, the flats are transferred to a cold frame and treated in the same manner as seeds which have been in a greenhouse for this same period of time.

If seeds are to be planted out of doors and grown on without the help of artificial heat, they may be sown in flats in June or July. This gives them their initial three months at approximately 70 degrees and the coming of winter provides the second cold period. Leaf growth ensues during the following spring.

This last method approximates germination of lily seeds of this type in the wild. Some lilies, *L. martagon album* and *L. szovitsianum,* have been known to produce seed which germinated the same season the seed ripened, probably because they do not require a temperature as high as 70 degrees. It is possible, however, that they were misled by a very warm autumn, since seeds of these species ripen early. In no case, however, did the leaves appear before the following spring, so that it may be assumed that the six-weeks' cold period is an absolute necessity.

SUMMARY

Four sowing methods are available for seeds of the delayed hypogeal type:

1) Sow in flats five months before greenhouse space is available. Water, and repeat as necessary, for three months at 70 degrees in an incubator, and six weeks in a cool room at 40 degrees. Bring into the greenhouse and leaf growth will start within two weeks.

2) Incubate the seeds at 70 degrees in moist vermiculite in screw-top jars, plastic bags, or larger receptacles. After the seeds have grown and been cooled off as above, sow them with the

vermiculite in prepared flats. Most of them will come up well, but not quite so strongly, since the main roots have not had soil to feed them and the plant's reserves are at a low ebb.

3) Incubate as above, and sow the seeds in a prepared bed outside, covering half an inch deep only and providing lath house or similar shelter from frost and hot sun. This must be timed to catch good weather.

4) Sow outside in June, water and weed the beds all summer and autumn and provide lath-house shelter, as above, before leaf growth takes place, since the leaves swell early and are very vulnerable to frost injury at this stage.

Since these lilies make but little growth in their first year, except under the best greenhouse conditions, it is better not to disturb them until the end of the second year's growth. Furthermore, we have already seen that germination is very irregular and can be either the first or second year. It frequently pays to leave them undisturbed a third year for the sake of seeds which germinate later.

Many lilies of this class do not produce stem roots, and these especially benefit from being left alone. Provided one can keep the foliage healthy and the beds well fed and watered, enormous crops can be raised from a small area.

Finally, when the bulbs have attained a reasonable size, transplant them fairly early in the autumn so that their new roots take hold before the cold weather sets in.

Growing Seeds under Glass. The starting of lily seedlings under glass is usually limited to new hybrids or valuable crosses and rare species. In the case of new hybrids, there is a double advantage in starting the seeds under glass.

1) Germination is much higher and mortality from diseases and insects can be reduced.

2) By starting the seeds early in the winter, or late in the fall, the plants will be large enough to be set out in beds or rows early in the spring. By leaving them in this bed for two full years, enough bulbs will flower the second year to give the grower a good idea of what he may expect from succeeding crosses.

Recent experiments have shown that the earlier the seed is planted in the fall, the better is the germination. As a matter of fact, some growers go so far as to say that green seed gives them

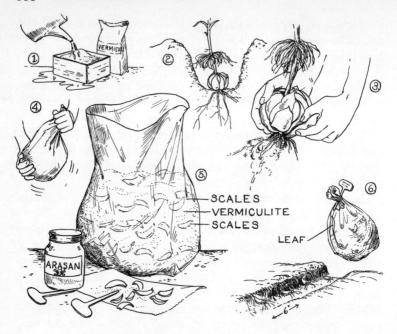

Method of propagating from scales.

the best results. This has been verified in the case of certain varieties. By collecting the seed pods early in the fall, before they are fully mature and while they are still green, removing the seed and planting it immediately, it is possible to have husky little plants up under glass before the short, dark winter days set in. By handling seeds in this manner, most varieties and most hybrid seed, will produce a high percentage of flowers on good-sized plants the second year.

PROPAGATION BY SCALES

The most rapid vegetative means of propagation of most lilies is by means of scales. This is the method most practical for amateurs and for all who grow lilies on a small scale. In many cases it is the only possible procedure. It consists simply of peeling

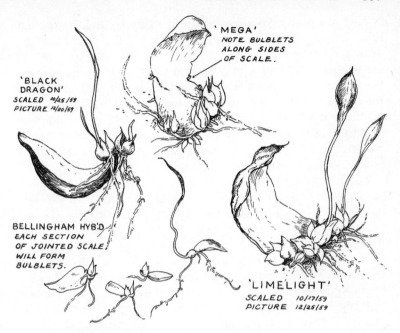

'MEGA'
NOTE BULBLETS
ALONG SIDES
OF SCALE.

'BLACK
DRAGON'
SCALED 10/25/59
PICTURE 12/20/59

BELLINGHAM HYB'D.
EACH SECTION
OF JOINTED SCALE
WILL FORM
BULBLETS.

'LIMELIGHT'
SCALED   10/17/59
PICTURE 12/25/59

Scales incubated indoors showing bulblets formed after two months.

off some of the outer scales of the lily bulb, placing them in suitable conditions of moisture and temperature and waiting for them to form small bulbs. These eventually produce roots and basal leaves.

As with everything else, this basic procedure has to be modified to suit various conditions and climates. Take, for example, the simplest case of an amateur with a few bulbs he wishes to increase in number. Sometime just before, during, or just after flowering, he should obtain a supply of vermiculite, polyethylene bags, labels, and Arasan or a similar fungicide.

The dry vermiculite is placed in a clean receptacle with drainage holes and flooded thoroughly for a few minutes. It is then allowed to stand and absorb all the moisture it can, while the excess drains off. Next day it will be in perfect condition, every grain full of water, yet no surplus remains to prevent aeration between the grains. If watered again, it will become sodden and useless.

Then the bulb may either be lifted or dug around to expose it fully, leaving the basal roots undisturbed. After discarding the dead and partly decayed outer scales, which usually are present, the next layer or layers, may be broken off carefully as near the base as possible. Since their arrangement is spiral, one has to go round and round the bulb to accomplish this. Up to half the weight of the bulb may be removed. If large and healthy, it will flower again the next year, though perhaps not so well as formerly. It may be dusted lightly with Arasan and replanted, or the soil replaced, as the case may be.

The scales are placed in a bag, with a pinch of Arasan, and are shaken gently till all raw surfaces are lightly coated. Then alternate layers of moist vermiculite and lily scales carefully spaced are placed in a polyethylene bag, which is then tied up and labeled. If this is kept at around 70 degrees, small bulbs will soon be formed on the broken bases of the scales. These will soon root and eventually send out leaves. Progress is easily observed through the polyethylene, whereas moisture is not lost. As soon as the first leaf begins to show and weather permits, the scales should be planted if possible. If planting is not possible, the bag should be cooled off to 40 to 45 degrees and held at this temperature till spring. It is best to plant each scale with bulblets and roots as one unit. Space scales six inches apart. The crop should be grown as rapidly as possible. One can often lift the two-year-old bulbs, at 9 to 10 inches circumference, and scale them again.

Commercial Methods

For larger quantities, the procedure is virtually the same, except that one has to dig the bulbs and replant the cores in an orderly manner, allowing them plenty of room. If well treated the bulbs will have developed sufficiently to permit scaling again in the second year.

When planted in the field, some stocks produce leaves by the beginning of September and sizable, well-established bulbs by winter. Frequently a small percentage will flower the next summer. For most varieties the best time to take the scales is approximately at the time the plant is in flower. Of the very late-flowering varieties, such as *L. speciosum,* it is advisable to take the scales

The operation of "scaling" consists in carefully removing the scales, by breaking them off where they are attached at the base. If the heart of the bulb is left intact, it may be replanted and will soon reestablish itself.

The removed scales are inserted in a suitable rooting medium. In a few weeks they will have begun to form new bulblets, often two or more to a scale. So, in a sense, the lily grower will have eaten his cake and still have it!

earlier. For the very early flowering forms, such as the *umbellatum-dauricum-elegans* group and their hybrids, it is advisable to take the scales later on in the summer, around the middle of July. In general, the scales should be taken early enough so that the young newly formed bulblets have time to make a good root growth in the field before the advent of winter.

Immediately after scaling, the scales should be dusted or dipped in a fungicide, such as Arasan, and planted. It is preferable to plant them where they can remain for at least another year. They will have time to make new root growth before fall, grow all the next year and can either be harvested then or be allowed to grow one more year.

An alternative method is to take the scales as soon as they have been removed from the bulbs and have been treated and pack them into trays, flats, or boxes in some rooting medium such as sand, peat moss, sphagnum, or vermiculite. The packing medium, again, should be moist, but not wet. These boxes can then be set in an incubator or in any location where there is a constant temperature of 65–70 degrees.

The boxes are examined four to five weeks after they have been in the incubator and, as soon as the roots start to form on the small bulblets, they may be sorted out and planted in the field. By using this procedure those scales which have not fully developed can be put back into the incubator. Plant out into the field only those which have well-developed roots and bulbs.

Although this method is somewhat safer than the method of planting directly into the open field, it is too costly in large commercial operations. The incubator method develops bulblets somewhat faster than field planting. It also eliminates the danger of the scales becoming too wet in the open field before they have calloused over or started to form bulblets. Temperature and moisture conditions can be carefully controlled in the incubator and the bulblets set out at exactly the right time.

A variation of the incubator system which produces plants even more quickly, is to incubate the scales and as soon as bulblets and roots are formed, to pot them up or put them into flats in plant bands in the greenhouse. In this method most varieties will make a leaf growth late in the fall and by spring will be husky little plants. When handled in this manner, many of the new hybrids will flower well the first year from scales.

IMPROVEMENT BY SELECTION: *From fifteen acres of Olympic Hybrids some five hundred extra fine plants are picked out to be used for scale propagation. These selected plants are dug when in full flower and carried out of the field.*

Here they are massed, and lug boxes are made ready to hold the scales.
Finally each bulb is scaled down to the core. The scales are then either
stored to incubate, or planted in shallow field rows. The stems, with cores
and roots attached, are heeled in to make new growth.

After lilies selected for scaling have been removed, the remaining plants are "topped" to remove flowers and so prevent seed production. This results in the plant's entire strength being used for bulb development. The topped plants have three months in which to make maximum development before winter.

Delayed Scaling. If it is undesirable to dig up the mother plants to scale, the scaling can be delayed until fall. At that time it is a simple matter to remove a few extra scales from the bulbs before the stock is replanted. Growth, however, is somewhat slower and the results are not so good as if the scales had been taken in the middle of the summer.

When scale propagation is done in the fall, the scales must be placed in a container and held over the winter in a warm room, since, if planted directly out of doors at that time of year, there is a great risk of loss from rot.

A combination of seminal and vegetative propagation is sometimes employed. First a large number of seedlings are raised. These are rigidly selected when in flower and only the very best plants are dug at that time. These are immediately scaled. Thus the stock of good plants can be increased twentyfold. By repeating this process from time to time continued improvement can be made and the high quality of a strain can be maintained.

PROPAGATION BY BULBILS

Some lilies, notably *L. tigrinum, L. bulbiferum, L. sargentiae,* and *L. sulphureum,* normally produce bulbils (small aerial bulbs) in the axils of their leaves. Concurrently, the growth of the underground bulb is less, for clearly the food cannot be deposited in two places at once. So, instead of scaling them, it is a general custom to grow them from the natural means of propagation provided by the bulbils.

In practice we immediately hit a snag, for most of these bulbils do not, till too late in the autumn, attain a size at which they can be planted. They then have too little time to root deeply enough in the ground to hold them securely against frost and heaving. If planted deeper, the tiny leaves fail to come up in the spring. Low-priced lilies, such as most of those that form bulbils, will not repay the cost of greenhouse culture on a commercial scale. Therefore, the bulbils usually have to be treated as seeds in beds and carefully protected through the first winter. Most of these species, however, have been superseded by their hybrid children, which pay much better for the necessary extra care and attention involved.

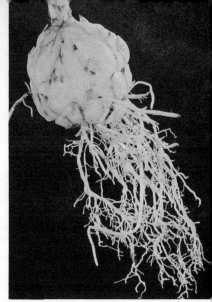

Base rooting and stem rooting bulbs.

Fortunately, special methods to stimulate the early production of larger bulbils have been evolved and applied even to some species not usually counted as bulbil producers and to their hybrids. *L. centifolium,* for instance, can be made to produce copious and large bulbils. Many of the Aurelian hybrids, particularly those based on *L. x aurelianense,* are potentially bulbil-bearing. We constantly find indications of bulbils in the Aurelian stocks and allied lilies.

Such lilies that do not readily produce normal bulbils can be propagated under glass from scales to produce small bulbs of just under flowering size. These, in turn, are started as early as possible in a warm, moist, shaded greenhouse and fed freely to produce vigorous growth. The result is an abundant and rapid production of bulbils on the small stems which can be left to reach a good size. In July or August these bulbils are sown in outside beds in time to establish themselves well before winter. All form strong roots and many produce leaves in September. They fatten appreciably before frost curtails growth above ground.

In these marginal bulbil-producing types, the production of a flower greatly reduces the bulbil-bearing potential. In this case the growing point should be pinched out when the stem is about two-thirds grown. Cutting the flower buds, however small, is too late, as but few and small bulbils will then be formed.

The largest bulbils planted in flats in July quickly make leaves in the current year and the best bulbil-bearing stems in the succeeding year.

Another outstanding advantage is that the greenhouse-grown stock, if clean to start with, can much more easily be maintained free from virus inside the greenhouse, if a normal routine of spraying and general supervision is maintained.

This method is of the greatest value for the rapid early propagation of appropriate select clones into mother stocks, after which cheaper forms of propagation may be used for actual commercial production. It is worth trying on any first class lily hybrid which has a bulbiliferous ancestor.

PROPAGATION BY NATURAL DIVISION

It is usual for all healthy lilies to reach a maximum size for the clone and then to form two noses, two growths; and a year or so later, two separate bulbs. Some, like *L. hansoni*, will separate into three or four noses or new bulbs, and multiply faster.

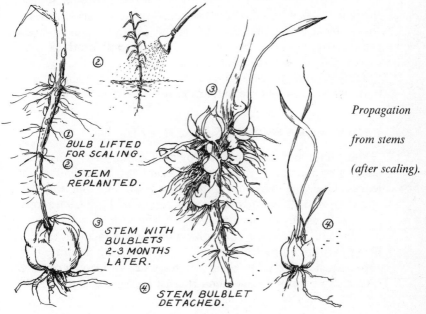

① BULB LIFTED FOR SCALING.

② STEM REPLANTED.

③ STEM WITH BULBLETS 2-3 MONTHS LATER.

④ STEM BULBLET DETACHED.

Propagation

from stems

(after scaling).

Others, when growing extremely fast, will produce smaller bulbs inside the main one, like the branches of a twig, and these in turn split off into separate bulbs.

Some of rhizomatous types, *L. pardalinum* particularly, divide very freely and each point may be separated, by cutting. Each part will then grow satisfactorily and new bulbs form in the following year.

PROPAGATION BY STEMS—NATURAL

Most lilies, but by no means all of them, naturally produce a few or many small bulbs or bulblets on the under-ground stem between bulb and point of emergence. These represent one of the main means of propagation of the most widely grown commercial lilies. Commonly, the bulblets are lifted with the main crop when it is mature, graded, and—according to size—replanted for one or more years.

Also, when bulbs are lifted in July or August for scaling, the stems with these bulblets on them may be replanted and established by watering. Since the leaves and main stem roots soon resume their function of good collection, but the main storehouse—the bulb—is gone, all the food manufactured by the leaves goes to the bulblets, which often by this means attain in their first year the size of two-year-olds. Frequently they will produce basal leaves of their own and flourish anew.

This method, be it noted, is complementary to scaling, but is only successful where the bulblets have already started.

PROPAGATION BY STEMS—ARTIFICIAL

Some lilies may be propagated by pulling out their stems intact just before blooming, removing buds and the lower half of the leaves and laying the stems in the ground with only the leafy part above ground. *L. candidum* and *L. x testaceum* have been propagated successfully in this manner.

There are, however, serious objections to this method, the first being that the bulbs are deprived of all their carbohydrate food supply, just at the time when they have drawn heavily on their reserves to build the leafy stem. It must be remembered that the roots of a plant provide only water and minerals in solution, and the leaves supply the carbohydrates so necessary to complete the food essential to growth. The one complements the other. When the leaves are removed, new growth ceases, though some of the remaining reserves are transferred from older scales to the young center bulb.

Secondly, when small bulbs are produced on the stripped parts of the stems, they are very small and, if left in the ground, are often too deeply covered to come up. If disturbed by lifting late in the autumn, and relocated at a depth suitable to their size, they require special care to avoid heaving.

The scaling method is infinitely preferable to the artificial stimulation of bulb production on stems.

PROPAGATION BY OTHER METHODS

It is possible to propagate some lilies by cutting off leaves with a small heel containing a potential bud. These are placed in light sandy soil in a cutting frame and treated as cuttings—shaded, kept moist, and fairly close. If in the particular variety or species concerned, the bud is sufficiently developed, it may be stimulated into growth and will make the equivalent of a stem bulbil. This, in turn, roots and produces leaves.

Lilies with a tendency to produce stem bulbils naturally are amenable to this method, even though there is no sign of bulbils in the axils of the leaves taken. In many others this bud does not develop fully enough ever to make a bulbil.

Another, somewhat similar method, is to cut up a lily stem into joints of four leaves and then remove all but one leaf. The stem is buried in sand in a propagating case. Success depends on the state of the axillary buds. These methods are useless for mass production, but valuable as a "last resort," when one is left with only the stem of a precious lily.

SUMMARY

In all the foregoing methods of propagation, it is most desirable to avoid any check to growth while the plant is small. With the least degree of adverse weather after transplanting, the initial push

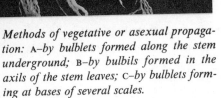

Methods of vegetative or asexual propagation: A–*by bulblets formed along the stem underground;* B–*by bulbils formed in the axils of the stem leaves;* C–*by bulblets forming at bases of several scales.*

is lost and the tiny bulb falters and ceases growth, instead of producing a steady succession of leaves and later a much larger bulb. Therefore, except where scales or seeds are started or germinated in vermiculite, as already described, and then planted out in specially protected beds, it is desirable that they should not be disturbed in their first year. Room should be allowed for this in sowing or planting of scales.

Considerable emphasis has been placed on the prevention and control of botrytis. In a rainy climate this is of paramount importance.

*It takes a highly improbable combination of many
mutations to produce a genius but a single mutation
may produce a mental defective. The likelihood of
transmission of genius to future generations is
minute compared with that of transmission of idiocy.*

AKE GUSTAFSON (1955)

LILY BREEDING

In breeding work three factors are of prime importance—the quality of the pollen used, the treatment of the seed, and control of diseases.

First, it is essential that good, clean, and "live" or viable, pollen be available. This is easily done when the two lilies we want to cross with one another are in flower on the same day. On the other hand, many lilies with characteristics that we should like to combine, flower on different days, weeks, and even months. A great deal of experimentation has recently been done with the pollen of lilies and it has been discovered that, if stored at low temperature in a dark and dry place, it can be kept alive long enough to fertilize the latest flowering lilies from the earliest varieties. This method was not known to earlier hybridizers, who consequently had to fall back on the less efficient means of forcing, that is, artificially advancing or retarding the flowering period in order to have ripe pollen. While feasible on a small scale, such systems obviously preclude mass hybridizing.

Another factor in the production of hybrid lilies is that of seed treatment to produce the greatest possible percentage of germination. Seeds of many lilies will germinate as soon as planted and throw up little shoots. Seeds of other species produce small bulbs, but make no top growth until the second year. It has been found that the latter seeds require storage for from three to six months at a temperature of about 68 degrees for the growth of the root. If then placed at a much lower temperature of 35–50 degrees for from six weeks to three months and then again at normal greenhouse temperature, the top growth appears promptly. Practically speaking, this simply means that many seeds need a warm period followed by a cold period before any top growth will form. Until recently these facts were not known to lily growers in general and hence much valuable seed, perhaps even good hybrid seed, was not treated correctly and consequently lost.

The last factor is the control of plant diseases. Briefly, virus or mosaic diseases can be so dangerous that, unless the new seedlings are grown far away from other lilies, the disease can infect the little seedlings and prevent their successful growth to maturity. Complete isolation has been found to be essential at this early stage. This is a recent discovery and one which has been of the greatest importance in the production of hybrid lilies. Still other new methods of growing seedlings have aided materially in the production of quantities of healthy plants. This applies especially to the new controls to prevent "damping off," the use of sprays and chemicals against fungus attacks, new media of growth, and methods of insect control.

Genetics

Of equal importance is our comparatively recent knowledge of the fascinating science of genetics. It is obvious that it is difficult to make the first crosses between species genetically far removed from one another. The devoted work of many amateur lily growers has shown us the possibilities inherent in these combinations. More than that, this work by lily specialists and fanciers in different parts of the world has provided the "bridges," the avenues of approach, which subsequent workers have used to obtain still better hybrids. When any one of these workers produced a genuine hybrid, a step forward was made. Backcrossed with either parent, crossed with still other species or varieties, such hybrids produced new colors and new forms, and, as explained in our chapter on hybrid lilies, often new hardiness and disease resistance.

The full use of all the new techniques of hybridizing and growing made mass production possible. Then, out of millions of individual plants raised, a small number of mutations, new combinations of characteristics could be expected; sports that paved the way to different and often better lilies. From mass-production methods has stemmed the great progress made in our own new garden lilies. Large scale growing again depends on the availability of generous quantities of lilies of any given species to provide enough seed so that inevitable losses can easily be made good or, at any rate, are not catastrophic. Quantities of seed are also necessary to obtain the maximum number of segregants, lilies that vary as much as possible from the type.

For gardeners the history of the hybrid lily is important because it shows when and how it became possible to raise good varieties for garden use. The discovery of *L. davidi* and its introduction into Europe in 1895 only then made it possible to use this fine lily in hybridization. Soon after it was used most successfully by Miss Preston in the production of many of her best hybrid lilies. The much later discovery of the fact that *L. davidi* is almost immune, or at least highly resistant, to virus diseases made its value as a potential parent of our garden lilies even greater than its pleasing form, color, and habit would have indicated. The emergence of lily hybrids resistant or immune to lily diseases is at least as important as their beauty.

Why the New Lilies Are Better

It is especially in their larger tolerances that the newer strains of garden lilies show their merits. Through selection of the sturdier species as seed or pollen parents, through years of testing and elimination of the weaker, or less hardy, plants, many new hybrid strains will grow and perform well where one, or sometimes both, of the parents may be grown only with the greatest difficulty, if at all. This characteristic of seedlings of hybrid origin thriving where the parents, at best, grow weakly, is typical of what we call "hybrid vigor." Like the mule that has more strength and endurance than either of its parents, many of the hybrid lilies show more stamina and persistence than that commonly found among their ancestors.

Hybridization, the breeding of new lilies, then, is not an idle pastime of the curious gardener or of the grower who wants to cross two lilies and raise the seed to the flowering stage just to see what will happen. It is a deliberate attempt to raise hardier lilies, more able to endure adverse conditions, more adapted to the garden; flowers which should retain many of the virtues of both parents, but lack most of the bad qualities. The ideal solution, that of combining *all* the good qualities and eliminating all the faults, shall probably never be attained. In many of the new lilies, however, so much improvement has been made that the value of hybrid lily strains, as compared to the true species, has been proved to the satisfaction of all experts and gardeners.

The Element of "Linkage"

If one were to list all the characteristics that make up a lily plant—its habits, form, color, fragrance, the length of the roots, the type of bulb, its resistance to diseases, and the many large and small details in which it differs from other lilies—a longer chapter than this would be necessary. Cross a lily endowed with many of these innumerable variants with one with a similar number of largely different factors, and an infinite number of other combinations is possible. The resulting seedlings will, of course, all be new lilies. Many of the characteristics, such as type of bulb, tolerances to temperature, disease, light, and moisture may often be so nearly equal in both parents that the seedling offspring cannot be much different from either one. In actual practice we often find that many qualities seem to have such an affinity that they stay together, even if transferred from a species lily to its hybrid child.

This habit of characteristics staying together we call "linkage." In some lilies it is especially strong. We might find, for instance, that the tendencies to be white, fragrant, and late-flowering are all inherited *together* and not separately. As plant breeders we may be anxious to have two, but not all three, of these qualities in our new lilies. It becomes a challenge to try and break this linkage and to obtain one of the characteristics in our new lilies without the others.

In other lily combinations there seems to be no linkage at all and the resulting seedlings will vary in the most charming way, every one differing from the other in minute or larger details. If only a few seedlings are grown, this is not so obvious, but if some fifty or hundred thousand seedlings are grown from one particular combination of parents, then the infinite variation that may result becomes apparent.

Most people seem to believe that, in order to develop a better plant of entirely new aspect, the plant breeder must accomplish some great change in the material with which he is working. Though it is true that such striking variations do result on occasion, the majority of improvements are apt to be of a less spectacular nature. It is the slight variations in flowers that make one plant better than another. Frequently, the most desirable improvements are those of a seemingly minor sort, variation in form and color, or in season and habit of the plant. Sometimes we see more radical changes.

In lilies, for instance, it is infrequent that the red does not completely overshadow the yellow, yet in some of the *L. umbellatum-tigrinum* hybrid seedlings it appears that the red color of some types was broken up to the point where the two pigments are more nearly balanced. The result is here that the yellow is not overwhelmed, but sometimes even dominant, producing lilies of a nearly shell pink color or of a deep raspberry shade, with many intermediate hues. These are both amazingly beautiful and quite surprising. Equally extraordinary is still another new shade in lilies and in a type where one usually expects no color at all. For instance, red-anthered forms of *L. candidum* have been raised, most striking in appearance.

As is readily seen, lilies of the *L. regale, L. sargentiae,* or *L. centifolium* type are never pure white. There is always some color in the flower. There may be a suggestion of red at the stem or it may be broad red or brown markings on the outside of the trumpet. True albinism, or the total absence of color, is extremely rare and nearly always fatal to a plant. In most white flowers numerous factors for color are present.

The Human Element in Plant Breeding

In articles about plant breeding the mechanics of the process are explained. Usually a lot of information is given about the plant material to be used as parental stock. Also, methods of growing and caring for the progeny are discussed. Nothing is said, however, about the qualities that the plant breeder himself should have.

Plant breeding is an art as well as a science, and the personality of the breeder will be reflected in the varieties he produces, as certainly as the personality of the artist may be seen in his works, or that of a composer in his musi` Like all artists, a plant breeder must first be a good technician and have a thorough knowledge of

LEFT: *Birth of a new lily! Jan de Graaff and Earl Hornback evaluate its qualities.* RIGHT: *Sometimes the towering stalks present a problem to the photographer.*

his material. He must be methodical and persistent in following his breeding lines to their logical conclusion, yet highly imaginative and constantly inspired by intuitive glimpses into the future. It is certainly true that the highly imaginative person is rarely methodical and the thorough, the methodical person is often uninspired, and that all the good qualities are rarely found in one individual. The answer to this problem is in the co-operation of two or more persons with complementary personalities. This is why teamwork in plant breeding is often so successful.

CHAPTER *15. Exhibiting Lilies*

The bright consummate flower
JOHN MILTON (1608–1674)

Sooner or later the time comes when every gardener wants to display some of his most prized flowers at a show. This may be an informal local affair, in which case the grower can walk out into the garden, cut a spike at its best, carry it to the show in one hand, and win a blue ribbon. Or it may be more formal, sponsored by a horticultural society or other large organization. In this case it could involve—for the commercial grower—cutting hundreds of spikes, holding them in cool storage, packing and transporting them hundreds, even thousands, of miles, and presenting them in top condition to the judges. In either case, excitement runs high, competition is keen, and the winner is rewarded by a great sense of achievement.

CUTTING AND AFTERCARE

Effect of Cutting the Flowers. One of the questions most frequently asked is whether any harm is done to lily plants by cutting the flowers. The amount of harm depends entirely on the number and amount of green leaves and stem taken with the blooms. To remove just the flower and pedicel, (the little stem of a single flower), is in no way harmful. In fact, it may strengthen the lily plant by eliminating the need for it to feed and mature the inflorescence. If any of the main stem is taken, however, the plant is injured in direct proportion to the amount of foliage and stem cut off. If as much as half the stem and half the foliage is removed,

208

Good stage of development at which to cut for a nearby show. If lilies must travel far, cutting at a somewhat earlier stage is desirable.

then it is safe to assume that the lily receives a serious setback, one that will show up the next year in stunted or, at least, less luxuriant growth.

Yet, when the entire stem is cut and no foliage remains on the plant, the bulb usually does not die, but will make new growth the next season. If left undisturbed, it may even flower that year or the next. This again depends upon the stage of development of the plant when the stalk is cut. Thus, if we figure that the growing period of the lily bulb is at the halfway point when the flower opens, then the bulb loses about half its normal annual growth, if the entire stem is cut at that time. Actually, there is a great deal of difference in the reaction of various lily species to cutting. It is impossible to lay down any hard and fast rules.

While it may hurt both the gardener and the lily to cut flowers from a good stand in the garden, it must be remembered that the cost of the bulbs is not prohibitive and that at the florist's shop a bouquet of equally fine flowers would probably cost a great deal more than it would to replace the bulbs. Lilies left undisturbed for a few years in the garden will grow into nice big clumps and throw up many stalks. A few of them can always be cut without harm to the planting as a whole.

Cutting Garden. If many flowers are required, however, either for the house or for showing, then it is well to make a special planting for cutting purposes. Small bulbs, proportionately cheaper, should be bought and given a chance to develop for two or three years. The new bulbil-bearing hybrids are especially useful, as each year new plantings can be started from the little bulbs forming along the stem and a multitude of good cut flowers can soon be raised. As a rule it is most convenient to place them in rows in a special cutting garden, where care can be minimized by the use of cultivators, fertilizer distributors, etc.

How and When to Cut. The best stage at which to cut lilies is when the lower flowers are fully open. Once the stalk is cut and placed in water, the upper buds will open successively. For very long-distance shipping, stems may be cut with even the lower flowers in bud.

Early morning is the best time to cut lilies, before the anthers have split open, ready to spill the pollen. If the pollen is already loose, early-morning dew will make it adhere to the anthers suffi-

Flowers evenly spaced around stalk, and all buds in undamaged condition, are factors that help win prizes.

ciently so that the flowers can be cut and, if carefully handled, taken indoors without undue staining of the petals.

Hardening. The amateur who is going to show some of his lily blooms should take deep containers of cool water with him into the garden and place stems in them as soon as cut. The cut stalks, in their containers of water, are then placed in a cool, dark place like a damp cellar, to "harden" overnight.

When commercial growers are cutting hundreds of blooms from the fields for a big show, some hours may elapse between cutting and placing the stems in water. In this case the flowers and the pedicels which support them may wilt a little. If this occurs, an inch should be taken from the base of each main stem just before they are set in deep pails of cool water in the basement or other dark spot where they are to "harden" overnight.

General Care. The greatest care should be taken at all times, from the moment the stalks are cut, to prevent the blooms from touching each other or rubbing against the container. Each flower must be perfect and unblemished in order to win a blue ribbon.

Removing Anthers. It may sometimes be necessary to remove the anthers, if the flowers have to be shipped or taken to a show at a distance, because otherwise pollen may stain the perianth. As the beauty of most lilies is enhanced by the sharply contrasting colors of anthers and pollen, this practice should be avoided, if at all possible.

When showing lilies in arrangement classes, the anthers already opened should be removed, as otherwise pollen is almost sure to cause stains while the flowers are being handled and placed. Buds opening after the arrangement is made will have their anthers intact and will show the true character of the blooms.

Pollen stains can easily be removed from fabrics by letting them dry thoroughly and then brushing them vigorously. It is fresh pollen that is sticky and adheres to materials for a short time. Dry pollen can also be removed from a flower with a small pad of cotton, but if stuck down with nectar, it is better not to attempt removal, as a small stain may then easily be enlarged into an ugly blemish.

For show purposes in specimen classes the anthers should be present, even at the risk of having the open flower stained.

Packing. Where cut lilies must be packed for transportation to a show by train, truck, or plane, there are a number of problems to be solved.

Sometimes it is possible to cut in bud, with the first flower just about to open, pack dry and let the flowers open after arrival. In this case, the blooms and pedicels are slightly limp during transportation, development being inhibited by lack of water. This reduces the danger of breakage, bruising, or distortion and makes it possible to pack a greater number of stalks in each box. If they can be chilled to about 40 degrees, this is helpful. Arrival at the show should be timed about three days before the opening. The stalks are placed in deep water and kept at a temperature of 55–65 degrees after the stems are recut, about an inch being removed. Development is then resumed and the flowers should be wide open and fresh for staging on the opening day.

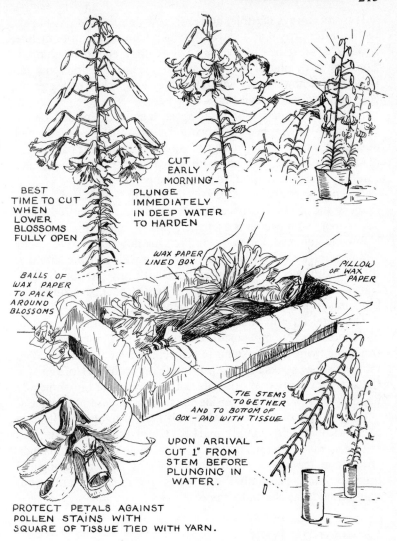

BEST
TIME TO CUT
WHEN
LOWER
BLOSSOMS
FULLY OPEN

CUT
EARLY
MORNING –
PLUNGE
IMMEDIATELY
IN DEEP WATER
TO HARDEN

BALLS OF
WAX PAPER
TO PACK
AROUND
BLOSSOMS

WAX PAPER
LINED BOX

PILLOW
OF WAX
PAPER

TIE STEMS
TOGETHER
AND TO BOTTOM OF
BOX – PAD WITH TISSUE

UPON ARRIVAL –
CUT 1" FROM
STEM BEFORE
PLUNGING IN
WATER.

PROTECT PETALS AGAINST
POLLEN STAINS WITH
SQUARE OF TISSUE TIED WITH YARN.

Cutting and packing lilies for showing.

It is not always feasible, however, to bring the blooms to perfection after arrival at a show, in which case much more mature
specimens must be cut the day before they are to be shipped.
These must be placed in water as soon as cut, for otherwise the
fully opened flowers may wilt. Then they are packed with greatest
care and kept cool at all times.

Preserving Anthers. For showing, anthers must be left on, so
each group is wrapped in a two-inch square of tissue and tied
once with a contrasting strand of wool. After the lilies are put in
place, these strings are cut with sharp scissors and the tissues
carefully removed without touching the petals.

Packing in Boxes. The box is lined with wax paper, as this
reduces the friction between flower and box. A pad of rolled
newspaper, wrapped in wax paper, placed under the neck just
below the inflorescence, serves to hold the flowers up so that they
will not touch the bottom of the box. In packing, make sure that
the actual flowers are not in contact with any part of the box.
Loose balls of wax tissue may be gently packed around the
blossoms to prevent this from happening.

The stems have to be tied (with large, soft twine) to the bottom
of the box to avoid movement. Pads of tissue or paper are put between the twine and the stems to protect them from bruising. With
most varieties stalks can be inserted from both ends of the box,
the stems being tied at opposite corners from the blossoms and
padded to prevent their bruising the flowers in case of contact.

If more than one box is needed, it is helpful to attach a label to
each, with contents plainly marked. On arrival, unpacking and
setting up may then proceed much faster and in an orderly manner.
Often more damage occurs during unpacking than in packing and
transportation, especially if one is engaged in conversation with
many friends, as is usually the case!

SHOWING IN POTS

One advantage of showing in pots is that a valuable plant may
be shown and brought home again without loss of foliage and
therefore without weakening the bulb. When exhibited after being
pot-grown under glass, the plants are not quite as vigorous and

perfect as when grown outdoors, though the flowers are often more softly colored and more perfect than when exposed to wind and rain.

Where flower show rules permit, lilies from the garden can be dug at the bud stage and potted. They must then be watched carefully, watered regularly from time to time, and fed either with cow manure extract or an ounce of nitrate of soda dissolved in a gallon of rain water. If handled carefully, so that they suffer minimum root damage, and if watered judiciously, such late-potted lilies will flower beautifully, often with more vigor and larger flowers than lilies which have made their entire growth in the confinement of the usual pot.

Packing Potted Plants. When potted lilies are to be packed for shipping, no better method can be followed than that employed for the purpose at the special Royal Horticultural Society Lily Shows. Here may be seen the finest displays of lilies ever assembled in one place. A short review of British shipping methods follows:

Each stem in each pot is staked separately with a thin, tapered green cane tied with raffia, the stakes just the right lengths to support the flower heads. Much longer, stouter white canes are used above them, and each flower is held to one of them by a chin strap of soft tissue paper. The anther cluster of each open flower is wrapped in a small square of tissue tied with colored wool and wads of cotton are placed between the blooms to prevent chafing.

Every pot is then bedded in hay or excelsior on the floor of the transportation truck, each line of pots secured by a board and the top of each white cane tied securely to a transverse rod in the van. Tall and short plants are alternated to prevent the flowers from touching one another.

Smaller lots are fitted into a crate packed with excelsior, strong uprights nailed to the corners, cross members nailed to them, and the tall white canes tied to the cross members. We have had plants thus packed travel by truck and rail without a mark on the flowers. The plants arrive two or three days before the show, when they are unpacked, untied, and permitted to develop naturally. By the day of the show they have reached perfection.

EXHIBITING

In showing lilies, whether at a small show or a very large one of national or international importance, there are three basic rules to be followed:

1) Select the best material available.

2) Get it to the show in perfect condition and display it to the best possible advantage.

3) Label each species or variety correctly and legibly.

These rules may sound so obvious that it would seem quite superfluous to state them here. They are, nevertheless, honored more in the breach than in the observance.

The interest in lilies is keener now than it has ever been. Whenever lilies, especially the new hybrids and varieties, are displayed at a flower show, they are bound to be the center of interest. If the display is made up of perfect specimens, attractively displayed and correctly labeled as required by the flower show schedule, the exhibitor can feel a just pride in his accomplishment and knows that each viewer can learn, by reading the labels, the names of these new garden beauties, so that he too can acquire them. (A complete show schedule will be found on page 222.)

Lilies in Competition. In specimen classes, the lilies are judged according to their merits in each of the following qualities: condition, vigor, arrangement on stem, substance, shape, and color. The show committee sets a definite maximum point value for each quality listed, the possible total of the point scale not to exceed one hundred.

Condition. Here one aims to have each spike of flowers, bearing as many open blooms as possible, but with none faded and with many unopened buds. Flowers should be fresh, clean, undamaged in any way, and the inflorescence undistorted. No disease should be present. Such perfection is attained by correct culture, *good timing,* and by careful packing and unpacking.

Vigor includes the size and strength of the stem, abundance of good healthy foliage and a maximum number and size of flowers and buds for a bloom in its particular class. An exhibitor should never show a distorted, flattened, or fasciated stem, if he expects to win an award.

Arrangement of flowers on stem varies with the species, but the ideal is to have the flowers so spaced that the lower flowers do not touch, even though they may be in a loose whorl, the others spirally arranged above them. Length of pedicels is important here. They may be too long or too short to be ideal for the particular lily shown.

Substance. Here the solidity of the perianth segments is considered. Cutting and packing have worked a hardship and, if lasting quality and recuperative power are lacking, faults are sure to show up in a bloom displayed under these circumstances. Strong substance in a perianth also helps to produce a well-shaped flower.

Shape. Flowers must be relatively large and of ideal shape for the kind shown. The shape of the blooms is the lily's greatest beauty, whether it be trumpet, martagon, or upright in form. In general, the flower should be regular, the petals having bold unbroken curves, not unduly twisted or rolled, and relatively broad. Width tends to give an air of solidity to the bloom, but like many characteristics, it can be overdone. Most other flowers can vie with the lily in color, comparatively few in shape or form. Size also counts in this, and many people consider ten points too few for so important a section of the scale.

Color is, of course, relative to the species or variety being judged, but it should be clear and bright, not mottled or unduly shaded. Good color is influenced by the amount of light, temperature, nourishment of the plant, and sometimes by the amount of iron in the soil.

SETTING UP THE DISPLAY

Unpacking. Before opening the lily boxes, or removing stalks from pails of water if they have been transported by car, it is well to have beside you the water-filled containers in which your lilies are to be displayed in the show. If possible, these should be tall, narrow-necked and of heavy glass or other material for displaying single specimens; and large, deep containers, if more than one stalk is to be shown in a single vase.

Remove each stem from the box, if they have been packed dry; hold the end of the stem under water in the vase; cut off an inch,

When a number of stems are to be placed in one container, avoid over-crowding!

and sink it to the bottom without again exposing it to the air. If there is any danger of tipping, place shot or sand in bottom of vase.

If transported in pails, and in perfect condition, stems need not be recut.

Setting Up. After placing each specimen in its containers and taking it to the table where it is to be displayed, wrapping can be removed from anthers and other paper protectors or supports taken off.

Where show schedule permits the use of other flowers with lilies, be sure that the lilies predominate.

If a group is to be shown in one container, be sure it is not crowded. Regardless of the type of vase used and the number of stems prescribed by the show program, every stem and every flower should be seen to advantage. This is often difficult to achieve, but by cutting a few stems short and by leaving others longer, it is possible to place the flowers at different heights and so show to best advantage the type of each stem and its inflorescence, its habit of growth and flowering.

Arrangement Class. If the class calls for lilies in combination with other flowers, then see to it that the lily is displayed at its best. It need not dominate the arrangement, but it should preserve the lily's true character. Crowded together in a mixed bouquet, lilies lose their individuality and can do no more than provide a color accent which, of course, is hardly the purpose for which we grow or cut them.

In the cut flower and flower arrangement classes care should be taken to remove all foliage that would be under water. Lily foliage is particularly tender and rots easily when submerged for any

In making arrangements, species and hybrid lilies with flowers of moderate size are often much more effective than larger types.

length of time. To keep the water sweet and clean in the vase it is usual to rinse the stems, and remove any impurity or soil that might pollute it. It is helpful to use the special proprietary substances, such as "Floralife," which aid in keeping flowers fresh for a long time.

It is not easy to subordinate so conspicuous a flower as the lily to harmonize with others in a bouquet, rather than to dominate the whole arrangement. It is more readily accomplished with the smaller lilies—such as *L. martagon, L. pumilum,* and *L. concolor*—than with the larger types. In this connection do not overlook the fact that many of the larger lilies furnish us with smaller-sized flowers from young bulbs. It is here again that the bulbil-bearing new *L. hollandicum-tigrinum* hybrids are especially valuable.

A lily like Enchantment, for instance, may in its maturity overshadow any other flowers in an arrangement, but from one-year-old bulbils it gives a graceful, prettily spaced, small inflorescence which is easier to arrange gracefully than almost any other flower.

The larger upright lilies like Tabasco deserve a container all to themselves. They are very easy to arrange and require no supplementary foliage as some of the stems can be cut short to furnish color at the base of the arrangement. If desired, an entire bowl or vase can be filled so that it presents an almost solid mass of flowers.

Since it is so beautiful, *L. candidum* is often shown by itself. The new strains are resistant to botrytis and hence have good, clean foliage of which no one need be ashamed. On the other hand, there are many lilies that are set off to advantage by the use of dark green foliage, such as rhododendron, *Magnolia grandiflora* or English Laurel. The need for either narrow-necked containers or very strong, heavy frogs for long-stemmed lilies is obvious. In showing arranged lilies over a period of years we have found that open bowls with good, heavy frogs in the center provide the best method of displaying them to their fullest advantage. For the lighter, thin-stemmed types pin holders with lead bases are recommended. The largest lilies obviously need the heaviest frogs. A friend of ours who is an amateur potter has made up a series of vases in all sizes which look rather like a straight-sided glazed drainage tile. Weighted with lead shot they are quite stable. The inconspicuous glazes used, a neutral gray-green, a dark brown and a soft yellow blend well with the flowers and foliage.

During Exhibition. After lilies have stood one or two days in a vase, it is advisable to change the water and shorten the stems a little to insure unimpeded flow of water to the flowers. This applies especially to stems bearing a large number of blooms. These lilies take up an astonishing amount of water.

"LILIES ON PARADE"
Information for Exhibitors and Class Schedules as proposed by The North American Lily Society

The following schedule of classes, schedule for judging, rules for exhibitors and definitions are based on those used for the Annual Lily Show.

INFORMATION FOR EXHIBITORS

1. Exhibits are open to any grower of lilies except for classes designated otherwise. Lilies in competitive classes have been grown by, or under the supervision of, the exhibitor.
2. Amateur—one who does not engage in the sale of bulbs or plants for any part of his livelihood and does not accept pay as a gardener or garden consultant.
3. Commercial grower—one who grows bulbs, plants, or flowers for sale.
4. Collection—several species or varieties of lilies entered in the same class, each stem in a separate container.
5. Display—an exhibit of lilies arranged for decorative effect. Accessories, including foliage and foliage plants, are permitted.
6. Clone—a group of plants propagated vegetatively from a single parent plant. A recognized clone is designated by a "fancy" name. Clone is often synonymous with "variety" in horticulture.
7. Intraspecific origin—refers to a seedling selected from a group of seedlings derived from a single species.
8. Interspecific origin—refers to seedlings derived from hybridizing or crossing two or more species.
9. All entries are to be correctly named and labeled by the exhibitor. Cards will be provided.
10. Unnamed seedlings should be designated by number and/or parentage, if known.
11. Abnormalities, such as fasciated stems, should not be entered in competitive classes.
12. The anthers of lilies may be removed to prevent staining petals during transportation. It is preferable to leave them on when this is possible.

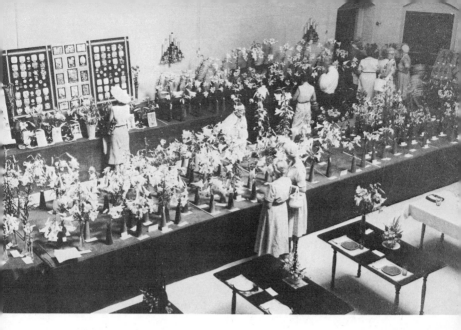

Two views of the Lily Show annually held at Worcester, Massachusetts, by the New England Lily Society. A great deal of practical information is to be obtained from the educational exhibits featured at such shows.

13. Entries should be made on forms provided and preferably sent in to the secretary of the show prior to the first day of the exhibit. The secretary of the show should be notified that an exhibit is to be entered so that space may be planned. Exhibits sent in from some distance and not to be set up by the exhibitor should have the class of the entry plainly marked on each stalk and surely arrive a day in advance of the show.

14. Exhibits should be entered in their proper classes. On the day of the show, there will be someone on hand to help exhibitors identify their material and designate to what class it belongs.

15. First, second, and third prize certificates and ribbons will be awarded in each class. Special awards will be given as indicated.

JUDGING INFORMATION

Lilies will be judged according to the following schedule:

	POINTS
Condition	30
Vigor	20
Placement on stem	20
Substance of flowers	10
Form of flowers	10
Color of flowers	10
	100

Condition includes the stage of maturity. Generally it is considered that a spike of lilies is in the best condition when the lower flowers are open, but not faded and the upper ones still in bud. The larger number of open flowers the better, provided the old ones have not begun to fade. The flowers should not be bleached in the sun, wilted, or otherwise in poor condition. The plants should also be free from disease of all kinds. The anthers should preferably be present, although it is recognized that, if open flowers are to be shipped, the anthers should be removed rather than have the petals smeared with colored pollen.

Vigor refers to the length and strength of the stem, the number and size of the flowers and the size and attractiveness of the foliage. In cutting lilies about one-third of the foliage is left with the bulb.

PLATE 17

Harlequin hybrids (above), *a new, fairly uniform but many colored group, extremely hardy and vigorous, and useful both for garden display and for cutting.*

PLATE 18

A group of Rainbow hybrid lilies, an early flowering group which brings a flood of cheerful color to the border that is beginning to "sag" as the late spring-flowering perennials fade.

PLATE 19

Golden Splendor, with its huge, gracefully formed recurving trumpets, coppery in reverse, is one of the most dramatic of all lilies, and a vigorous grower.

PLATE 20

Golden Sunburst strain, a vigorous, broad-petaled sunny yellow of Aurelian Hybrid parentage.

PLATE 21

*In this reproduction of
an illustration from
Hexandrian Plants, the
lilies shown, top to
bottom, are:*
L. martagon album
(white); L. martagon
(lilac); L. pyrenaicum
(yellow), and
L. chalcedonicum *(red).*

PLATE 22

L. auratum *Red Band
strain. Among the most
spectacular of lilies,
these are not hybrids but
a strain produced by
the selection from large
plantings of seedlings
of* L. auratum, *all
seedlings producing
red-banded flowers. By
intercrossing these
individuals, the red color
factor has been greatly
strengthened.*

PLATE 23

A collection of species lilies.
1. L. martagon album, *white*
2. L. pumilum, *red*
3. L. martagon, *lilac*
4. L. concolor, *red*
5. L. pumilum *Golden Gleam, orange*
6. L. concolor *var. Coridion, yellow*
7. L. amabile, *red*
8. L. amabile luteum, *yellow*

PLATE 24

L. szovitsianum. *This picture shows the great variety of form, color and substance found in any group of wild lilies raised from seed. By selecting the finest flowers for further breeding, strains of great individuality can be raised.*

Placement of flowers refers to their arrangement on the stem. In general separation spirally on the stem vertically, rather than crowded at the same level, is an advantage. They should also be spaced in such a way that the individual flowers do not interfere with each other. With hybrids competing against each other, the separation of the flowers and the attractiveness of the appearance as related to the angle on the pedicel may be considered.

Substance of the flowers refers to the thickness of the petals. Firm texture which withstands exposure is desirable.

Form of the flower is judged on the basis of its conformity with the typical form of the species or variety, or with attractiveness of form in comparing different species or varieties.

Color of flowers should be clear and attractive rather than muddy. This is particularly important in hybrids which have no recognized typical color.

Only worthy exhibits will be given awards. The opinion of the judges will be final. In placing the entries in *collections* the quality of flowers, the number of species shown—except where the number is limited—and the horticultural difficulty of raising the kinds of lilies will also be considered.

SCHEDULE OF CLASSES

Section A. *Lilium* species and their varieties.

CLASS 1.   Collection of six different kinds. One stem of each.
  (*a*) Open to amateurs only.
  (*b*) Open to commercial growers only.

CLASS 2.   *Lilium* species in season. The judges may at their discretion set up other classes if the entries warrant doing so.
  (*a*) *Lilium candidum.* Single stem.
  (*b*) *L. canadense.* Single stem.
  (*c*) *L. martagon.* Single stem.
  (*d*) *L. amabile.* Single stem.
  (*e*) *L. davidi (L. willmottiae).* Single stem.
  (*f*) *L. hansoni.* Single stem.
  (*g*) *L. pumilum.* Single stem.
  (*h*) Any other *Lilium* species. Competing at discretion of the judges.

CLASS 3.　Collection of three native American species. One stem of each.

SECTION B.　*Named* clones of *intra*specific origin.

CLASS 4.　*Lilium,* nodding flowers with reflexed petals (Martagon type). Specimen. One stem.

CLASS 5.　*Lilium,* erect flowering type. Specimen. One stem.

CLASS 6.　*Lilium,* trumpet type except those in class 16. Specimen. One stem.

CLASS 7.　*Lilium,* outward facing type. Specimen. One stem.

SECTION C.　*Named* clones of *Lilium* of *inter*specific hybrid origin.

CLASS 8.　Collection of six. One stem of each.

CLASS 9.　*Lilium,* nodding flowers with reflexed petals (Martagon type).
　　　　(*a*)　Collection of three. One stem of each.
　　　　(*b*)　Specimen. One stem.

CLASS 10.　*Lilium,* erect flowering type.
　　　　(*a*)　Collection of three. One stem of each.
　　　　(*b*)　Specimen. One stem.

CLASS 11.　*Lilium,* trumpet type, except those in Class 16.
　　　　(*a*)　Collection of three. One stem of each.
　　　　(*b*)　Specimen. One stem.

CLASS 12.　*Lilium,* outward facing type.
　　　　(*a*)　Collection of three. One stem of each.
　　　　(*b*)　Specimen. One stem.

SECTION D.　New seedlings. No limit to the number of entries.

CLASS 13.　Single stem of intraspecific origin, *unnamed.*
　　　　(*a*)　*Lilium,* nodding flowers with reflexed petals.
　　　　(*b*)　*Lilium,* erect flowering type.
　　　　(*c*)　*Lilium,* trumpet type.
　　　　(*d*)　*Lilium,* outward facing type.

CLASS 14.　Single stems of interspecific origin.
　　　　(*a*)　*Lilium,* nodding flowers with reflexed petals.
　　　　(*b*)　*Lilium,* erect flowering type.
　　　　(*c*)　*Lilium,* trumpet type.
　　　　(*d*)　*Lilium,* outward facing type.

CLASS 15. Single stems of any origin named and/or introduced since the last show.

    (*a*) *Lilium,* nodding flowers with reflexed petals.

    (*b*) *Lilium,* erect flowering type.

    (*c*) *Lilium,* trumpet type.

    (*d*) *Lilium,* outward facing type.

SECTION E. Types given special recognition (named or unnamed seedlings or clones).

CLASS 16. *Lilium, L. regale* type to include *L. regale, L. centifolium, L. sulphureum, L. sargentiae, L. leucanthum* and hybrids among them.

    (*a*) Collection of three. One stem of each. May be same clone.

    (*b*) Specimen. One stem.

CLASS 17. *L. auratum* and its hybrids.

    (*a*) Specimen. One stem.

CLASS 18. *L. speciosum* and its varieties. Specimen. One stem.

CLASS 19. *L. henryi* and its hybrids including *L. x aurelianense* and Havemeyer. Specimen. One stem.

CLASS 20. Bellingham Hybrids. Specimen. One stem.

CLASS 21. "Stenographer" type hybrids. Specimen. One stem.

CLASS 22. Martagon-hansoni Hybrids. Specimen. One stem.

SECTION F. Displays.

CLASS 23. Display of *Lilium,* twelve kinds or more arranged for effect. Suitable foliage and accessories permitted, but award will be made mainly on number of kinds, quality of bloom, and horticultural value of species or clones.

    (*a*) Open to all.

    (*b*) Restricted to amateurs only.

Part Three

THE LILY WORLD

CHAPTER *16.* *The History of Lilies*

The blessed damozel leaned out
From the gold bar of Heaven.
Her eyes were deeper than the depth
Of waters stilled at even;
She had three lilies in her hand,
And the stars in her hair were seven.

DANTE GABRIEL ROSSETTI
(1828–1882)

The Lily in Legend and Early History

Everybody knows that certain flowers have a symbolic significance. In its many forms, more than any other flower, the lily is
associated with religion, both ancient and modern.

In the first garden of all, according to the Talmud, there dwelt
with Adam, before Eve was sent to comfort him, a certain soul-
less, golden-haired woman named Lilith, whose fatal charm lay in
her honey-colored hair. Her emblem was a lily.

The sweet white Candidum Lily, found wild in what is now
Palestine, Asia Minor, and Syria, was cherished for its food and
medicinal value by the ancient nomadic tribes of the Near East
who carried it on their travels and planted it in their gardens. A
lily bulb was found in an Egyptian mummy case now in a museum
in Paris, placed there to provide nourishment for the deceased.
The lily was held equally sacred by the early Cretans.

In classic Greece, the lily was cherished both as food and for its
beauty. *L. candidum* is depicted on early urns and vases and
appears in low relief on many pieces of exquisite Greek sculpture.

231

The Madonna Lily
(L. candidum), *which has been in cultivation since before the time of Pharaoh is still an unchallenged favorite in gardens of today.*

Artemis, cool as moonlight; Aphrodite, goddess of love and beauty; Hera, the queen of heaven—all had the white lily as their flower.

From Greece it traveled to Rome, where it became the symbol of the goddesses Diana, Venus, and Juno. The lily was used freely in ceremonies and rites sacred to these deities. At weddings the priest was supplied with two chaplets, one composed of lilies, the other of sheaves of grain, which he placed on the heads of the bride and groom to typify purity and abundance. Today we still decorate our churches with lilies.

When the Romans conquered Gaul and Britain, the lily went with them, used as a salve for wounds and for the skin, as well as cherished for its blooms. When they built villas by the waters of the Loire and the Moselle, and on English soil as well, they surrounded them with gardens full of southern shrubs and flowers, including the Madonna Lily.

At the time of the Teutonic invasion, when the Roman Empire fell, sweeping away villas and gardens and laying waste the entire countryside, the lily was lost to civilization, only to creep back in the wake of Christianity.

In the Bible, references to the lily are frequent, always symbolizing sweetness and purity. The temple of Solomon was decorated with sculptured lilies and pomegranates. From the days of the earliest Crusades, pilgrims to Palestine sought that lily before which even the glory of Solomon faded. In Hebrew, the name Susannah literally means lily.

The advent of Christianity brought a new importance to the Candidum Lily, for it became the symbol of the Virgin Mary, of St. Joseph, and of St. Anthony of Padua. Wandering through the catacombs of Rome, one often finds this flower—signifying chastity —carved on the tombs of Christian maidens. It appears in many religious paintings of the early Christian era.

The prophetess who announces the Incarnation holds a lily; St. Joseph bears one in his hand; and, in representations of the Last Judgment, a lily is depicted on one side of the Judge and a sword on the other. In fourteenth and fifteenth century paintings of the Annunciation, Madonna Lilies stand in vases or are held in the hand of the Virgin or the Angel. It is always used, too, at the Feast of the Visitation on July 2, instituted by Pope Urban VI in 1389 in commemoration of the visit paid by the Virgin Mary to her cousin Elizabeth, mother of John the Baptist.

During the Dark Ages nothing is known of the fate of the Madonna Lily, but it undoubtedly continued to flourish wherever it found congenial surroundings. In this period it must have multiplied well in northern Europe and in England, for the herbalists John Gerard and John Parkinson seem to regard it as a native plant and give it scant attention.

The Crusaders brought lily bulbs back with them during the eleventh, twelfth, and thirteenth centuries, spreading its fame as a medicine and a symbol of purity. It thus became one of the cherished flowers of convent and monastery gardens. The monks were skilled gardeners, for their diet was largely vegetable, and food gardens were therefore an absolute necessity. Its beauty and religious significance, however, caused it to be grown also as a blossoming plant. Even in times of war the convents and monasteries were respected and protected. Their gardens survived and with them the lily, which gradually spread to secular gardens.

The lily has often been chosen, too, as the emblem of religious orders or societies. One of the very earliest was "The Order of the Lily of Navarre," instituted by Prince García, the sixth of that name, in the city of Nagera, 1048 A.D. Here the image of the Virgin Mary issuing out of a lily was discovered in the time of the illness of the king who thereupon suddenly recovered his health, and, in token of gratitude, instituted the Order of the Knights of St. Mary of the Lily, consisting of eight and thirty knights whereof he was chief. "Each of these weareth a lily on his breast, made of silver and a double chain of gold interlaced with the Gothish letter M, which stands for Mary. At the end of the chain hangeth a lily carrying the same letter crowned."

In 1234, King Louis IX of France instituted an order of knighthood, each member of which wore a chain of broom flowers intertwined with white lilies, signifying humility and purity. On a cross suspended from the chain were inscribed the words: "He exalteth the humble." The lily has long been used in heraldry, as well, it being the flower of France's Royal House of Bourbon, which reigned from 1589 until the French Revolution.

In following the Madonna Lily through its long road down the path of history, it is easy to see that from the earliest times it has been considered a choice flower; inspiring to people of all times as a religious symbol; useful as food and medicine; and so beautiful in itself that it was carried from the Near East to southern Europe; from there over the Alps into northern Europe; and from England and Holland to the New World. Even today it is one of the prize assets of any well-planned garden.

Another lily, not as widely grown, but even so cherished by early gardeners all over northern Europe, is *L. chalcedonicum*. This lovely, brilliant, and dazzling red lily was described by John Parkinson in 1629 as the "Red Martagon of Constantinople." It is known in some rural districts in England as "Turn again, Gentlemen," a nickname of quite obvious origin, for who could resist a second look at this vividly colored lily?

From America came, quite soon after the discovery of our country, the lovely *L. canadense*. Its graceful nodding flowers and rich coloring must have attracted the early explorers of our continent and it is not surprising that this lovely lily received a great deal of attention both in France and in England. By 1629, when British herbalist John Parkinson wrote his famous book on English garden flowers, *L. canadense* was already well known to English gardeners.

During the eighteenth century, *L. superbum* and *L. philadelphicum* first bloomed in Europe. The Western American lilies, of course, crossed the Atlantic only after the exploration of the West, that is, after 1846.

Asiatic lilies arrived in Europe as China and Japan were gradually explored by the Dutch and English traders of the eighteenth and nineteenth centuries. Only *L. pumilum* and *L. dauricum* were brought in during the eighteenth century. *L. tigrinum, L. concolor, L. elegans,* and *L. hansoni* all reached there during the earlier part of the nineteenth century, while *L. auratum, L. speciosum rubrum* and *album* arrived around 1850. Still later, almost at the end of the century, came *L. henryi* and *L. leucanthum.* It was E. H. Wilson who, on one of his trips to China, discovered *L. regale, L. davidi,* and *L. sargentiae.* Seed of these fine lilies was made available to both American and European growers around 1908. *L. amabile* was discovered in 1905 and *L. cernuum* in 1910, while other lilies are of still later discovery.

The Lily as a Garden Plant

In the history of the lily as a garden plant we can discern five important periods. The first is the one of the Madonna Lily, which, as we have seen, became widely known because of its nutritious and medicinal properties and later because of its religious and aesthetic values. It still is one of the most widely distributed species lilies in our gardens.

The second important period was during the nineteenth century when *L. speciosum* and then *L. auratum* were flowered in England. These magnificent lilies created a furor and caused a great increase in the attention given to all lilies. The space devoted to them in publications of that period shows clearly the sensational character of this first showing of these Oriental species.

The third stage in lily history came with the introduction of *Lilium regale,* which flowered first in England in 1905 and was

Our native L. superbum *is America's most valued contribution to the world of lilydom. It reached European gardens during the eighteenth century. This striking colony of it was photographed at Windsor.*

introduced into the United States between 1908 and 1910. The importance of *Lilium regale* in the history of garden lilies can hardly be overestimated. It is easily grown from seed and, probably more than anything else, this factor is responsible for its remarkable performance in our gardens. Growers selected the finest and strongest plants as seed and pollen parents and constantly improved the strain. Raised from seed, the lilies were only nursery-grown for a comparatively short period, rarely more than three or four years, and hence the chances of contamination with virus diseases were minimized. *Lilium regale* thus provided our gardens with a cheap, virtually indestructible, lily, representative of Asiatic lilies in all their glory. No wonder that the Regal Lily took America by storm and that, in a short time, it became one of the most widely planted lilies. That it is now being replaced by better and stronger hybrids is only natural and not to be regretted. A strain of *L. leucanthum* seedlings, such as the Olympic Hybrids, is far superior in size and form, in drought and virus resistance and in beauty.

The fourth period is that of the Easter Lily, the Croft Lily, to be more specific. Its popularity, which took on the proportions of a real boom, a bright bubble that grew and burst in only a few years, was the direct result of the tragedy at Pearl Harbor and the ensuing war. In 1942, an Easter Lily craze struck the coast sections of California and Oregon, between Eureka and Astoria. In 1948, the boom was over, leaving in its wake untold misery and losses.

When, in 1928, Sidney Croft, a keen gardener of Bandon, Oregon, received some Easter Lilies from Dr. Griffiths, who had raised them from seed at the experimental station of the United States Department of Agriculture at Bellingham, Washington, nobody could have predicted that fourteen years later this gift would reach a value of many millions of dollars. In those days our Easter Lilies were imported from abroad where they could be grown much more cheaply than in this country. As a matter of fact, the bulbs were becoming too cheap and the quality was suffering.

The lilies that Croft received from Dr. Griffiths were healthy and multiplied at an astounding rate. They had been tested by commercial growers and florists and had already found a limited market on the Pacific Coast at the time World War II began. When, in 1941, no more lilies could be imported and this country reached the fullest employment ever known, the demand for cut flowers also attained unheard-of proportions. Shortages of flowers, heavy demand, and a public willing and able to pay caused the prices of the Croft Lilies to rise to astonishing heights.

Attracted by fantastic newspaper stories, by often inaccurate magazine articles and by the emphasis given to the economic possibilities of the Croft Lily by local boosters, many people were induced to invest in this "bonanza" and along the West Coast land prices rose from twenty-five or fifty dollars to one thousand dollars an acre and even higher. The price of planting stock went up to over a dollar a bulb. It was the demand for planting stock, developed by these new growers, that kept the available bulbs from the legitimate market and caused a still greater, entirely artificial, shortage and high prices when the normal demand was already oversupplied.

Considering that, through bulblets and scales, the Croft Lily can be increased at the rate of fifty-to-one in one year and remembering that Croft was mainly in demand for only one day each year, Easter Sunday, it soon became obvious to all insiders that the bubble must eventually burst. From a few bulbs in 1928 to some ten million in 1947 was an increase large enough to oversaturate any market.

Sidney Croft died early in the nineteen thirties. His widow lived to see the boom, but neither one shared in any of the profits—nor did the thousands of investors who arrived late on the scene. It was only the small band of pioneer growers, and perhaps some among the large group of dealers and gamblers who followed in their wake, who made money out of the boom. Now that its boom period has subsided, the Easter Lily will remain a standard crop for experienced growers, something which, like any other agricultural crop, provides for the serious operator a living, but no fortune.

The new era of lily culture, the fifth state, begins with the introduction of hybrid lilies into our gardens. Like *L. x testaceum* and that beautiful variety, Lillian Cummings, raised by Miss Preston, several of the earlier hybrids had already convinced many gardeners that it was worthwhile to give these new lilies a trial. The history of the still newer hybrids, made possible by the advance in science and research described in Chapter 14, begins only now. Developing along the lines of increased knowledge on the breeders' part, these new lilies are finding an honored place in the plantings of specialist and amateur alike, in this age of suburban and rural living, with its deepening appreciation of choice garden subjects. Although they have their origin in the remote wildernesses of Asia or India, or in the mountain regions of Europe; although they may come to us after long sojourns in the nurseries of England or the Netherlands or Japan, they are now being transformed into typically American plants.

The conditions to which our lilies are exposed in suburban gardens are often as difficult for them to take as the impact of the noisy waterfronts and crowded slums of Boston and New York must have been on our immigrants when they arrived in the United States. As the latter have found their bearings, have acclimated themselves and been assimilated, and as they have learned to love the land of their adoption, so the older lilies are adapting themselves and the new hybrids are claiming this country as their native land. Through hybridization by the American growers and gardeners, the best and the finest qualities of these lilies have been fused and those traits that might have made them unsuitable for our gardens are being eliminated.

We are entering upon a new era. The species, the wild lilies, are still being grown and sold, but their role has been played and their importance to gardeners is rapidly diminishing. Endowed with new vigor and easily propagated, the new hybrids are rapidly increasing or, in many instances, have already replaced the species from which they were derived. As with roses and tulips, iris and peonies, the day is not far off when hybrids will be the accepted lilies for all our gardens and species will be of interest only to the specialist and the breeder.

for Your Garden

The species are good to see. I like them better than the hybrids, for they are what nature made them to be. The species have characters that separate them one from another, that express countries and climates and suggest surprising histories in long lines of worthy books. Yet I do not eliminate the hybrids, because all lilies are adorable. Much of the glow of the world would disappear if lilies were lost.

L. H. BAILEY (1858–1954)

The lily species that have been tried and have proved themselves come in many types. As they were discovered in our mountain regions and on our plains, and as they came from Europe and Asia, they found a home in many a garden and were welcome guests. Bulbs selected from good strains of wild lilies gradually produced vigorous clumps and multiplied. Such bulbs were often given away or sold. As the interest in gardening increased and as these lilies became more popular, they eventually spread over an increasingly larger area. Among our older gardeners there will be few who recall the gardens of their youth without remembering the Tiger Lilies, the Madonna Lilies, and the upright Candlestick Lilies so well loved in those days, as well as many a clump of *L. superbum, L. canadense, L. washingtonianum, L. pardalinum,* and many another American native cherished by old-time gardeners.

In this chapter we shall discuss the wild lilies from all over the Northern Hemisphere. With a little care and attention, most, if not all, can be grown by you. We have found that many lilies listed in older literature as tender or half-hardy grew well for us in Oregon. Similar lilies, *L. nepalense* to cite an especially extreme example, flowered in New England. From Winnipeg, Manitoba, comes word of the repeated flowering and survival in hard winters of several trumpet lilies. From Sweden, Norway, and Scotland come similar reports. Definitely, the lilies are hardier than we knew.

The wild lilies have been listed here in alphabetical order. For every one we have given the currently correct name, the country or region of its origin, and other pertinent data. Our indebtedness to Wilson's great book, *Lilies of Eastern Asia,* to Grove and Cotton's *Supplement to Elwes' Monograph,* to Professor George L. Slate's *Lilies for American Gardens,* and to Woodcock and Stearn's *Lilies of the World* is gratefully acknowledged. Students seeking further information should turn to these sources for more complete data.

We have included the lilies given specific standing by Beane and Vollmer, as published on December 30, 1955, in the Contributions from the Dudley Herbarium. It should be distinctly understood, however, that our purpose here is not to give a critical, botanical review of the entire range of the lily species. We have tried to give a complete listing of the wild lilies of the world in terms understandable to the layman and have assessed these species as to their horticultural value, actual or potential. The genera Cardiocrinum, Notholirion, and Korolkowia have not been discussed. Interesting as they are, specialists and keen amateurs will find the information in readily accessible form in Woodcock and Stearn's excellent book. We have no experience with these plants and could add nothing to the fund of knowledge and experience available in England.

L. amabile

A nodding, grenadine-red, late June-flowering lily, found throughout Korea. The brilliant red flowers, nicely spotted and dotted with black, are carried on strong but slender stems, from three to four feet tall. Because of its free-flowering habit, few bulbs are needed to make a vivid display of color in the garden. *L. amabile* does well in the full sun and will stand considerable drought. The intense color does not fade in direct sunlight. The bulbs are white, high-crowned, and composed of relatively few large scales. Plant five inches deep in porous soils, more shallowly in clay and adobe. Stem roots are sparse and often entirely lacking; basal roots heavy and contractile. Under-ground bulblets are formed in profusion, especially on the smaller stems. It is also easily raised from seed. Its rather strong scent is resented by some and, while usually not objectionable in the garden, may be a trifle too fragrant in the house, when the flowers are used in quantity. *L. amabile* was first flowered in cultivation in 1913. In 1918 R. H. Wilson sent seeds to the Arnold Arboretum, by which they were distributed.

L. amabile var. luteum. This lovely yellow form appeared in 1933 in Holland and a similar one was found in England's famous Kew Gardens near London in 1934. Here in America a number of growers have raised considerable quantities from seed which comes true to color, but shows a great deal of variation. The best plants among them have been selected and are now on the market. The bulbs are similar to those of *L. amabile,* but run somewhat smaller in size.

L. amoenum

A dwarf and attractive pink-flowered lily from Yunnan Province in China—looking rather like a narrow-leaved and small flowered *L. rubellum.* It flowered in cultivation for the first time in 1938. The bulb is small. The slender stem grows to about 12 inches tall and bears from one to three, slightly drooping, bowl-shaped flowers of a deep rose-pink color. It grows in China at an elevation of from 6000 to 7200 feet and, consequently, we believe that, once a little stock of this lily has become established and selected plants can be made to produce seed, it may well be possible to build up a stock that will be hardy in many parts of the United States and Europe.

L. arboricola

A lily which grows in trees—not as a parasite and not receiving nourishment from it—but having a habit of growth that seems to make it dependent on the air and moisture available in the branches of trees in the forests of Northern Burma. Discovered by Frank Kingdon-Ward in 1953, this rare lily flowered in England in

1954 and it was shown in May of that year at the Chelsea Flower Show. This lily, which comes close to *L. primulinum var. ochraceum* differs from it in the form of the bulb and the flower, as well as in the size of the leaves. The flower is notable for its color, being a clear apple-green, the petals recurving from the base. Obviously this rarest of all lilies is not one for our gardens, nor is it a prospect for hybridizing. It is listed here solely because of its curiosity value.

L. auratum, *the so-called Gold-band Lily of Japan, reached England and Massachusetts simultaneously in 1862—only about one hundred years ago. Its blood is evident in many of the finest new hybrids.*

L. auratum

The "Gold Band" or "golden-rayed" lily of Japan. This magnificent lily seems to have been introduced simultaneously in England, where the famous firm of Veitch showed it in 1862, and in our country, where Francis Parkman of Jamaica Plains, near

Boston, Massachusetts, flowered it from bulbs sent to him from Japan. The Auratum Lily is, without doubt, the most magnificent representative of the entire lily family. It flowers from early August to the middle of September; sometimes even into October, depending on the strain and type. The flowers range in color from ivory-white, with only a few slight golden speckles, to almost solid carmine-red, a variation that has given rise to the erroneous belief that such highly colored lilies are of hybrid origin.

L. AURATUM

Growers distinguish two main types of this species. The first to flower is *L. auratum var. praecox,* an alpine type that bears very big flowers on rather thin short stems. The other type, *L. auratum var. platyphyllum,* or broad-leafed, grows to a maximum height of twelve feet and will bear as many as thirty flowers when full-sized. The *platyphyllum* type is the best for American gardens and American production has been concentrated on this form.

L. auratum is not more difficult to grow than any other lily. Failure in the garden must be ascribed to the use of faulty bulbs, to virus diseases, and to errors in planting and handling. In spite of many opinions to the contrary, *L. auratum* need *not* be planted nine to twelve inches deep. Experiments with thousands of bulbs have convinced us that a six inch depth is more than sufficient and that a well-drained, well-aerated soil and a good, airy, sunny location is what this lily prefers. Also, contrary to the opinion expressed in many books, this lily is a gross feeder and needs a rich soil. Incorporated with the soil some time before planting, old well-rotted cow manure and a generous mulching with compost and rich leafmold are most beneficial. Thus grown, these lilies will make an abundant increase.

Imported by the millions between the period of their first showing in this country and 1941, Japanese bulbs were at first of excellent quality. Roughly speaking, we can say that between 1862 and 1912, from Japan there came no bulbs but those actually found growing in the wild on mountain slopes, harvested there, packed and shipped without an intervening stay in nurseries or bulb farms.

After 1912 the demand for these lilies grew to such proportions that the Japanese began to produce them commercially. The larger concentrations of bulbs on their farms, together with the total absence of any protection against the spread of virus diseases, soon caused a widespread infection of the bulbs. Removing the roots before shipping the bulbs facilitated packing and handling, lowered the weight, and hence the shipping costs, but certainly did not help to improve the quality of the stock nor its adaptability to our gardens.

Such imported and mutilated bulbs usually flowered once, only to succumb to virus or bulb rot. It is immaterial whether this handling method was used by design or through ignorance. It was one of the strongest factors in leading American gardeners to brand all lilies, and especially *L. auratum,* as difficult to grow. That this was entirely undeserved has been shown quite amply by the great success of American-grown seedling strains.

Several color types have been segregated, such as *L. auratum var. rubro-vittatum,* with deep crimson stripes. There are ivory-colored types known as *L. auratum var. virginale* and one called *pictum* in which the flower is heavily spotted with crimson. These so-called varieties are color variants selected from seedling Auratums. The differences have been accentuated by further crossing of selected and desirable types. Such lilies are not of hybrid character and merely represent selected strains of greater or lesser uniformity.

L. bakerianum

A species described by E. H. Wilson and by Grove and Cotton as "one of the most variable of lilies." The type we have grown is the one from the Shan State of northern Burma. The stem is from 2 to 3 feet tall and bears large, pendulous, bell-shaped flowers of a soft, creamy-white color, spotted with red on the inside. The stem has roots above the bulb and wanders under ground before emerging; the leaves are narrow and scattered. The stamens have brownish anthers and orange pollen. *L. bakerianum* is named after the noted British botanist, John Gilbert Baker (1834–1920) who worked at Kew. The *L. bakerianum,* described above, is probably the type—*L. bakerianum var. typicum.* Other variants have been named *yunnanense, rubrum, delavayi,* and *aureum.* It is quite possible that among these variants there are some new species. It is to be hoped that they will soon be introduced again so that they can be studied and described from material grown under garden conditions. The names suggest some delightful color variations which, combined with the lovely bell shape of the flower and its delicious scent, may well be of great value to hybridizers.

L. bolanderi

An attractive and exotic-looking little lily from the Siskiyou Mountains of southern Oregon and northern California. The smooth, bluish-green stem carries several whorls of leaves. The flowers are bell-shaped and hang down. They have a suggestion of a "bloom," like that found on grapes. The outside color is a strange brick-red with a marked bluish cast to it; the inside is pale crimson and conspicuously dotted with red. As many as seven flowers are carried on a stem. This charming little lily was named after Henry Nicholas Bolander, a noted botanist, who in his later years taught at Portland, Oregon. In our garden this little lily has persisted with no care whatsoever, but it has not multiplied.

L. BROWNI

L. browni var. browni

This lily is said to have been introduced into England about 1835, and to have first flowered with F. E. Brown at Slough, near Windsor, in 1837; about that date he gave three bulbs to M. Miellez, a French horticulturist of Lille. In 1838 it was introduced into Belgium and Holland, and in 1841 made its public debut at a Horticultural Exposition held in Lille. It was at once acclaimed and its cultivation in Belgium and Holland assiduously entered upon. Where Brown obtained his bulbs from is unknown. According to Spae, von Siebold ventured the opinion that it might be a native of Nepal and also of China and Japan. To date no such lily as *L. browni* F. E. Brown is known from Nepal. At the time of its introduction only the Dutch had trade with Japan, and no lily exactly like it has been found in Japan, though the variety *colchesteri* Wils. is cultivated there. In China at that date only Macao and Canton were open to trade (except that Spanish ships had a right to call at Amoy), but the British East India Company maintained a brisk trade with Canton and their ships continually brought back plants which notably enriched English gardens.

L. browni is a beautiful trumpet lily, bearing large, horizontally placed trumpet flowers of a pure, creamy-white color inside; dark purple, sometimes tinged with green, on the outside. The specimens we have grown carried only from one to three flowers on stems of from two to three feet tall.

L. browni var. australe. This is the narrow-leaved type that occurs in Hong Kong and the Yunnan district. It emerges very late and flowers late, thus suggesting that it found its origin in rather high and cold regions. This variety grows much taller than the type. The flowers we have raised here were of a generally lighter color and the shape even more elegant and refined than those on *L. browni* itself. We believe that *L. browni var. australe* may have great potential as a parent plant for special races of trumpet lilies.

L. bulbiferum

An upright-flowering lily with red or orange-red flowers and bearing stem bulbils in the axils of the leaves. In our experience this bulbil-bearing characteristic is not of great importance as a means of botanical identification. Many lilies raised by us will produce stem bulbils, if disbudded at an early stage or when damaged in some way. Under normal circumstances they do not produce bulbils. Production of stem bulbils is, therefore, not a reliable characteristic.

L. bulbiferum var. croceum. This brilliantly orange-colored, upright-flowering lily has been the pride of many a cottage garden. As the Orange Lily it is cultivated in Great Britain. In Germany it is known as the Fire Lily (Feuerlilie) and in the United States it is sometimes known as the Russian Lily or Red Russian Lily. It is hardy, stem-rooting, multiplies rapidly and lasts well even in completely neglected gardens. *L. bulbiferum var. croceum* crosses readily with *L. dauricum* and its varieties, as well as with many other species, and imparts to the offspring its vigor and hardiness.

L. callosum

From a package of seed received from a friend in Japan, we raised a large stock of this very lovely, elegant, and refined little lily, only to find that no demand existed and no great interest was aroused by it among the gardeners who viewed it. On slender stems from five to fifteen little bell-shaped flowers are borne with the segments cohering for about one third of their length. From this little tube they curve outward and reveal the soft orange-red color of the inside of the bell and the orange-red pollen. The outside is a dull red. The foliage is narrow and scattered. These little lilies are very easy to raise from seed. They are exotic and unusual in appearance and the amateur gardener would make no mistake in raising a few for planting out in the rock garden or in some other sheltered spot where they may reproduce themselves from seed. To our knowledge no one has tried to use this lily in hybridizing.

L. canadense

The commonest and most widely distributed lily of eastern North America was also the first American lily to become known in Europe. The stems are from two to five feet tall, smooth and green; the foliage is arranged in whorls and the graceful bell-shaped flowers open in July in a color range that varies from pure canary yellow to a deep and distinct reddish crimson. The species has been subdivided according to its color forms and varieties such as *L. canadense var. coccineum* (dark red); *var. editorum* found in drier regions and *var. flavum,* clear yellow, and *var. immaculatum,* clear warm unspotted yellow, are sometimes offered.

L. candidum

This lovely pure white lily, a symbol of our religion and often the highlight of the June garden, has been cultivated for thousands of years. The clones that have persisted are invariably infected with a mild virus disease which, in turn, seems to open the way to damage by botrytis, basal rot, and other pests and diseases. We have raised large stocks of disease-free *L. candidum.* By selection of the finest individual plants and by using them as the parents of further generations, we were able to produce a race, the Cascade Strain, far superior to any of the older *L. candidum* now in our gardens or imported from abroad. Since, even though this race of lilies was indubitably superior, it had to compete on the basis of price with any and all cheap stocks of unknown provenance, it was impossible to continue its commercial production. All bulbs from the approximately five acres of healthy stock were sold and for several years we abandoned any idea of producing more. Recently a new interest in healthy *L. candidum* of the Cascade Strain type is appearing and, consequently, we may reintroduce the strain. In addition to these Cascade Strain lilies, we are also now growing a strain of seedlings, from seed collected for us in Palestine, that show remarkable vigor.

As has been noted elsewhere, this lily is different from all others, in that it must be planted almost even with the soil and certainly never with more than an inch of soil over the bulb. Flowering in June, it will die down and start making new leaves almost before, or as the old foliage dies down. For best results August planting is indicated. *L. candidum* needs lime and does well in a fairly moist, rich, well-drained garden soil.

L. candidum varieties. A number of varieties or strains of *L. candidum* have been offered. A silver or gold-edged leaf variant is seen from time to time. This may not be a virus-caused color variant, but rather due to a sport or mutation. While a plant like this may be a curiosity, it has no great value for horticultural purposes.

L. candidum Cascade Strain—a strain raised in Oregon from seed originally sent over by the Abbé Souillet of Milly-sur-Gennes, France. Through selection of better and better seed and pollen parents a fine strain was built up. Due to the difficulties of competing with cheap foreign offers, from stocks accumulated during the war years, the American production of this fine strain had to be abandoned. It was resumed in 1960.

L. candidum var. *cernuum*—a form with smaller, rather star-shaped flowers. It occurs in various sections of the United States and we have found sizable groups in Oregon gardens. It has no advantage over other *L. candidum* types.

L. candidum var. *plenum*—a monstrosity for which there should be no room in the garden. This is a double Madonna Lily, a mutation already described and pictured in a four-page German tract, dated 1662.

L. candidum var. *purpureum*—a variety with both bulbs and flowers streaked with purple-red. It was known in the year 1700. The discoloration may be due to virus infection.

L. candidum var. salonikae—an early flowering form of *L. candidum,* similar in many respects to *L. candidum var. cernuum.* The original bulbs of this strain were collected in Greek Macedonia in the winter of 1916–17. At one time thought to be botrytis-resistant and stronger-growing than the type, it soon succumbed to virus and, at present, is no longer offered in the trade.

L. carniolicum

A typical martagon lily with five or more vivid red flowers. It was described by John Parkinson as the "Bright Red Martagon of Hungarie." It grows wild in northern Italy, western Rumania, and in Hungary down to southern Yugoslavia. It grows in well-drained loam, in meadows and hedgerows, and is an attractive lily which is closely related to *L. chalcedonicum.* The varieties *albanicum* and *Jankae* are subspecies and often occur with bright yellow petals usually spotted with black.

L. catesbaei

This is the lily which grows profusely in the slash pines and acid swamps of the Southeast. It is an upright flowering lily with narrow yellow and scarlet petals that blooms a month later than *L. superbum.* It is the only American lily, except *L. philadelphicum,* with erect flowers.

L. cernuum

A most attractive, diminutive lily from Manchuria and Korea, has lilac-tinted, recurved flowers, often dotted with wine-purple spots. This charming little lily resembles *L. pumilum* in all but color and is as easy to raise as that coral-red lily.

Several growers in this country have built up stocks and, through the usual process of selecting the strongest-growing types for further propagation, it has become readily available in dependable quality. This is one of the prettiest of small lilies and possesses a color most desirable and rare in the summer garden.

L. cernuum does well in full sun and does not seem to have any special requirements. It flowered for the first time in England in 1915 in the famous nursery of Amos Perry of Enfield. It is from

*L. cernuum is a dainty
Korean species noted for its
pink-orchid color and dark
markings.*

12 to 20 inches high and sets seed readily. Interesting hybrids between this odd-colored lily and several other species have been
raised and are now available. (See Patterson and Harlequin
Hybrids.)

L. chalcedonicum

This is probably the most dazzlingly brilliant red lily in existence. Its intense color, further heightened by an almost lacquer-
like sheen, highlights any garden corner. The nodding flowers are
two to five in number. Flowering in early July, the plants grow
about three feet tall with numerous, light green leaves closely held
to the stem. It has no stem roots and the bulbs should be given
the same shallow planting as Madonna Lilies. They prefer to be
left undisturbed for many years and will form charming clumps in
the garden. As usual in all lilies, there is some variation in the
color and spotting of the flowers and no doubt vigorous types can
be selected from any group of seedlings. This is the lily described
by Parkinson as the "Red Martagon of Constantinople."

L. chalcedonicum is the seed parent of the famous cross with *L.
candidum* which produced the beautiful *L. x testaceum.*

L. columbianum

Our Oregon native, it looks like a miniature *L. humboldti*. It grows wild in great profusion from northern California through Oregon, Washington, western Idaho, and southern British Columbia. It is a graceful little lily which, when well suited, may produce as many as thirty flowers. First collected and sent to Europe in 1873.

L. CONCOLOR

L. concolor

Is one of the best species lilies for garden effect and for cutting. The vivid red, star-shaped flowers hold their own in arrangements with other flowers and lend unusual distinction to any mixed bouquet. For this reason alone, if for no other, it should be more widely grown. The solid bulbs are sound, creamy-white in color, turning pink when exposed to light and should be planted three to four inches deep.

L. concolor var. coridion. A bright yellow form of this lovely lily. It has been used by us in the production of several interesting hybrids.

L. dauricum

Is an upright, yellow to deep red, cup-shaped lily which flowers quite early. It will be found in many old gardens and used to be available in varieties, such as *L. dauricum luteum,* a clear yellow and *L. dauricum* E. H. Wilson, a clear apricot. Both varieties were used in the production of the Tiger Lily Hybrids described elsewhere. Whereas the Dauricum Lilies have now been surpassed by more recent introductions, they are, nevertheless, still very attractive. When available, good healthy stocks of them should be cherished.

L. davidi *(formerly* L. willmottiae*) bears up to forty or more small pendant red flowers on a tall wiry stem.*

L. davidi

This name belongs to a wide group of lilies, formerly sold as *L. willmottiae, L. sutchuenense,* etc. It is essentially a tall, cinnabarred lily with as many as forty or even fifty flowers borne on a tall, wiry stem which often rises to a height of six feet. The bulb is white and flattened out, consisting of but a few large substantial scales. Found in western China and often grown in that country for its nutritional value, it was first introduced by E. H. Wilson in 1904. Various forms or varieties have been raised, such as the one known in the trade as *L. willmottiae unicolor,* the variety or selection called *L. maxwill,* and one called *L. davidi* Queen Charlotte.

These named varieties are now of little importance since, based mainly on the best forms of *L. davidi* as mother plants and a wide group of pollen parents (including *L. dauricum* and *L. amabile*), some much improved hybrids have been raised and are readily available as Fiesta Hybrids.

L. distichum

Is a little lily from Manchuria and Korea, essentially a plant of the moist and shady woodlands. It is a stem-rooter, grows from one to three feet tall and has its leaves arranged in whorls. The flowers are arranged in a raceme, are pale orange-red with dark spots and the anthers are orange-red. It is like *L. medeoloides,* but more vigorous. To the best of our knowledge it has little to recommend itself, either for hybridizing or for the garden. Possibly, there may be a place for it in the rock garden.

L. duchartrei

A lovely, nodding, little lily with white flowers, delicately spotted with purple. It was first discovered by the French missionary, Armand David, in 1869, but was not cultivated until 1903 when E. H. Wilson sent some bulbs to England. The *L. duchartrei* now in cultivation probably all came from the collection of Reginald John Farrer (1880–1920) who also found his plants in western China and called it the "Marble Martagon." We have grown a small stock of this lily without difficulty and believe it will be as easy to produce and to flower as *L. lankongense,* which it resembles.

L. fairchildi

A lily from the Palomar and Laguna Mountains in San Diego County, California. It is very close to *L. ocellatum.* The leaves are narrower and brighter green than in *L. ocellatum* and according to Lawrence Beane, who has described it, it is unique and quite distinct. Neither as a garden plant, nor in hybridizing, does it hold promise as a plant of outstanding value.

L. FORMOSANUM

L. formosanum

A tall, white, very late-flowering trumpet lily, raised very easily from seed, is also so highly subject to virus diseases that its presence in our gardens is a doubtful asset. A dwarf form, known as Price's Variety, is very attractive. The tall form, which reaches a height of better than six feet, is magnificent. Because of its habit of flowering from October to November, it has great appeal and distinction. *L. formosanum* will flower within 18 months from seed. While it is so susceptible to virus diseases that it is difficult to maintain a stock of it in the garden, the symptoms of the disease are readily apparent and a careful gardener can keep the stock healthy by vigorously roguing out the sick plants. New stock can easily be raised from seed or bought cheaply from reliable sources. The dwarf form, Price's Variety, breeds true from seed.

In the trade the tall, late-flowering *L. formosanum* has been offered under the name of St. Louis Strain. This name stems from the fact that for many years this outstanding lily was raised by Mr. and Mrs. Mortimer Burroughs of St. Louis. Through careful selection they built up a tall, strong-growing strain of great beauty and refinement. *L. formosanum var. wilsoni,* while not selected with such a personal taste, is a fine, tall, and beautiful strain. *L. formosanum var. pricei* is the early flowering, short-stemmed strain, attractive in borders. Another group, selected by the late Mr. Wallace of Tunbridge Wells, England, is now being marketed as Wallace's Selection. The flowers are all-white, mid-season and about five feet tall when well grown.

L. grayi

This small, graceful lily from Virginia, Tennessee, and North Carolina, where it grows in woods and in mountain glades, is possibly a subspecies of *L. canadense.* Since it is less vigorous than *L. canadense* and rather variable, there seems to be little advantage in recommending it. The name commemorates Asa Gray (1810–1888), for many years Professor of Natural History at Harvard University.

L. hansoni

Is a strong-growing, sturdy, vigorous lily with a great number of nodding thick, waxy, slightly recurved, orange flowers nicely spotted with brown. The plant grows four feet tall in the garden, taller in semishade. It is one of the few lilies that definitely must have shade to give its best performance and to set seed. The bulbs are white, tinged pink upon exposure to light. It is a stem-rooter and should be given about five inches of soil over the top of the bulb. Strangely enough, for a lily which grows readily from scales, it is hard to obtain. It will set seed with pollen from *L. martagon,* but very rarely with its own pollen. It is strongly resistant, perhaps immune, to virus and is therefore most welcome in our garden. When crosed with *L. martagon,* it produces magnificent hybrids, all of which are charming garden ornaments.

L. harrisianum (See *L. pardalinum var. giganteum.*)

L. henrici

Is a border-line lily, in that many botanists look upon it as a *Nomocharis* and not as a true lily. It is a July-flowering plant with three foot stems on which it carries from one to five, white or faintly rose-tinted, open flowers on long pedicels. The spreading segments have a narrow, triangular smooth green nectary furrow typical of many true lilies. Different forms have been found, including the variety *typicum* which has pansy-purple patches at the base of each petal. In the variety *maculatum* the petals are marked at the base with a few scattered, but rather large and well defined, crimson-purple spots. To the best of our knowledge, this little lily has not yet been used in hybridizing.

L. henryi

One of the finest lilies from China, bears as many as twenty bright orange, nodding flowers on tall, swaying stems. The shiny, broad leaves are of a dark green color and are closely spaced. The flowers have a tendency to bleach in the sun and, therefore, are grown to best advantage in light shade.

E. H. Wilson sent large shipments of the lily to this country in 1900 and from that date on it has become a popular garden lily. A beautiful lemon form appeared, at approximately the same time, in several nurseries; and while it has been called a hybrid, it is undoubtedly a mutation or sport. Several growers own stocks of this yellow lily under the name of *L. henryi var. citrinum.*

As stated in other chapters, *L. henryi* will cross with various trumpet lilies to produce magnificent hybrids, endowed with great vigor and fine coloring, and with many new and interesting intermediate flower types.

The bulbs of *L. henryi* and its hybrids are dark purple. It is a stem-rooting lily, bearing numerous bulblets under the ground. This habit can be exploited to advantage by packing the bulbs in moist peat moss and by letting them sprout while in storage. The sprouts can be kept growing till they have attained a length of several feet. By planting the bulb on its side, laying the stem carefully in a five-inch-deep trench, made for that purpose, many more bulblets will form and the flowering of the lily is in no way impaired. This method can also be followed with other lilies which have a pronounced bulblet-forming habit.

L. humboldti

An extremely variable, but very beautiful, species from the Sierra Nevada range of central and northern California. It grows in open woodlands at an elevation of from 2000–4000 feet. The fine, nodding, reflexed flowers are bright orange, strongly spotted with large maroon dots. The large, purplish anthers have dark-orange pollen. Dr. Griffiths remarked, "In the experimental planting at Bellingham, Washington, consisting of close to 2000 bulbs grown mainly from seed, it is difficult to find two plants upon which the flowers are alike. The vegetative portions of the plants are nearly as variable and the bulbs scarcely seem to belong to the same species." We have also grown a large number of these fine lilies and have found Dr. Griffiths' statement to be true. The leaves of *L. humboldti* are spatulate, dull green and carried in irregular whorls and the inner perianth segments do not show the crested claws found in the closely related species *L. ocellatum* and *L. ocellatum var. bloomerianum.*

L. iridollae

The "Pot of Gold Lily," belongs to the *L. superbum-L. canadense* group. It grows in meadows and sphagnum bogs in southern Alabama and northwest Florida, not far from the Gulf of Mexico. This lily was discovered, as recently as October 1940 by Mrs. J. Norman Henry of Gladwyne, Pennsylvania. The lily bears pendulous, usually solitary, flowers with strongly reflexed petals of a golden yellow or warm buff-orange color. An unusual feature of this lily is that it makes new foliage growth in August and stays green over winter. This habit suggests that it might best be transplanted immediately after flowering. *L. iridollae* is not a lily for the average gardener, nor does it offer much for the hybridizer. It is possible, however, that in its growth characteristics there may be special habits that could be of value.

L. japonicum

The Bamboo Lily of Japan, bears long, nicely trumpet or funnel-shaped flowers in June. The stem is from two to three feet tall, the foliage sparse. According to English garden experts it is a tender lily, but in Oregon it grows without any protection and has lived through several very cold winters without injury.

L. japonicum is susceptible to virus diseases and imported bulbs have been most disappointing in quality. Domestic stocks of this fine lily are now available. It is, however, a very slow grower and may well remain on the "difficult to grow" list.

L. kelloggi

This is one of the very prettiest of all American lilies, sweet-scented and of lovely form and color, the Turk's-cap flowers ivory-white when first opening, but soon turning to pink and pinkish mauve, deepening to dull purple. Often there is a yellow stripe at the base of each petal; and maroon or wine-red dots sometimes appear. The anthers are reddish and the pollen orange. Usually from two to four feet tall, specimens have been found as tall as eight feet and carrying seventy blooms instead of the usual ten to fifteen. We have grown considerable stocks of this lily from seed collected for us by Boyd Kline of Medford, Oregon. There seems to be a very good chance that it will hybridize with other Pacific Coast species.

L. lankongense

Like L. duchartrei, a native of western China, this is a very easy lily to raise from seed and is extremely attractive in the garden. The flowers are of the recurved martagon type and the petals are a soft pinkish-rose that deepens with age. Sometimes spotted quite heavily with purple, it will also come almost without spots. It has done well in any of our newly cleared soils and seems to be able to withstand considerable drought and heat.

L. leichtlini

Is a rather rare lily, also difficult to grow. The variety *maximowiczi* is much easier and should be ordered in preference to the true type. Both are stem-rooting, with wandering stems sometimes traveling for several feet before emerging. The flowers, orange-yellow or orange-red in color, are heavily spotted with purple-brown dots. This lily, which in many respects resembles the Tiger Lily, flowers in July. It was used in the production of the Fiesta Hybrids.

L. leucanthum var. chloraster

Identical with *L. centifolium* and the latter name is to be preferred. (E. H. Wilson distinguished *L. leucanthum* by the greenish mark down the center of the perianth segments.) Many such lilies have shown up in large groups of *L. centifolium* hybrids and it may well be that the popular strain called Green Mountain Hybrids is a selection of the types recognized by Wilson as *L. leucanthum var. chloraster.*

L. longiflorum

The family to which all our Easter Lilies belong is, commercially at least, our most important lily. The long, funnel-shaped, pure-white flowers are borne on a short stem, covered with short, narrow green leaves. The lily is very fragrant, lends itself well to forcing and has excellent keeping qualities (See page 136). The United States Department of Agriculture is testing a number of new varieties which may replace the Croft, Ace, Kenyon-Davidson, and others now on the market.

L. mackliniae

A lovely little nodding lily with white or soft rose-purple campanulate flowers with a deep carmine stain at the base. Our plants do not grow more than 12 inches tall and carry but one or two flowers, but Frank Kingdon-Ward, who discovered the lily in

L. MACKLINIAE

January 1946, mentions that it will grow up to 36 inches in its wild state, with as many as five to eight flowers. It was found on Sirhoi Peak in Manipur and first flowered in England in 1948. Our little stock flowers well and we are raising a new crop from seed. Nothing is yet known about the hardiness of this little lily nor about its tolerance to adverse or different conditions. We have treated it as a half-hardy lily and have given our stock the protection of a cool greenhouse.

L. maritimum

A graceful, small-flowered lily from the northern California coast. On a stem that varies from three to seven feet, it carries up to ten small dark orange-red bell-shaped flowers on long pedicels that curve up and outward. It grows close to the sea near bogs and in meadows and would be difficult to establish in any areas where dry and hot conditions prevail. It is, we feel sure, a lily which must have a seaside habitat to thrive and would not be suitable either for the garden or for hybridizing. It should be pointed out that, even though this lily is found in or near swamps, it does not actually grow in the water, but rather on hummocks or between other plants that keep the bulb dry.

L. martagon album, *with its tall spires of moderate-sized pendant white flowers, is especially effective against evergreens or other shrubbery.*

L. martagon

This best known European lilies comes in two distinct colors. The purple form, the true type, is quite attractive, but the white form, *L. martagon album,* is of superlative beauty and grace. Both are from three to five feet tall, have their leaves arranged in whorls around the stem, and flower in June. They are not at all particular about soil and will thrive in a wide range of climates. Both lilies are comparatively easy to raise from seed and show charming variations in color. In particular, a very dark purple form of *L. martagon* is sometimes found, one that is especially attractive. When it is crossed with *L. hansoni,* hybrids of exceptional grace and beauty result. This cross was made by the late Mrs. R. O. Backhouse at Sutton Court, Hereford, England, and in a recent letter her son William tells of finding the lilies still in good condition after many years of neglect.

To the amateur lily breeder this group of lilies is strongly recommended as a most worthwhile and fruitful field of endeavor. *L. martagon* is one of the most permanent of all lilies. Once settled in the garden, it will increase from year to year, forming larger and finer spikes.

L. martagon var. cattaniae—the dark, burgundy red, completely unspotted form, originally found in woods near Mue, Dalmatia, by Maria de Cattani, a Dalmatian lady with botanical interests. The name *dalmaticum* has been used both for the variety *cattaniae* (unspotted, dark burgundy red) and for *sanguineo-purpureum*—a name used by British writers for the slightly spotted maroon-purple form.

L. medeoloides

The "Wheel Lily" of Japan, so named for the whorls of foliage which distinguish this plant. It is closely related to *L. distichum* and *L. tsingtauense*. *L. medeoloides* grows from Honshu, the main island of Japan, northward. In south Kamchatka it is a common plant, found in the meadows and birch forests. The bulbs are used for food. The nodding flowers range from apricot to scarlet, spotted with black but plants can also be found with unspotted flowers. Dr. Skinner of Manitoba, Canada, has used this lily in hybridizing, crossing it with *L. hansoni*. Since he reports that the resulting seedlings suffer less from spring frost than *L. hansoni*, there may be value in repeating this cross.

L. michauxi

The southern counterpart of *L. superbum*, growing from southern Virginia southward to Florida. Mrs. Henry reports that it grows in well-drained soil, usually on a hillside, often in a ravine but always well above the smallest stream. It is distinguished botanically from *L. superbum* by its smaller stature and by some other rather unimportant characteristics—unimportant to the gardener, if not to the botanist. The lily commemorates its discoverer, the French botanist André Michaux (1746–1802).

L. michiganense

Closely related to *L. canadense,* it carries from one to eight, often more, long-pedicelled, pendulous flowers of a beautiful orange-red, spotted toward the base with deep maroon. There is a great deal of variation in size and color and pure, golden yellow forms have been found.

L. monadelphum

One of the very first lilies to bloom on our farms, this lovely lemon-yellow lily with large scented, pendulous flowers is of great value for the specialist's garden. It will grow well in light shade and needs a woodland-type of soil, plenty of humus, perfect drainage. Its natural habitat is the north Caucasus, where it grows among shrubs and along mountain woods, up to 6000 feet. This is an easy lily to grow from seed. It resents transplanting and bulbs received from dealers may often, if not always, stay dormant for a year before making above-ground growth. Once established, it will be a major ornament to any garden. Its value in hybridizing has not been established, although crosses with *L. bulbiferum* and *L. maculatum* have been recorded.

L. neilgherrense

From southern India, where it grows among low shrubs and grasses at an altitude of from 6000 to 8500 feet. The long, narrow, almost tubular, trumpets may measure up to twelve inches long. They are of a very pure white, flushed with yellow within and strongly scented. Plants with almost solid yellow color have been found and are sometimes listed as *L. neilgherrense var. flavum.* The stem of young plants runs under ground for one or two feet before emerging above ground. While we have grown this lovely lily only in the cool greenhouse, we believe that it holds promise for the southern part of the United States. It flowers in August and September out of doors, but in the greenhouse it has flowered in June.

L. NEPALENSE

L. nepalense

A very beautiful and impressive lily from Nepal, with large, pendulous, pod-green flowers with the inside stained a deep wine-purple. We have grown it for years without any losses due to winter injury. We also have good reports on it from other parts of the country. Obviously, then, it is not a tender lily, but will grow when its normal growth habits coincide with the seasons. Late emerging, it needs warm, moist weather to come into bloom and warm, but not hot and dry, weather to complete its normal growth. Large plants raised by us went up to four feet tall and carried as many as five large flowers, well spaced on short pedicels along the stem. A selection, grown from seed, has been offered as *L. nepalense var. robustum.* There seems to be no foundation for this distinction. Another type, *L. nepalense var. concolor,* with self-colored yellow flowers has been reported and should be of great interest. It is to be hoped that seed of this variety can be obtained so that it can take its place along with its green variety.

L. nevadense

A small-flowered lily from the Sierra Nevada of California, closely resembling *L. pardalinum.* A number of varieties are recognized, such as *shastense.* This latter variety has now been raised to specific rank and should be listed, according to Beane and Vollmer, as *L. shastense.* Having had the privilege and pleasure of growing a number of these little lily variants, the thought remains with us that the slight differences that are noticeable are of little interest to the gardener or hybridizer. As Dr. Griffiths has repeatedly pointed out, any large population of any of the Pacific Coast species raised from seed, shows great differences in color, form, and even flowering season. We believe that merely regional variations should not be taken too seriously, as long as from selfed seed of *L. shastense,* one can raise *L. nevadense* or its exact duplicates.

L. nobilissimum

This interesting little lily with pure-white, often erect, flowers comes from the Ryukyu Archipelago south of Japan. It was shown at the International Lily Show in Seattle in 1954, the flowers being flown directly from Japan. Since it frequently has erect flowers, it may have great importance in hybridizing but, to date, no success with such attempts has been reported.

L. ocellatum

A very showy and lovely lily that occurs in Santa Barbara County, California. It is very closely related to *L. humboldti* but, according to Beane and Vollmer, it possesses so many distinct and unique characteristics that it should be considered as a separate species. The basic color of this lily is cadmium orange and the tips of the petals are splashed with crimson. The same authors also recognize *L. ocellatum var. bloomerianum*—a smaller, fewer-flowered and not so richly colored variant.

L. occidentale

The most western of American lilies, growing along the coast of Humboldt County in northern California and also in the coastal region of southern Oregon. It is closely related to *L. maritimum* and has pendulous, reflexed flowers of orange with maroon-purple spots, crimson tips and purple anthers with orange-red pollen.

L. ochraceum

An interesting lily from Yunnan, of which we received bulbs and seeds from the J. F. Rock collection in 1946. Our plants carried from one to two, strongly recurved, pendulous flowers of a curious greenish-yellow color, with deep purple in the throat and a rusty brown pollen. These lilies were never more than 12 inches tall and, judging by their appearance and the difficulties we had to keep them alive, we doubt if this plant will ever be of value to gardeners. *L. primulinum var. ochraceum* may be a variant. Also, *L. primulinum var. burmanicum,* however interesting to the expert, seems to have little value for the hybridizer or gardener. For those who can raise and show these lilies, they may well be a source of great pleasure and interest.

L.PAPILLIFERUM

L. papilliferum

Is another of the choice, little lilies that are the delight of the fanciers and the despair of the gardener who buys them for color effect in the garden and expects a show for his considerable expenditure of time and money. We raise a flat or two of *L. papilliferum* in a cool greenhouse without any difficulty and find in its fragrant, dark and deep crimson-purple, almost black, flowers a fine topic of conversation. This lily comes from warm and dry locations in northwestern Yunnan Province. With us it never exceeds 12 inches in height and carries at most two flowers, strongly reflexed and neatly offset by vivid orange pollen.

L. pardalinum giganteum *Sunset. This, the finest of the panther lilies, is held by some authorities to be a clone of the species, by others to be a lost, and later rediscovered hybrid originated by Burbank; by still others to be a natural hybrid between* L. humboldti *and* L. pardalinum; *in any event, a grand lily.*

L. pardalinum

The Leopard Lily of California, which has become widely distributed in gardens all over the Northwest. *L. pardalinum* will grow almost anywhere and multiplies so rapidly that substantial colonies of it can be found in the gardens of summer homes along the Northwestern mountain ranges. *L. pardalinum* is again a variable species. It carries many scentless Turk's-cap blooms, much recurved and of bright crimson toward the tips, with lighter centers and many brown spots. Similar lilies are now the *L. nevadense, L. fresnense,* and *L. shastense* species. A variant with orange flowers, small anthers and unbranched rhizomes is recognized as the distinct species *L. vollmeri.*

L. pardalinum var. giganteum. A new name, proposed by Beane and Vollmer for this lily, is *L. harrisianum.* This magnificent lily, also known as the Sunset, Red Giant, and Chinook Lily, has long been considered by the noted authority, Carl Purdy, and others, as a hybrid between *L. pardalinum* and *L. humboldti.* Beane and Vollmer report finding the lily along the Van Duzen River in northern California, where a Mr. Lee Harris had observed its growing on the banks prior to 1890. They report: "The old stage-coach road has followed this river for many years and directly in front of an inn and station these lilies were plentiful. Many lily bulbs must have been taken from this spot by travelers and transplanted to their own gardens." In our opinion this is no proof of the true origin of this lovely lily. Rather, we believe, that it is a hybrid remaining from those raised by Luther Burbank. It is not generally known that, beginning in 1875, Luther Burbank carried on an extensive hybridizing program. Purdy reports that "the start was made with the wild *L. pardalinum,* which was cultivated and the seeds planted. Extreme types of these seedlings were selected and cross-fertilized, the process being repeated several times. Variation in the offspring was wonderful to behold. In a collection of an estimated four hundred hybrids, every intermediate form could be found, from giants nine feet tall to dwarfs from six inches to a foot in height, while the flowers ranged in color from yellow centers and scarlet tips through orange to light yellow centers with pale red tips."

Knowing how readily outstanding, vigorous growing, new hybrids can travel, it is not surprising at all to find one of Burbank's early achievements growing in the gardens of an inn, on a stagecoach road leading from Burbank's Santa Rosa to northern California and Oregon. The rapid dissemination of new hybrid lilies in a wider and wider circle around our nurseries has always been a matter of concern to us. There is no doubt in our minds that Burbank must have had the same difficulties in keeping control of his many originations. To us, the conclusion is inescapable —travelers with gardening interests spread these lilies. We are dealing here either with one of Burbank's hybrids or with an unusually strong-growing mutation of *L. pardalinum,* one noted and selected by Burbank. In our opinion, the name *L. harrisianum* cannot be defended.

L. parryi

The Lemon Lily of California and Arizona, a lovely, scented, and delicately lemon-colored lily that is of great importance as one of the parents of the new clear-colored, scented Bellingham Hybrid Strains. *L. parryi* is difficult to establish, but colonies of it, such as we have seen in England and in our own gardens, lead us to believe that selected strains can be raised that should do well in most areas. The large, funnel-shaped, clear-lemon or butter-yellow flowers are borne on long pedicels. We have grown considerable numbers of this lily from seed. Like all American lilies, *L. parryi* should be transplanted immediately after, or even during, its flowering period. The bulbs cannot be stored and shipped later with any reasonable expectancy of success.

L. parvum

An alpine species, from the Sierra Nevada and Cascade Mountains of Oregon and California. It grows along mountain streams and, as Purdy relates, prefers a granite sand mixed liberally with humus. Again, like all lilies, it delights in good drainage, a soil filled with humus and a good supply of moisture at all times. The color of the lily varies according to the elevation at which it grows, from pure yellow to dark red, all spotted maroon. It reaches a height of from five to six feet and, while small, the attractive, bell-shaped, ascending blooms make a bright patch of color in the garden. It is easily propagated from scales.

L. philippinense

A truly tropical lily from the mountains of northern Luzon in the Philippine Islands. It is a rather short, up to three feet, trumpet lily with one to two purest white, long and narrow funnel-shaped flowers per stem. This lily, which to the best of our knowledge is not now produced in the United States, might be of great value for the subtropical gardens of Florida.

L. philadelphicum

The Wood, Glade, or Flame Lily widespread in eastern North America. The flowers are of a vivid orange-scarlet, slightly lighter at the base and spotted with dark maroon. The flowers stand wide open and upright. Many color variants exist, some of them named.

L. pitkinense

Another of the Beane and Vollmer new species. This lily was found in the Pitkin Marsh, in Sonoma County, California. It grows from three to six feet tall, from a short, almost round, stoloniferous rhizome; the leaves are whorled. The flowers are scarlet-vermilion in color, with a well-defined zone of yellow extending to the base of the petals and with small black spots confined mostly to the yellow zone.

L. POLYPHYLLUM

L. polyphyllum

A beautiful lily from the western Himalaya range where it was found at heights of 6000 to 12,000 feet. The narrow, bell-shaped flowers are creamy white, spotted, and streaked with lilac. In nature it grows up to six feet tall and carries as many as thirty flowers. The leaves are scattered. As reported by Woodcock and Stearn, in its color this lily resembles *L. duchartrei,* and in form, the Caucasian *L. monadelphum* group. The fleshy roots go down several feet and if bulbs are collected in the wild, when in flower or shortly after, the roots dry out and have great difficulty in becoming established again. Obviously then, this is a lily which does not like being disturbed. Its lovely coloring and the fine form of its flowers make it appear to be quite desirable as a potential parent plant in hybridizing experiments. Its apparently close relationship to *L. monadelphum* and, again, the relationship between *L. monadelphum* and *L. bulbiferum* suggest that possibly *L. polyphyllum* might be used in connection with such complicated hybrids as the Mid-Century group, to produce white and lilac-tinged flowers of upright or outward-facing form.

New seed of this lovely species reached us through the courtesy of Elgin T. Gates of Surfside, California. Traveling in the high valleys of Hunza, near the Chinese border, Mr. Gates had found these lilies and collected the seeds. It reached us in December 1959 and by May 1960, it was well up in the greenhouse and gave every promise of producing a clean and healthy stock.

L. pomponium

This lily forms with *L. chalcedonicum, L. carniolicum,* and *L. pyranaicum,* a group of closely allied species. *L. pomponium* is found on the southern face of the Maritime Alps of southern France. On stems of from twelve to eighteen inches in height five to ten nodding, recurved blooms are borne, with a rather unpleasant scent, but a brilliant grenadine-red color. Its merit in the garden is limited, as *L. pumilum* and *L. amabile* will give the same general effect and are easier to grow.

L. ponticum

Differs from *L. monadelphum* and *L. szovitsianum* in being smaller and less attractive. The flowers are primrose-yellow, pendulous and have a well-marked purple zone in the throat. The plant is said to have an unpleasant scent and, according to all we have learned about it, it has no value either for the garden or in hybridization.

L. primulinum

And its varieties *burmanicum* and *ochraceum* are all handsome lilies from southwestern China. We have grown a number of these, but find them definitely of interest only to the advanced specialist. The entire group is variable. It differs from *L. nepalense* in having shorter, more recurved flowers. The flowers are usually greenish-yellow with conspicuous purple blotches down the throat. A self-colored form, unblotched and of a lovely primrose yellow color, is called *L. primulinum var. primulinum.*

L. pumilum

This used to be called *L. tenuifolium* and is also known as the Coral Lily. It is one of the smallest lily plants, not much more than two feet tall when full-grown. Its brilliant scarlet flowers are very much recurved and borne in large numbers on stems covered with narrow, grasslike foliage, very much like that of *L. cernuum.* Its home is in China, Siberia, and Korea. *L. pumilum* flowers readily from seed in from one to two years. The bulbs are small and, when allowed to set seed, the plant sometimes exhausts its strength in seed production and dies. A fine orange-colored form is called Golden Gleam. It is as vigorous as *L. pumilum* and can be used to obtain interesting color effects. A yellow sport of *L. pumilum* was found in Canada and has been sold under the name of Yellow Bunting. It does not seem to be as strong as its deeper colored relatives and may well be a true albino form. Attempts are being made now to build up, through careful breeding, this yellow form. The time should not be too far distant when brilliant red, true soft orange, and clear yellow forms of *L. pumilum* will be generally available.

L. pyrenaicum

Although from northern Spain and southwestern France, this lily is very much at home in English gardens and grew very readily in Oregon. It is extremely early and suffers sometimes from late spring frosts. The yellow flowers, spotted black, set off its vivid orange anthers. A red form is sometimes available under the name of *L. pyrenaicum var. rubrum.*

L. regale, *the Regal Lily, discovered in 1903 by "Chinese" Wilson, has undoubtedly done more to popularize lilies for the home gardener than any other species in the world. It is now available in new colors, and in hybrid forms.*

L. regale

The ubiquitous Regal Lily of our gardens and of the bulb catalogs is probably the hardiest and most adaptable lily. Discovered by E. H. Wilson in 1903, it was introduced into this country in 1908 by the Arnold Arboretum. Later it was taken up by the Wayside Gardens of Mentor, Ohio, and distributed in large numbers directly to the gardeners of our country, so that it rapidly became well-established and popular. The Regal Lily shall forever stand as a glorious memorial to E. H. Wilson.

A description of this lily may be superfluous for most readers. It will grow up to six feet tall, each stem bearing as many as twenty flowers, of true trumpet or funnel shape, pure white inside and rose-purple on the reverse. Leaves are numerous, narrow, and scattered along the stem. Stem-rooting, it makes bulblets on the under-ground portion of the stem. It needs no mulch or special attention.

L. rubellum

A lovely, delicately formed and colored pink trumpet lily from the main island of Japan. It is extremely early and forces well. Because of its lovely color and early flowering, we have used this lily extensively in crosses with the finest specimens of *L. auratum var. platyphyllum, L. speciosum var. rubrum,* and *L. japonicum var. platyfolium,* which in itself may well be a hybrid between *L. japonicum* and *L. rubellum.* Imported bulbs are usually in such poor condition that only a small percentage may survive. Imported seed likewise has given us much difficulty and it was not until we had our own Oregon-grown strains established that we realized that this was an unexpectedly easy and rather hardy lily. Because of the slow-growing habit, it will always be an expensive lily, but the gardener who is so fortunate as to obtain a few bulbs can raise them in a deep flat or large pot in a cool house and soon have a crop of seed and subsequent crops of *L. rubellum* bulbs of his own. There is no lily which gives so much pleasure, color, scent, and refinement of form in the cool greenhouse as this lovely plant. *L. rubellum var. album* has shown up in our own seedlings in Oregon. It, no doubt, is an albino and not as strong as the darker pink-colored form.

L. rubescens

Closely related to *L. washingtonianum* (the Mount Hood Lily of Oregon), *L. rubescens* is found in the California coast ranges from Santa Cruz County in the south to Siskiyou County in the north. The stems grow up to six feet tall and carry as many as thirty trumpet-type flowers in a loose raceme. The flowers are white, when first open, but soon turn to pinkish purple, spotted with tiny dark purple dots. Nicely scented and with attractive, whorled foliage, *L. rubescens* is an appealing garden plant and not too difficult to establish. Its potential in hybridizing has not been established.

L. sargentiae

A beautiful trumpet lily from western China, is similar to *L. regale,* but bears a profuse crop of bulbils in the axils of the leaves. It flowers later than *L. regale* and has larger flowers with a more intensely colored reverse. It is fragrant and sets seed readily. *L. sargentiae* also was discovered by E. H. Wilson, in 1903. It is one of the parents of the important Aurelian Hybrids and will readily cross with many other lilies, often imparting its bulbil-bearing characteristic to its offspring. It is perfectly hardy and disease-resistant and we can recommend it to all gardeners who want to extend the flowering season of good trumpet lilies. Starting with *L. regale,* the sequence is *L. centifolium* Olympic Hybrids, *L. centifolium* Green Mountain Strain, *L. centifolium* Green Dragon Strain, *L. sargentiae,* with *L. sulphureum* and *L. formosanum* as the latest to bloom.

L. sempervivoideum

Is another little lily from Yunnan Province, close to *L. amoenum.* It has not yet been introduced and we doubt that it would have any special merit, either in the garden or for hybridizing.

L. shastense

This lily was raised to specific rank by Vollmer and Beane. We have grown it from specimens collected for us on Mount Shasta and it does not appear to be of great value to any but lily specialists. It looks very much like a small *L. pardalinum* and, as such, is a pretty little plant in our rock garden.

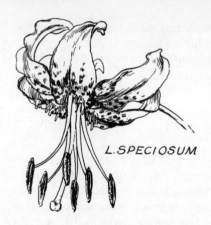

L.SPECIOSUM

L. speciosum

One of the most richly colored lilies in existence, the large, very fragrant, well-recurved, and often prettily twisted petals are essentially white-margined, heavily stained with rich rose-pink and spotted with crimson-red raised dots. It is a stem-rooter and produces numerous bulblets on the under-ground part of the stem. Deep planting gives a larger crop of bulblets. The stem-roots need a cool, moist topsoil to give maximum support to the stem, and a mulch of rich leafmold and compost is recommended. Well-established bulbs throw stalks of five feet or more with as many as thirty flowers. *L. speciosum* is available in several selections and varieties. The one called "Red Champion" was grown from one bulb imported from Japan in 1876. Stocks currently imported from both Japan and Holland are largely diseased. Hybrids between this lily and *L. auratum* have produced flowers of surpassing beauty.

L. speciosum album is the pure-white form of the above. It is a lily of ethereal beauty and, while it is not as strong as its gaily colored relative, the disease-free stocks now available thrive under ordinary garden conditions. This variety is usually sterile and will rarely set seed.

L. speciosum var. album-novum is a pure white, large-flowered form that may have merit for florist's and garden use. It is bound to be surpassed by the new white hybrids disseminated by the U. S. Department of Agriculture Experiment Station at Beltsville, Maryland.

L. speciosum "Gilrey"—a fine ruby-red form introduced by

Gilbert Errey of Lilydale, Victoria, Australia, and one of the parents of "Jillian Wallace."

L. speciosum var. gloriosoides; var. Kraetzeri; var. "Lucie Wilson"; var. "Red Champion," "Oregon Giant," "Melpomene," *punctatum, roseum, rubrum* are all clonal selections. All of them will soon be replaced by hybrid forms of greater disease-resistance, hardiness, and beauty.

L. sulphureum

Formerly known as *L. myriophyllum var. superbum,* this is a rather rare, but worthwhile trumpet lily with very fragrant flowers that vary from ivory-white to rich sulphur-yellow. It is stem-rooting, emerging very late in the spring and flowering in late September. Its pollen has been used freely in producing some interesting hybrids, valuable both for their coloring and their late-flowering habit. *L. sulphureum* is reported to be tender, but in Oregon has proved to be perfectly hardy. Its late emergence may indicate that it can stand even the coldest temperatures that our country can offer. Having reports on supposedly tender lilies such as *L. centifolium* from Saskatoon, Saskatchewan, from northern New York, and from other regions where temperatures go far below zero, we believe that with the right soil and exposure, all such lilies are perfectly hardy. Drainage, sun, and a free flow of air are what these lilies need. Given these conditions, they thrive in cool weather and can stand any amount of winter frost.

L. superbum

Is often called the Wild Tiger Lily and its usually orange, reflexed Turk's-cap flowers, with their strongly maroon-spotted petals, are one of the gayest and finest sights to behold in the summer landscape. *L. superbum* flowers in July and August. Its habitat is from eastern Massachusetts to southern Indiana and all the way south to northwestern Florida and Alabama. It prefers moisture and will grow in quite acid soils. *L. superbum* is not difficult to raise in the garden, but requires, as do all lilies, a great deal of humus, moisture, and little competition with stronger-growing shrubs or plants. Mrs. J. Norman Henry has found some delightful color variants and this suggests that it should not be difficult to raise this lily in a series of true colors, ranging from soft canary-yellow to deep red.

L. szovitsianum

Closely related to *L. monadelphum,* this is a lily which should be seen more frequently in our gardens. It grows wild in southern Georgia and in northeastern Asia Minor. The yellow bell-shaped flowers, carried on stems from two to three feet tall, are often spotted with minute black dots. As shown under *L. monadelphum,* this lily (and the also closely related *L. kesselringianum*) may well cross with *L. bulbiferum* and with *L. polyphyllum* to provide us with a wide range of attractive garden lilies in colors that might vary from white, through lilac to maroon-red; and in forms from the pure, pendulous, bell-shape to outward-facing and upright-flowering. *L. szovitsianum* commemorates Johann Nepomuk Szovits, a Hungarian apothecary at Odessa, who in 1828 and 1829 collected seeds and bulbs in the Caucasus and Armenia for the Leningrad Botanic Garden. According to Woodcock and Stearn, he is credited with the introduction of this lovely lily. Because of its early flowering habit it should be much more widely grown.

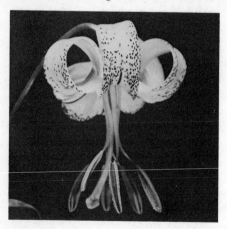

L. taliense *is a fragrant white, dark spotted lily with extremely recurved petals, which has proven valuable in hybridizing.*

L. taliense

Is closely related to *L. wardi* and *L. duchartrei.* We have grown it extensively from seed and found it varied in color and size. *L. taliense* is named after the Tali Range in northeastern Yunnan Province and flowered for the first time in England in 1935. For us it has been an easy lily to grow, and because of its white color, good form and general attractive appearance, we have used it in hybridizing experiments with several other lilies. That it can be crossed with the *L. cernuum* x Mid-Century Hybrids seems extremely likely. With us it grows up to five feet tall and carries numerous (as many as twenty) flowers in a racemose inflorescence. It is sweet-scented and has bright yellow pollen. It is a lily for which we have great hopes. Both as the true species and eventually, in hybrid form, it should be widely tested in our gardens.

L. tigrinum

This, the true Chinese Tiger Lily, is one of the common ingredients of the Chinese, Korean, and Japanese diet. The bulbs, which are cooked until soft, taste somewhat like artichoke hearts and do not appeal to the Western palate. The fact that it can be eaten and has a definite food value made it one of the most widely cultivated lilies of Eastern Asia, antedating, perhaps, *L. candidum* of the Mediterranean region as a garden lily. *L. tigrinum* has a four-foot tall, stiff stem covered with white, woolly hairs and rather short, dark-green, glossy leaves. In the axil of each leaf a small black bulbil will grow, as many as thirty from one single strong stalk. The flowers, which appear in late August, are strongly recurved, of a glowing pinkish-orange color, heavily spotted with black. As many as twenty flowers are sometimes produced on one stem. This lily is one of the strongest growers and seems equally at home in the South and in the Middle-West or the East. It can stand strong feeding, in fact, requires it for best performance. The little bulbils can be detached, when showing signs of maturity, and then planted. One can thus easily and cheaply use this lily in large numbers for naturalized plantings. It is a stem-rooter and loves a good mulch of leafmold or humus.

L. tigrinum is one of the parents of the Mid-Century Hybrids and has imparted to most of them its bulbil-bearing characteristic. Its color factors, in particular its tendency to produce pinkish-orange flowers, combine with those of other lilies to produce brilliantly tinted offspring. A double form exists, but has little or no value.

L. tigrinum fortunei is a very late strain.

L. tsingtauense

Is a lily from eastern China, where, according to Wilson, it grows in thin woods, margins of thickets and among tall grasses. We have raised it on several occasions from seed sent to us from China. The lily grows no more than two feet tall and carries three to five scentless, orange, widely opening flowers and has orange filaments, anthers, and pollen. Color variants have been reported with red flowers (*L. tsingtauense var. carneum*) and with pure-yellow flowers (*L. tsingtauense var. flavum*). Neither in its growth habits, nor in its coloring or form did we see any potential for hybridization and consequently abandoned our little stock of this lily.

L. vollmeri

Is one of the attractive *L. pardalinum*-type plants to which now specific standing has been given. It lacks the vigor of *L. pardalinum* and thus has little to recommend it for the gardener who likes to have a few lilies of this color and form in this collection. Grown from seed *L. pardalinum* will vary considerably, so that the amateur lily grower can soon raise a number of variants, which are bound to include lilies very much like it, if not identical in every respect. *L. vollmeri* is named after Albert Michael Vollmer, M.D., of San Francisco, California, whose research and reports on West Coast lilies have been invaluable. Dr. Vollmer's support of the lily industry in its early phases will always be gratefully remembered by those of us who benefitted from his wise counsel. His colored photographs and movies of lilies in their natural habitat have been a highlight of many a lily growers' meeting.

L. wallichianum

Another Himalayan trumpet lily, closely related to *L. neilgher-rense*, *L. wallichianum* bears on smooth, green stems three to six feet tall, narrow funnel-shaped flowers of a creamy, almost greenish white. The pollen is yellow. It is a stem-rooter and wanders. It

L. WALLICHIANUM

can be propagated from the numerous stem-bulbils that form just under the surface of the soil. A very lovely, scented trumpet lily of transcending beauty that may well have great value in sub-tropical gardens.

L. wardi, *like* L. taliense, *has extremely recurved petals and is very fragrant; pale to rose-pink with deep carmine spots.*

L. wardi

A most attractive lilac lily from southeastern Tibet. It was discovered and introduced by Frank Kingdon-Ward and first grown in England in 1927. We have a nice stock of this lily, from seed sent to us from New Zealand. The pendulous, small, strongly re-curved little flowers are sweetly scented.

L. washingtonianum

The Mount Hood Lily of Oregon grows from the Yosemite Valley northward, along the Cascade Mountains as far north as the Canadian border. The large, funnel-shaped blooms are pure white, but turn purple with age. It grows up to seven feet tall, with as many as thirty flowers, delightfully fragrant.

L. wigginsi

Collected and named by Vollmer and Beane, this yellow, purple-spotted lily grows in the Siskiyou Mountains near the Oregon-California border. It grows up to four feet tall from a thick, non-branching rhizome. The flowers are borne horizontal or nodding and the perianth segments reflect from the middle; the pollen is yellow.

L. WILSONI

L. wilsoni

This, and its yellow form *L. wilsoni var. flavum*—which obtained an Award of Merit from the Royal Horticultural Society under the name of "Marlyn Ross"—are natives of Japan. We have found the orange form to be invariably present in wild collected stocks of *L. auratum var. platyphyllum.* Its presence among those bulbs suggests that the lily is of true species origin. It flowers in August and will cross readily with earlier flowering Mid-Century Hybrids, with *L. bulbiferum* and others. Because of its late-flowering, it decidedly has a place in the garden.

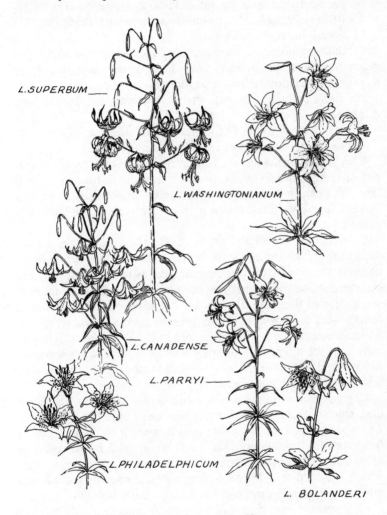

Native American species lilies

CARDIOCRINUM

A close relative of the true lilies—formerly classified as *lilium*—is the cardiocrinum, now considered a separate genus. The differences distinguishing cardiocrinum from the genus lilium are:

1) Broad, heart-shaped leaves.

2) Bulbs monocarpic: producing but one flower stalk after bulbs reach maximum size. Bulblets formed among the basal roots go on to produce new flowers and fruit, the process taking three to four years from bulblet to bloom. After flowering, the parent bulb disappears.

3) Fruit capsules with fibrous teeth along the openings.

There are three species of cardiocrinum.

C. cathayanum, the Cathay Lily, a Chinese species, produces kidney-shaped stem leaves and flower stems one to four and a half feet tall, bearing horizontally, one to five funnel-shaped, whitish flowers sparsely dotted inside with purple. This is the least decorative species.

C. cordatum, the Old Woman or Heartleaf Lily comes from Japan and grows from four to six feet in height, the stem bare for at least one third its lower length. Leaves to one foot long are scattered above with sometimes one crowded whorl of foliage near the center of the stem. Leaves are broadly cordate to a foot in length with long petiols. From four to twenty or more cream-white, fragrant trumpets to six inches in length are borne horizontally near the top of the flowering stem. The three lower segments are marked at the throat with red-brown spots and are streaked near the base with golden-yellow.

C. giganteum is a native of the Himalayas of Burma and Tibet and, true to its name, produces a very large bulb (6 to 7 inches). From this rises a six to twelve foot flowering stalk, a rosette of long-stalked, broadly cordate leaves to one and a half feet long at its base. Lesser leaves are scattered along the flowering stem which bears up to twenty six-inch, white, funnel-shaped blooms striped with purple on the inside and greenish without.

C. giganteum yunnanense is a variety from central and western China, differing from *C. giganteum* only in its smaller size (five to seven feet), its foliage which is deep bronze when young; its dark

Cardiocrinum giganteum, (*formerly classified as* L. giganteum) *is taller and more spectacular than any lily but difficult and much less satisfactory as a garden plant. (Supreme as a conversation piece, for those who take the trouble to grow it!)*

stem; and flowers pure white inside and out except for red markings within.

All the cardiocrinums are woodland plants which thrive in cool part shade in fibrous, loose, well-drained soil enriched by well-rotted manure. They are gross feeders.

The tips of the bulbs are set just below soil level and plantings should be protected in winter by evergreen boughs or other loose mulching material, to prevent early frost injury to the foliage.

After flowering, the parent bulb dies and the small offsets which form among the basal roots should, in the fall, be dug up and replanted to grow on. Three to four years are needed for these to reach flowering size.

Notholirion, nomocharis, and *korolkowia,* all closely resembling *lilum* and *fritillaria* are separate genuses sufficiently unlike true lilies to render unnecessary further discussion of them here.

PLATE 25

Continued crossing and intercrossing, with lilies as with other flowers, frequently brings undreamed of results, such as the crushed raspberry tint of this new hybrid from L. auratum tricolor, *crossed with an* L. japonicum *x* auratum *hybrid.*

Below is L. auratum, *variety* tricolor.

PLATE 26

PLATE 27

Red Gold strain, one of an entirely new group of lilies resulting from cross-ing yellow L. regale *Royal Gold with a pink-flowered* L. regale *clone.*
BELOW: *Stardust, an Aurelian hybrid clone with flat-opening two-toned flowers, is a choice lily for use in arrangements and corsages.*

PLATE 28

PLATE 29

Paisley Hybrids in a border planting, with the lower growing L. martagon
album *in the foreground.*

PLATE 30

Cinnabar, one of the most brilliantly colored of the Mid-Century hybrids.

L. x Enchantment (below) *unexcelled as an all-around, general-purpose lily for the amateur. Merits a place in every beginner's first order for bulbs.*

PLATE 31

CHAPTER *18. Hybrid Lilies—*
a New Era Begins

> *I may be charged by the botanist with making confusion in the genus, but I, as a florist, cannot agree with him, for I believe that in obtaining new varieties I am only developing the latent beauties of nature, which are thus wisely hidden, to excite us to further industry.*
>
> HENRY GROOM
> *Early Lily Hybridizer*

After discussing the wild lilies, the species from all over the Northern Hemisphere, it is logical that we consider the history, the present and future of *hybrid* lilies. With a few notable exceptions this is a story of today and of the future. Until very recently hybrids in the genus *Lilum* have been rare indeed.

Whereas in almost all other garden plants many good hybrids were already available long before the turn of the century, this was not true of lilies. Turning to the catalogs and lily literature of the past, we do, however, find descriptions of a number of hybrids which must have been attractive and of definite value to the gardeners of those days. Most of these early introductions are now lost, but one exception remains with us, the lovely *L. x testaceum,* the result of a cross between *L. chalcedonium* and *L. candidum.* Unfortunately its true hybrid character was not recognized, and in its early years it was sold as a new lily from Japan. Apparently an accidental hybrid, it was first found in 1835 in a bed of lilies growing in Germany.

L. x testaceum is important. Because of its hybrid vigor it has spread all over the world and has done well in many gardens. Its

289

beauty has advertised all lilies as much as did the exciting later arrivals on the European garden scene, *L. auratum* and *L. speciosum* from Japan. Finally, its comparatively easy multiplication has given many an amateur gardener his first chance to propagate some new plants of his own. We shall discuss *L. x testaceum* again further on in this chapter.

Even before *L. x testaceum* was known, there were in Dutch gardens a large group of hybrid lilies, imported from Japan around 1830 by the well-known plant explorer, von Siebold. It seems likely that these lilies were hybrids between *L. dauricum* and *L. concolor.* They are upright-flowering, usually quite short-stemmed, and come in many colors, both spotted and clear. One of these lilies, the variety called *L. x maculatum astrosanguineum,* was used by the London nurseryman Henry Groom, who between 1830 and 1840 raised a number of fine hybrids. We can quote his own story, as reported in the *Gardener's Chronicle* in 1841: "I crossed *L. bulbiferum* with *L. x maculatum atrosanguineum* and have obtained some beautiful varieties, most having very brilliant colors and many being finely blotched with the deep color of *L. atrosanguineum . . . "*

If we have to credit Japanese growers with the earliest successful hybridization of lilies, there can be little doubt that Henry Groom is the first breeder on record in our part of the world. It is quite evident that the large group of lilies, now classed as *L. x hollandicum* hybrids, found its origin in the Groom nursery. Hovey, the Boston, Massachusetts nurseryman, visited Groom and bought a set of eighteen hybrids from him in 1844. His visit to Groom led him to try his own hand at hybridizing lilies.

Hovey, who was, undoubtedly, the first American lily breeder, started hybridizing in 1846 and raised some attractive specimens of the same types as Groom was introducing. From seed of *L. speciosum var. rubrum,* of which he bought some bulbs from Groom, he raised a vigorous strain of high quality. When, in 1862, the first *L. auratum* were sent from Japan to the American historian Francis Parkman in Jamaica Plain, Massachusetts, he and Hovey used them to produce the lovely hybrid *L. x parkmanni. L. auratum* was the pollen parent and we can well assume that Parkman selected the finest *L. speciosum* that he could find among Hovey's seedlings as the seed parent.

Backhouse Hybrids. *This group, developed by the world-famous English gardener Mrs. R. O. Backhouse, gave a new impetus to the breeding of lilies for general garden use.*

L. auratum was shown in 1862 at the Royal Horticultural Society in London, England, by the famous firm of Veitch. In 1867 there was exhibited in Rotterdam, Holland, a lily under the name of *L. wittei.* Examination of contemporary records and illustrations reveals that we are dealing here with the first recorded hybrid between *L. auratum* (possibly *L. auratum var. platyphyllum*) and *L. japonicum. L. x wittei* has a large, bowl-shaped flower of pure, smooth white. No papillae are present nor are there any spots, both so typical of all *L. auratum.* Our identification of *L. wittei* as a hybrid is further substantiated by the fact that identical hybrids have shown up in controlled crosses made by us between *L. auratum var. virginale* and *tricolor* and *L. japonicum.* The strain now grown under the name of White Pearl looks in every respect identical with the illustration of the famous *L. wittei,* published by Messrs. E. H. Krelage & Son of Haarlem, Holland.

The new American hybrid *L. x parkmanni* was shown in London in 1875 and by 1879 it was illustrated in full color in the *Gardener's Chronicle*. Unfortunately, the lily was not long-lived. Due perhaps to overpropagation and consequent weakening of the bulbs, or to virus, the stock became subject to basal rot. Before the turn of the century all trace of it had been lost.

Another group of lilies had better luck and persists, though in small quantities, to the present day. It is the group of hybrids between *L. martagon var. album* and *L. hansoni,* raised by the late Mrs. R. O. Backhouse at Sutton Court, Hereford, England. Already at an earlier date similar hybrids had been raised by C. Baden Powell of Southborough, England, and by Messrs. van Tubergen of Haarlem, Holland. It was Mrs. Backhouse, however, who persisted with her work and who, around the turn of the century, built up named clones that are still with us.

One more historical hybrid lily deserves mention here. It is *L. x kewense,* a hybrid raised by an unknown gardener at the Royal Botanic Gardens at Kew, England. Using *L. leucanthum* as the seed parent and *L. henryi* as the pollen parent, he raised some viable seed, which in July of the year 1900 produced a plant of hybrid character that in habit, foliage, size, and form of flower was very like *L. auratum.* There is no doubt that this plant soon succumbed to virus, but Monsieur Debras of Orléans, France, has stated that knowledge of this successful cross prompted him to try and raise similar hybrids. Debras flowered his first hybrids in 1928. We shall discuss his lilies later.

At approximately the same time, Dr. David Griffiths of the United States Department of Agriculture, flowered a large group of colorful lilies of undoubted hybrid nature from seed purchased in 1919 from Carl Purdy of Ukiah, California. These lilies, the foundation of the famous Bellingham Hybrid Strain, exemplify the West Coast American lilies at their best. The gardens and parks of the United States and Great Britain have been immensely enriched by the lovely clones and the mixtures of hybrids, all stemming from these original Bellingham stocks.

It is not until approximately 1925 that a concerted effort was made in many parts of the world to produce new and better lilies of hybrid ancestry. When we survey the lily hybrids of today, it becomes obvious that already now, only thirty-five years after

Bellingham Hybrids, *developed by Dr. David Griffiths of the U.S.D.A. added to the interest in lily growing in America.*

attempts were first being made in many parts of the world to improve the lily, the number of new varieties that have been named is greater than we could discuss in this book. We shall, therefore, confine ourselves to main groups and single out for special mention only those that are freely available. Rare hybrids there will always be and the amateur gardener will have no difficulty in locating them through the fine Yearbooks of the Royal Horticultural Society, the North American Lily Society and the lily dealers' catalogs.

Mid-Century Hybrids—First in popularity and easily the leader of all hybrid lilies, if for sheer numbers only, is L. x Enchantment. With its close relatives it belongs to the Mid-Century group. These hybrids are of complicated parentage and have a family tree that goes like this:

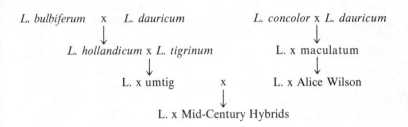

L. bulbiferum   x   *L. dauricum*   *L. concolor* x *L. dauricum*
                    ↓   ↓
        L. hollandicum x *L. tigrinum*   L. x maculatum
                    ↓   ↓
            L. x umtig   x   L. x Alice Wilson
                            ↓
                L. x Mid-Century Hybrids

The first Mid-Century Hybrids included varieties like Enchantment, Fireflame, and Valencia. Crossed with *L. davidi,* they in turn gave us more lovely hybrids of which Joan Evans is a good example. Crossing them with *L. amabile var. luteum* produced varieties like Destiny and Prosperity, as well as other fine seedlings.

The Mid-Century complex then includes basically factors from *L. bulbiferum, L. concolor, L. dauricum,* and *L. tigrinum* and, in the later stages, *L. amabile var. luteum* and *L. davidi,* as well. Continuing to build further on this good foundation, the addition of *L. cernuum* gave an even greater diversification of colors and forms to produce the lovely Harlequin Strain.

It should be emphasized that this type of lily hybridizing is by no means beyond the scope of the average gardener. The species involved are easily obtainable; the processes followed are simple and, once obtained, the seeds offer no difficulty at all in germinating and growing on to the flowering stage. The incredible variation possible in color, form, scent, and so many other factors will delight any gardener. If our large-scale experiments along these lines have convinced us of anything, then it is that we have by no means exhausted the potential inherent in these crosses. As with the hybrid tulips and daffodils, the combinations that can be obtained are without limit.

Oriental Hybrids. Another very large group of hybrids is that encompassed by the *L. auratum, L. speciosum, L. japonicum,* and *L. rubellum* group, all species from Japan. Three shining examples of the goals that can be achieved stand before us: *L. x parkmanni,* the result of but a single cross between *L. auratum* and *L. speciosum rubrum.* While this lily was lost, as well as a similar and very lovely hybrid called L. x Mrs. Anthony Waterer, we have a third great hybrid in L. x Jillian Wallace. This lovely lily, fortunately still with us and freely available, was raised by Roy M. Wallace of Warburton, Victoria, Australia. It is the result of crossing *L. speciosum* var. Gilrey with *L. auratum* var. Crimson Queen. Gilrey is a selected variety of the species and, so far as can be ascertained, not of hybrid origin. Crimson Queen, as we have known it, was a weak grower with virus, but partially resistant. We imported it year after year from Japan. It had narrow leaves, and *no indication* of speciosum blood. The color was essentially the dull *changing crimson* of pure auratum types. Wallace's argument

Jillian Wallace, *developed in Australia. This dramatic, large-flowered, flat opening red and white lily has become immensely popular.*

that the red "must have come from somewhere" and therefore from speciosum is outdated. We now know that the red auratum color is the diffusion of the spot coloring—a genetically sound mutation. Wilson in *Lilies of Eastern Asia,* noted the variation in color in the wild plant. Actually, there is much more color in auratum type seedlings than in *var. platyphyllum* seedlings.

In a search for disease-free plants and greater variety in color and type, this line of breeding was continued and L. x Jillian Wallace backcrossed to *L. auratum* var. Crimson Queen to produce the lovely Empress of India. Similar backcrosses of L. x Jillian Wallace to selected plants of *L. auratum var. virginale* gave us Empress of China and Empress of Japan. Backcrossed to selected plants of *L. speciosum var. album novum,* it produced a strain of pure white, large-sized, flat-flowered hybrids that have great merit for both garden and greenhouse.

The Empress Series; *a new group that has caused a sensation at lily shows. Top left: Empress of China, white; top right: Empress of India, deep red; bottom: Empress of Japan, striped.*

At Beltsville, Maryland, Dr. S. L. Emsweller has raised a number of similar fine hybrids between *L. speciosum var. rubrum* and good *L. auratum* selections, which have been introduced as Potomac Hybrids. Others, crosses between *L. speciosum var. album* and *L. auratum,* are of good size and pure white. These latter hybrids were introduced in 1960 and should make a welcome addition to the white lilies of that type for greenhouse and garden.

Building on these *L. speciosum x L. auratum* crosses, the introduction of *L. japonicum* and *L. rubellum* has been effected by several hybridizers. Miss Pfeiffer of the Boyce Thompson Institute in 1942 reported her success with *L. auratum x L. japonicum* and *L. auratum x L. rubellum* hybrids. Various other American hybridizers have raised equally attractive seedlings of similar type. It was obvious that attempts to combine all four species should be successful and events have proved this to be true.

An attractive new type of flower, with gracefully recurved, wavy petals, appears in this L. japonicum *x* L. auratum *cross. Arrangers will welcome it.*

In our work we were privileged to have access to large numbers of wild collected plants of *L. auratum var. platyphyllum* and stocks of *L. speciosum, L. japonicum,* and *L. rubellum,* the true species raised by us from seed. Selecting the finest specimens out of tens of thousands of such plants, our progress in hybridizing with them has been rapid, as well as rewarding. The acclaim given to our Empress series of hybrids, whenever shown, is proof that these magnificent lilies will find their way in the world. Mixed strains—the Imperial Silver, Imperial Gold, and Imperial Crimson Strains—are already on the market. In hardiness and tolerance to changed conditions, as well as in resistance to pests and diseases, they are a revolutionary step ahead. The new Jamboree Strain, essentially *L. auratum x L. speciosum,* is hardy, healthy, and more vigorous than either parent. It promises to be an ideal greenhouse strain, as well.

From the lovely Imperial Strains to improved soft pink and ethereal white lilies of the utmost refinement was an easy step. Backcrossing these giant varieties to selected *L. japonicum* and *L. rubellum,* both species and hybrids, gave us new forms—

Potomac Hybrids, *a new, distinctive group from the U.S.D.A. resulting from crossing* L. speciosum rubrum *with* L. auratum.

plants sturdy enough to stand severe winters and yet elegant, light, and lovely enough to stir the heart of any flower lover. To see these new hybrids, such as Pink Beauty, Pink Pearl, and Pink Diamond, in field rows is an unforgettable sight. The flowers look too refined, too gossamer, too light to live in the rough and tumble of the nursery, yet they thrive in such surroundings as they will find in gardens.

The last word in this line of breeding has by no means been spoken. Many amateur growers and professionals have chosen this field in which to work. There is no doubt that their efforts will be crowned with success. Already a further step seems indicated. A plant exists, which is, without doubt, the result of a cross between *L. speciosum var. rubrum* and *L. henryi.* While it is sterile, and thus further progress along these lines is for the moment closed, there is no doubt that this obstacle will, in time, be overcome. What will then happen is anybody's guess. A similar hybrid was already reported by Dr. Henry Nehrling some twenty-five years ago.

Fiesta Hybrids. Another line of breeding, and one which carries the touch of several fine breeders, is exemplified by the Fiesta Hy-

Fiesta Hybrids; *one of the early American hybrid groups, developed by Dr. F. Horsford Abel, and later improved by de Graaff.*

brids. From Dr. F. Horsford Abel of White Plains, New York, came a strain of lilies with unmistakable *L. davidi* and *L. leichtlini* parentage. Miss Isabella Preston at Ottawa, Canada, has followed a similar line of breeding, crossing *L. dauricum x maculatum* hybrids with *L. davidi*. This resulted in her lovely Stenographer series of lilies. The best known of these lilies are the named varieties, Lillian Cummings and Brenda Watts.

From this series Miss Preston developed some upright-flowering brilliantly colored lilies which show the *L. dauricum* parentage. In more recent years some good yellow lilies have been developed from this series. The catalogs of Canadian lily specialists offer a fine assortment of the best of Miss Preston's introductions.

Taking the best available selected plants from these breeders and crossing them with *L. amabile* resulted in the Fiesta Hybrids. Now, some ten years after their introduction, this strain is giving us delightful color variations. The pure yellow Citronella, the ruby-red Burgundy and the bronze-colored Bronzino Strain, all true-breeding from pollen and seed taken from certain selected stock plants, are easy to raise. They are very lovely garden plants.

Harlequin Hybrids, *a new, exceptionally colorful group with* L. cernuum *blood, developed by Dr. C. F. Patterson of the University of Saskatchewan; tall, vigorous growers.*

Harlequin Hybrids. An entirely different strain of lilies in colors, amazing even to the expert, has been raised by Dr. C. F. Patterson, head of the Department of Horticulture, University of Saskatchewan, Saskatoon, Canada. Intercrossing the species *L. tigrinum, L. cernuum, L. davidi* and its variety *Maxwill,* he obtained a race of lilies of lovely coloring, great hardiness and vigor. These tall lilies have up to fifteen martagon-type flowers on short pedicels scattered along the stem. They come in rose, ivory, pink, salmon, and other pastel colors. Varieties like Rose Queen, Edith Cecilia, Lemon Queen, White Princess, and Burnished Rose are bound to be of great interest to all lily growers and all gardeners, especially those in the prairie states where the extreme hardiness bred into them will be invaluable.

In order to see what could be achieved along similar, although somewhat different, lines, we have crossed *L. cernuum* with various Mid-Century Hybrids and have obtained a similar, vigorous group of complicated hybrids, introduced as the Harlequin Strain. There have been similar crosses with *L. wardi, L. taliense, L. lankongense,* and others with fascinating results. Here again the opportunity is wide open for all amateur gardeners. These crosses are not difficult to make. The results are bound to be interesting and pleasing.

Aurelian Hybrids. Of again entirely different parentage is the large group of hybrid lilies of which the prototype is *L. x kewense.* This was followed some twenty-eight years later by *L. x aurelianense* of Monsieur Debras of France. From there to keen hybridizers, like LaVerne Freimann of Washington, and others, was but a step. Tom Barry of Lambertville, New Jersey, raised his beautiful *L. henryi x L. sulphureum* hybrid clone, T. A. Havemeyer, in 1937. Shortly before his death in 1935, Dr. David Griffiths was making similar crosses; and, in Canada, Dr. E. Frank Palmer of Vineland, Ontario, and Miss Isabella Preston of Ottawa have raised hybrids of this parentage.

Our own work with this intriguing group started in 1938. At that time we flowered one thousand jumbo-sized plants of *L. henryi,* as well as a similarly sized stock of the true *L. leucanthum var. centifolium,* grown from seed contributed by Dr. Griffiths. We also had nice stocks of *L. sulphureum, L. sargentiae,* a few bulbs of Debras' *L. x aurelianense* and L. x T. A. Havemeyer. Enlisting the services of a most careful friend and neighbor, Mr. Werttemberger, a retired farm-machinery salesman, we hand-pollinated all the *L. henryi* flowers with pollen taken from the various trumpet lilies. Conversely, we pollinated all the trumpet lilies with pollen from the finest *L. henryi.* The resulting enormous batch of seed formed the basis for our first mass attack on the Aurelian complex. Exemplified by the hundreds of thousands of Golden Clarion, Sunburst, and Heart's Desire produced, the results are to be seen wherever lilies are grown. The Award of Merit, given to us in 1949 by the Royal Horticultural Society for our Lily Golden Clarion, the prototype of this new strain, dates the real breakthrough in golden-yellow trumpet lilies. From that date on we have refined and improved the strains, so that they are now true breeding and of uniformly high quality.

The Aurelian Hybrids are now the subject of intensive work on the part of many hybridizers. These growers not only raised many clones and strains, but have also launched their creations with fancy names. The point to remember in this connection is the fact that only if continually new crops are raised from parent plants with known and tested genetic potential, will such crops be clean, healthy, and vigorous. By continued testing of the finest plants a rapid and steady improvement in quality can be obtained.

Sunburst Strain, a selection from Aurelian Hybrids.

We have found that true-breeding variants of Golden Clarion can be raised in chartreuse-green to soft yellow self-colored flowers, or with deeper golden yellow hue and deep wine-red or brown stripes on the reverse of the petals. The self-colored, soft yellows, the Limelight Strain, and the darker Golden Splendor Strain, with strongly contrasting reverse of the petals, are our standard bearers in this Aurelian trumpet type of lily. Many clones have been selected by us. They are being tested, but not until they have been fully proved to be satisfactory in other regions, as well as in Oregon, do we intend to introduce them. Working with strains raised from selected parents, with proved genetic potential, our advance toward still better lilies is rapid. The time to name individual plants and increase them vegetatively is not yet here. We feel that the early naming of clones should not be encouraged unless their resistance to virus is fully established.

Hybrids of similar parentage that resemble the *L. henryi* parent more closely, with flaring, broad petals and in less formal inflorescence, are grouped together as the Sunburst Strain. These too come in true-breeding color groups, such as the Silver Sunburst, the Golden Sunburst (based on a yellow mutation of *L. henryi,* known as *L. henryi var. citrinum*) and, more recently, the Pink Sunburst strains.

Intermediate lilies, halfway between the trumpet and the Sun-

Early Centifolium Hybrids, forerunners of today's Olympic Hybrids.

burst types, are bowl-shaped. They often show an orange heart or center, often of a deep, flaming orange color, shading to cream at the slightly waved and recurved tips. This lovely and rather rare type has been named the Heart's Desire Strain. It shows every promise of becoming popular.

Among the Golden Clarion trumpet lilies, some have shown up with markedly pink or red veining and a much deeper than gold, almost orange, color throughout the petals. The loss of the factor that restricts the color only to the outside of the petals was to be expected. Soon it was found that, by carefully controlled hybridizing, this factor could be reinforced. The lilies now sold as the African Queen Strain come closest to a true orange trumpet type.

The Golden Regal Lily. Before discussing the next color variant, the true fuchsia-pink trumpet lilies, a word is in place about the

Golden Regal Lily. These very lovely, golden-yellow, early flowering trumpet lilies made their appearance at approximately the
same time in three very different locations. The type offered as
Butterfield originated in the East from seed supplied by the United
States Department of Agriculture at Beltsville, Maryland. Another
golden Regal originated in the garden of LaVerne Freimann at
Bellingham, Washington. Royal Gold, the third type, was found
in a field of *L. regale* on our farms.

All three have unmistakably *L. regale* characteristics. The
other parent, in our opinion, is *L. sulphureum.* Just as the Golden
Clarion trumpet lilies stem from a combination of *L. henryi* and
L. leucanthum factors, so does the yellow *L. regale* find its origin
in *L. sulphureum* and *L. regale.* In both Aurelian and Regal offspring the same change must have occurred. The factor restrain-
ing the yellow center to the base of the flower was lost; the color
became suffused throughout the entire flower. By intercrossing,
the color was strengthened and the golden trumpet lilies— Aurelian or Regal—were born.

It is interesting to note that the history of all three golden
Regals includes a little batch of seedlings sent by Luther Burbank
to Mr. Rait of Bellingham, Washington. From this, through
successive generations of seedlings, came *L. regale* var. Gold
Cup, bought and distributed by the Wayside Gardens of Mentor,
Ohio. From seed taken from Gold Cup and its sister seedlings
came successive batches of Regal Lilies, some of which had a
faint yellow tint and a slightly different, shining texture of the
petals. It is in seedlings from hand-pollinated selections of these
peculiar Regal Lilies that the golden yellow flowers suddenly
showed up.

Of the three types found and named, the Royal Gold threatens
to overshadow the others. Large-scale selective breeding has been
done with it. The individual crosses have been recorded and
scored and production of this lovely lily on a large scale has already produced it in numbers sufficient to supply the American
and European market. Without such mass production, the other
types, even if good, are bound to lose out. A further step toward
greater color diversification has already been taken. From slight
pink veining, sometimes found in *L. regale,* a more intense color
has been developed. Pink Regal Lilies are already a reality.

The Hybrid Trumpet Lilies

The wild trumpet lilies of China belong to several distinct species, of which *L. regale, L. sulphureum, L. sargentiae,* and *L. leucanthum* are those of greatest importance to our gardens. The *L. regale* species is tolerant to adverse conditions and, ever since its discovery in 1903 by E. H. Wilson, has made its way into the hearts of gardeners all over the world. With *L. tigrinum,* it undoubtedly shares the honor of being the most widely grown of all lily species.

L. sulphureum, by contrast, is very little grown. Since it emerges late in the spring and flowers late, it is an easy prey to aphids. Hence, virus disease in this species is almost inevitable. As far as can be ascertained, no nursery-grown stocks have escaped this always fatal infection. Yet, the beauty of the long, sulphur-yellow trumpet and its noble habit of growth make it a most desirable lily. There is a great temptation to use it in hybridizing work. Some of its characteristics, combined with those of the much earlier flowering and more resistant *L. regale,* are evident in the golden yellow Regal Lilies, such as Royal Gold.

Another cross along this line resulted in a hybrid called Sulphurgale. Dr. E. F. Palmer of Vineland, Ontario, Canada, used this hybrid, in connection with the true *L. sulphureum,* and raised a strain of late-blooming trumpet lilies, the Sulphur Hybrids. The entire group of seedlings, clones and selected strains, as we saw them in Dr. Palmer's garden a few years ago, was of surpassing beauty. Raised in but a small garden, Dr. Palmer's lilies are again proof that the exciting and rewarding hobby of lily breeding is easily within the realm of possibility for any gardener. The outlay of a few dollars for the original stock, plus a certain amount of patience and persistence, will soon pay dividends in increasingly better lilies, selected to suit one's taste.

The Sulphur Hybrids have been used by us in the production of several late-flowering strains of garden lilies of great beauty.

L. sargentiae, characterized by its habit of making bulbils in the axils of the leaves and by the greenish color of its long trumpet flowers, has been used a great deal in hybridizing. Crossed with *L. regale,* it produced *L. x imperiale,* the result of a chance cross in the nursery of Messrs. R. & J. Farquhar of Boston, Massachusetts. This hybrid flowered for the first time in 1916 and a description of it was published by E. H. Wilson in 1920. In 1916 Miss Preston of the Ontario Agricultural College at Guelph, Ontario, made a similar cross. Of the lilies so raised, one of the finest was named George C. Creelman after the president of the college. While stocks of trumpet lilies are still sold under this name, or as George C. Creelman Hybrids, it can safely be presumed that none of the original stock remains. *L. sargentiae* has been used in the production of the new Green Magic, Green Mountain, and Emerald Strains, lilies of great beauty and refinement.

The last lily of our group of four species is *L. leucanthum.* Several forms have been collected in China. An exceptionally good one reached the U.S.D.A. Bureau of Plant Introduction from an American missionary and was grown and distributed by Dr. David Griffiths of Bellingham, Washington, Experiment Station. It is this lily, which, grown from seed in large quantities, selected and reselected, is the foundation of the Olympic Hybrids. Through controlled breeding the pyramidal inflorescence, the color and form of these lilies have been accentuated. All of them have dark-brown reverse and pure white interiors of the flowers. They are tall, carry their flowers in stately candelabras and, even when raised from seed, have reached an astonishing uniformity. The finest types among them were selected and are now available as the Black Magic Strain. A clone, Black Dragon, has also been introduced.

Pink Trumpet Lilies. Growers of both the *L. regale x L. sargentiae* and of the *L. leucanthum var. centifolium* strains soon noticed among their seedlings a few plants that showed in the flowers distinct pink veining and pink margins. These were selected and intercrossed with the result that among the subsequent stocks of seedlings more such pink-veined and pink-margined lilies appeared. From such beginnings have been raised deep fuchsia-pink trumpet lilies, such as the Pink Perfection Strain.

While we might assume that in these new, dark trumpet lilies we are dealing with a mutation which released the color-restraining factor—the one that restricts the dark wine-red color to the center stripe on the reverse of each petal—there may also be another solution to this rather sudden emergence of deep- and dark-pink trumpet lilies. This may be in the possible contamination of pollen

An Olympic Hybrid.

Pink Perfection, a new strain similar to the Olympic Hybrids.

with that of Aurelian Hybrids grown on nearby fields. As we have seen in the Golden Clarion, the suffusion of golden color is due to the influence of the self-colored *L. henryi* and *L. sulphureum,* without color restricting factors. This characteristic may well have become part of the make-up of the pink lilies, thus permitting the wine-red color of the reverse of the petals to flow and suffuse throughout the bloom. Be that as it may, the fact remains that, either as pure trumpet lilies or with one or more factors derived from *L. henryi* or *L. sulphureum,* the pink trumpet lilies have become a reality. Already they have been tested in many parts of the world and universally admired.

L. candidum hybrids. L. candidum hybrids are among the most beautiful of all modern garden lilies. The classical example, *L. x testaceum,* is now a hundred and twenty-five years old. It is still being produced and, even though the stock has virus, it is growing well in many gardens. While the infection will definitely be a menace to other lilies and tulips grown nearby, in a larger garden it may be possible to isolate the plants and thus safely enjoy their beauty. A distance of three hundred feet, at least, seems to be indicated to safeguard against virus spread.

L. candidum x L. chalcedonicum is not a difficult cross to make and the resulting plants, most of them colored or white with red-colored pollen, are always attractive. Since it is more difficult to obtain *L. chalcedonicum* than it is to buy *L. x testaceum,* it is suggested that the latter be used in its place. Often the resulting seedlings will include a good red one, approaching the true *L. chalcedonicum* in color and form and excelling it in vigor. *L. candidum* is supposed to have been crossed with *L. szovitsianum* and even a cross with *L. parryi* has been reported. While we have not seen such hybrids and are rather dubious about them, the possibility that *L. candidum* will cross with lilies other than *L. chalcedonicum* must not be overlooked. Here again, a wonderful opportunity for the amateur lily breeder offers itself. The study of *L. candidum,* its distribution, history, symbolism and use in all forms of art, should be a fascinating pursuit for any amateur botanist.

Backhouse Hybrids. Fascinating as the *L. candidum* potential is, the *L. martagon* hybrids are no less so. The martagon lilies come in many colors, ranging from pure-white to deep wine-red and mahogany-purple. It has already been noted that these lilies will cross with *L. hansoni* and that, some sixty years ago, the lovely Backhouse Hybrids resulted from this combination. Since then, other breeders, notably Professor George L. Slate, have explored the possibilities of this cross. Raised by us in Oregon, the Paisley Strain is a richly colored group of such hybrids, all of them very vigorous, disease resistant, and lovely.

Other crosses with *L. martagon* are possible. *L. martagon x L. medeoloides* produced a hybrid to which the name L. x Marmed was given by E. H. Wilson. *L. martagon* also crossed with *L. pumilum,* and the resulting hybrid with *L. hansoni,* to produce a lily which we have grown for years under the name of L. x Pumarhan. This one in turn will cross with other, equally complex hybrids. To the persistent and patient hybridizer there seems to be no obstacle in combining some factors of half a dozen, or even more, distinct species in a complicated hybrid group. We have not pursued this line of breeding any further, as many of the lilies involved are slow-growing. The commercial advantage of bringing *L. martagon* and *L. hansoni* factors into the Mid-Century group, for instance, seem to be slight. All the more reason for a curious amateur breeder to try his hand at this line of breeding!

Rainbow Hybrids, *in various shades of yellow, orange and dark red, have up-facing, cuplike flowers.*

Rainbow Hybrids. A group of hybrids that will delight many a gardener is the early flowering, upright, cup-shaped family of hybrid lilies, the Rainbow Hybrids, in a wide range of colors, and the Golden Chalice Hybrids, a strain confined to golden yellow colors only, self-colored or spotted with maroon. They found their origin in stocks of *L. x maculatum* collected from various sources. Crossing the named clones with others, such as Alice Wilson, Leonard Joerg, and Golden Fleece, gave a wide variety of short and tall, variously colored lilies. All of them were upright-flowering and some had nicely shaped cups with wide overlapping petals. Singling out the best, intercrossing them and repeating this process several times produced a race of superior garden plants. They multiply rapidly and can easily be grown on vegetatively as named varieties. One of them, Spotlight, seems to have distinct merits as a pot plant.

Golden Tiger Lily, a distinct break in this widely grown and hardiest of garden lilies.

Tiger Hybrids. L. tigrinum as it appears in most gardens, is sterile. There are, however, fertile strains and hybrids of this lily, with *L. amabile, L. bulbiferum, L. x hollandicum, L. leichtlini,* and *L. x maculatum,* have been raised. As pointed out at the beginning of this chapter, many more combinations of them and other species, with *L. tigrinum* are possible. Here is a challenge, indeed, for any amateur lily breeder. The brilliant coloring of L. x Enchantment in flowers of *L. tigrinum* form and with *L. tigrinum* vigor is a pleasure to behold. New lemon yellow, salmon and pink-colored *L. tigrinum* hybrids have been raised. The problem with these hybrids is no longer how to raise them. Rather, it is what to do with them, this galaxy of colors and forms, once they are full-grown. They multiply so fast, are so vigorous and take up so much space in the nursery that they create a real problem for the commercial breeder. Again, we point out that with *L. tigrinum* as a starting point, a keen amateur can have real pleasure in building up an exciting group of hybrids. Should he produce a vigorously growing upright-flowering, white or pink lily, then a real service to the world of horticulture will have been performed.

Bellingham Hybrids. We shall close this chapter with what many gardeners consider the finest contribution of American lily hybridizers: Dr. David Griffiths' Bellingham Hybrids. It is true that the seed for this strain came from another fine American plantsman, Carl Purdy of Ukiah, California. It is now known that he, in turn, obtained it from Robert Kessler in Los Angeles. This does not detract from the importance of Dr. Griffiths' contribution. It was he who thought of planting the seed, raised it to flowering stage and, with unfailing taste, selected the clones to be named. It was, again, his enthusiasm that, on his constant travels and visits to farmers and bulb growers all over the country, spread the story of these fine lilies. From the time of the first distribution of the Bellingham Hybrids in 1932 to the present, these beautiful lilies have given pleasure to untold thousands of gardeners. They are one of the highlights of Sir Eric Savill's wonderful creation, the Savill Gardens in The Great Park, Windsor, England. New selections have been made and new species introduced into the hybrid strains. *L. bolanderi, L. kelloggi,* and other fine species are now imparting certain of their characteristics to this hybrid family. Slowly, the barriers that inhibit many an American wild lily from ready adaptation to changed conditions of soil and climate are disappearing. These Bellingham Lilies, ambassadors of beauty and good will, are finding a welcome home in countries the world over. They are as American as our Indians. They have the vigor of the pioneers who made our country great. If we had made no other contribution to the world of lilies than just these hybrids, we could well rest on our laurels. There are, however, other American lilies making their way and finding acceptance wherever people garden for pleasure and profit. There are still more to come!

Hybridizers in the United States and Canada join with those of all other countries to make this world of ours more beautiful. In the lily we have a plant of unsurpassed beauty in a wide variety of colors, forms, and seasons. Thirty-five years of concerted effort in breeding for greater tolerance and greater beauty has already brought substantial success. There is no doubt that the next thirty-five years, yes, even the next ten or even five, are going to bring us greater advances. The future is in the hands of the imaginative, the patient, and the persevering gardener. Raising new lilies, there seems to be no limit to what he may achieve!

Appendix

LISTS OF LILIES FOR VARIOUS PURPOSES
BY COLOR, BY HEIGHT, BY BLOOMING PERIODS

> *And because the breath of flowers is far sweeter in the air (where it comes and goes, like the warbling of music) than in the hand, therefore nothing is more fit for that delight than to know what be the flowers and plants that do best perfume the air.*
>
> FRANCIS BACON (1561–1626)

"Lilies" That Are Not Lilies.

Lily Registration

Schedule of Awards

Bibliography

Lily Societies.

LILIES FOR VARIOUS PURPOSES

FOR THE BEGINNER

Aurelian Hybrids
Bellingham Hybrids
L. canadense
L. candidum
L. concolor
L. davidi
Fiesta Hybrids

L. formosanum
Golden Chalice Hybrids
L. martagon and hybrids
Mid-Century Hybrids
Olympic Hybrids
L. rubellum
L. speciosum and hybrids

FOR THE SPECIALIST

L. amoenum	very rare
L. bakerianum	very rare
L. catesbaei	difficult
L. concolor coridion	rare but easy
L. duchartrei	rare
L. japonicum	difficult
L. kesselringianum	very rare
L. leichtlini	rare
L. mackliniae	rare
L. maritimum	difficult
L. martagon cattaniae	difficult
L. nobilissimum	rare; not garden material
L. occidentale	rare; little garden merit
L. papilliferum	scarce
L. parvum	rare
L. philadelphicum	difficult outside natural range
L. polyphyllum	rare
L. pomponium	attractive; not often seen
L. primulinum	scarce
L. tsingtauense	no garden merit
L. wardi	rare

FOR HYBRIDIZING

Aurelian Hybrids
African Queen Strain
L. candidum
L. cernuum
L. chalcedonicum
L. davidi

Paisley Hybrids
L. papilliferum
L. parryi
L. regale

Fiesta Hybrids
Firecrown
L. hansoni
L. henryi
L. lankongense
L. leichtlini
L. martagon

Red Gold Strain
L. sargentiae
L. sulphureum
L. taliense
L. tigrinum
L. wardi

PRIMARILY BASE-ROOTING LILIES
(balance have stem roots)

Bellingham Hybrids
L. bolanderi
L. canadense
L. candidum
L. catesbaei
L. chalcedonicum
L. columbianum
L. grayi
L. kelloggi
L. kesselringianum
L. maritimum
L. martagon
L. michauxi

L. michiganense
L. monadelphum
L. pardalinum
L. parryi
L. philadelphicum
L. pomponium
L. pyrenaicum
L. rubescens
L. superbum
L. szovitsianum
L. x testaceum
L. washingtonianum

FOR FULL SUN

L. *amabile*
L. *amabile luteum*
L. *canadense*
L. *cernuum* and hybrids
L. *concolor*
L. *concolor coridion*
L. *dauricum*

Dr. Abel
Fiesta Hybrids
L. *formosanum pricei*
L. *formosanum wilsoni*

Golden Chalice Hybrids
L. *longiflorum,* Croft's Variety
L. *longiflorum,* Estate Variety
L. *martagon album*

Mid-Century Hybrids
Mountaineer
L. *pardalinum giganteum*
L. *pumilum* and hybrids

Rainbow Hybrids
L. *regale*
L. *regale* Royal Gold

FOR PART SHADE

L. *amabile*
L. *aurantiacum*
L. *auratum*
Aurelian Hybrids
Bellingham Hybrids
L. *bolanderi*
L. *browni*
L. *canadense*
Copper King Strain
L. *davidi*
L. *distichum*
L. *duchartrei*
Emerald Isle
Golden Harvest Hybrids
L. *grayi*
L. *hansoni*
L. *henryi* and hybrids
L. *japonicum*
Jillian Wallace
L. *kelloggi*

L. *lankongense*
L. *leichtlini*
L. *mackliniae*
L. *martagon album*
L. *michiganense*
Olympic Hybrids
Painted Lady Hybrids
L. *pardalinum*
L. *parryi*
Pink Perfection Strain
L. *regale*
    Royal Gold
L. *rubellum*
L. *rubescens*
L. *speciosum* and hybrids
L. *superbum*
L. *tigrinum*
L. *tsingtauense*
L. *wardi*
L. *washingtonianum*

FOR COOL, MOIST, WELL-DRAINED SOIL

L. auratum platyphyllum and hybrids
Bellingham Hybrids
L. bolanderi
L. canadense
L. columbianum
L. distichum
L. grayi
L. lankongense
L. nepalense
L. parryi
Pink Perfection Strain
L. rubellum
L. superbum
L. vollmeri
L. wigginsi

FOR ACID SOIL

Bellingham Hybrids
L. catesbaei
L. lankongense
L. occidentale
L. philadelphicum

FOR HEAVY LOAM

L. browni
L. chalcedonicum
L. humboldti
L. ocellatum
L. parryi
L. tsingtauense

TOLERANT OF LIME

L. amabile
Backhouse Hybrids
L. browni
L. bulbiferum
L. callosum
L. candidum
L. carniolicum
L. cernuum
L. chalcedonicum
L. concolor
L. davidi
L. hansoni
L. henryi
L. hollandicum
L. leucanthum
L. longiflorum
L. martagon
L. monadelphum
L. pardalinum
L. parryi
L. pomponium
L. pyrenaicum
L. regale
L. szovitzianum

FOR CUTTING

L. *auratum* and hybrids
Aurelian Hybrids
L. *canadense*
L. *candidum*
L. *cernuum*
L. *concolor*
L. *dauricum*
L. *davidi*
Fiesta Hybrids
L. *formosanum*
Golden Chalice Hybrids
L. *henryi* and hybrids

L. *hollandicum*
L. *japonicum* and hybrids
L. *longiflorum* and varieties
Marlyn Ross
Mid-Century Hybrids
Olympic Hybrids
L. *pardalinum*
L. *pumilum*
L. *regale*
L. *speciosum* and hybrids
L. *x testaceum*
L. *tigrinum* and hybrids

FOR FRAGRANCE

L. *auratum*
Aurelian Hybrids
L. *bakerianum*
Bellingham Hybrids
L. *bolanderi*
L. *browni*
L. *candidum*
L. *cernuum*
L. *formosanum*
L. *grayi*
Green Dragon Hybrids
Green Mountain Hybrids
L. *henryi*
L. *humboldti*
Jillian Wallace
L. *kelloggi*
L. *kesselringianum*
L. *lankongense*
L. *leucanthum*
Olympic Hybrids
L. *monadelphum*

L. *neilgherrense*
L. *nepalense*
L. *nobilissimum*
L. *occidentale*
L. *papilliferum*
L. *philippinense*
L. *polyphyllum*
L. *primulinum*
L. *pumilum*
    Golden Gleam
L. *regale*
L. *rubellum*
L. *rubescens*
L. *sargentiae*
L. *sulphureum*
L. *superbum*
T. A. Havemeyer
L. *x testaceum*
L. *wallichianum*
L. *wardi*
L. *washingtonianum*

FOR POT CULTURE

L. auratum
L. auratum-speciosum Hybrids
    Jamboree Strain
    Potomac Hybrids
L. browni
L. candidum Cascade Strain
Fiesta Hybrids
Golden Chalice Hybrids
L. hansoni
Henryi Hybrids
Hollandicum-tigrinum Hybrids
L. longiflorum
    Ace
    Croft
    Estate
L. maculatum
L. martagon album
Mid-Century Hybrids
L. nepalense
L. pumilum
Rainbow Hybrids
L. speciosum, varieties and hybrids
L. x testaceum
Umbellatum-tigrinum Hybrids.

FOR THE ROCK GARDEN

L. amabile
L. bolanderi
L. bulbiferum chaixi
L. carniolicum
L. cernuum
L. columbianum
L. concolor
L. dauricum
L. formosanum pricei
L. hollandicum
L. kelloggi
L. medeoloides
L. papilliferum
L. philadelphicum
L. pomponium
L. pumilum
L. rubellum

WITH UNPLEASANT ODORS

L. amabile
L. carniolicum
L. martagon
L. pomponium
L. pyrenaicum

LILIES BY COLOR

GREEN

HEIGHT	NAME	COLOR	BLOOM
5–7′	Aurelian Hybrids Moonlight Strain	chartreuse and apple green	August
5–7′	Emerald Isle	yellow and emerald green reverse	July
5–7′	Emerald Strain	white flushed emerald green	July
5–7′	Green Dragon	chartreuse	July
5–7′	Green Magic Strain	same as Green Dragon	July
5–7′	Green Mountain Hybrids	ivory, green or green-bronze reverse	July
4–6′	Limelight	chartreuse	July
2–3′	*L. nepalense*	emerald green, wine center	July
5–7′	Olympic Hybrids	include greens	
5–7′	New Era	chartreuse and ivory	July
5–7′	Reflection Strain	includes greens	late July

LILAC, WINE, PURPLE AND MAHOGANY

1–2′	*L. bolanderi*	wine-red, purple dots	July
2–3′	*L. cernuum*	orchid-lilac	July
3–5′	Fiesta Hybrids Bronzino Strain	amber, sand, teak, chocolate, mahogany	July
5′	Harlequin Hybrids	ivory, lilac, old rose to purple	July

HEIGHT	NAME	COLOR	BLOOM
3–5'	*L. martagon cattaniae dalmaticum*	black-purple blood-purple	June–July
	Backhouse Hybrids	include dark colors	
	Paisley Hybrids	include lilac and mahogany	
3–5'	Mid-Century Hybrid Tabasco	chestnut-red, black spots	July
1–1½'	*L. papilliferum*	dull maroon	July

ORANGES

AND MIXTURES INCLUDING ORANGE

HEIGHT	NAME	COLOR	BLOOM
5–7'	Aurelian Hybrids:		August
	African Queen Strain	apricot and orange	
	Coraline	apricot	
	Heart's Desire	white, orange center	
	Sunburst Strain	white to orange	
4–5'	Backhouse Hybrids (martagon type)	cream, yellow, orange to red	June–July
5–7'	Bellingham Hybrids	yellow, orange to red, spotted	July
4'	Brandywine	red-orange, dotted	June
3–4'	*L. bulbiferum var. croceum*	orange, black spots	late June
3–4'	*L. callosum*	orange, spotted	late July
3–5'	*L. canadense*	orange, speckled	July
	Cavalier	red-orange	June
5–7'	Copper King Strain, trumpets	orange & apricot	
3–5'	Coral Hybrids	coral-apricot	June–July
4–6'	*L. davidi maxwill willmottiae*	orange vivid orange	July
3–5'	Fiesta Hybrids	straw, orange, maroon	July
2½–4'	Golden Chalice Hybrids	lemon to orange	June–July
4–6'	*L. hansoni*	orange, brown spots	June–July
	T. A. Havemeyer	buff-suffused apricot	August

HEIGHT	NAME	COLOR	BLOOM
5–8′	*L. henryi*	orange	August
3–4′	*L. hollandicum* and hybrids	red-orange	July
3–5′	Mid-Century Hybrids	yellow to red	July
4–5′	Orange Perfection	orange, black spots	July
3–5′	Paisley Hybrids (martagon type)	ivory, yellows, oranges, tangerine, mahogany; also lilac; maroon dots	June
3–5′	Preston Hybrids	yellow to red-orange	July
2–4′	*L. pumilum* Golden Gleam	light orange	June
2–4′	Rainbow Hybrids	golden yellow to mahogany	July
5–9′	*L. superbum*	bright orange	July–August
4–6′	*L. tigrinum*	reddish-orange	July–August
3–5′	*L. wilsoni*	apricot	July–Sept.

PINK

3–4′	*L. auratum platyphyllum —japonicum* hybrids	blush and pink, gold band	July
	Pink Diamond Strain	pink	
	Pink Pearl Strain	salmon pink, gold band	
3–5′	*L. auratum—speciosum* hybrids:		
	Jamboree Strain	deep pink	
3–5′	*L. auratum—speciosum— japonicum—rubellum* hybrid:		
	Pink Glory Strain	pink	
5–6′	Aurelian Hybrid Pink Trumpet	pink	July
2–4′	*L. japonicum*	shell to rose pink	June
2–4′	*L. japonicum platyfolium*	pink to rose	June
2–4′	*L. lankongense*	rose, spotted purple	August
2′	*L. mackliniae*	pale pink	May

HEIGHT	NAME	COLOR	BLOOM
5–7'	Olympic Hybrids:		July
	Pink Perfection Strain	fuchsia pink	
1½–2'	L. rubellum	rose pink	June
2–3'	L. wardi	pink spotted	July–Aug.

RED

HEIGHT	NAME	COLOR	BLOOM
3'	L. amabile	grenadine, black spots	June
5–7'	Afterglow	crimson, maroon spots	July
2–4'	L. bulbiferum	crimson, black spots	June
3–5'	L. canadense var. rubrum	red	
4–5'	Cardinal	fire red	July
2–3'	L. chalcedonicum	mandarin-red, vivid	July
3'	L. concolor	scarlet	June–July
	pulchellum	vermillion, purple spots	June–July
1–2'	L. dauricum	scarlet	June
2–3'	Fire King	red	June
4–6'	Hollywood Hybrids	orange-red to dark red	July
	Imperial Crimson	crimson	
3–5'	Mid-Century Hybrids		July
	Cinnabar	maroon	
	Enchantment	nasturtium-red	
	Firecrown	vermillion	
	Fireflame	crimson	
	Sunstar	vermillion	
	Tabasco	chestnut-red	
2–4'	L. medeoloides	scarlet, black spots	July
2–5'	L. michiganense	orange-red, maroon spots	June–July
3–4'	Mountaineer	capsicum-red	June
3–4'	Navajo	fire-red	June
1'	L. papilliferum	maroon	July

HEIGHT	NAME	COLOR	BLOOM
3–4′	Paprika	blood-red	July
	L. pardalinum giganteum	red, heavily spotted	July
1–3′	*L. philadelphicum*	orange-scarlet	June–July
1–2′	*L. pomponium*	lacquer-red	June–July
2–4′	*L. pumilum*	scarlet	June
2½–4′	Red Fortune	currant-red, dark spots	June
3–4′	Samarkand	dark red	July
3–3½′	Siam	scarlet	July
3–4′	Sirdar	dark red	July
3–4′	Valiant	bright red	July

WHITE WITH ROSE-RED OR PINK

HEIGHT	NAME	COLOR	BLOOM
4–7′	*L. auratum pictum*	white, crimson, red band	August–September
	rubrum	white, crimson center	
	rubro-vittatum	white, crimson ray, gold center	
3–5′	*L. speciosum*	white, with rose or red suffusion and spots	August–September
	magnificum		
	Oregon Giant		
	punctatum		early
	Red Champion		August

WHITE TO IVORY

HEIGHT	NAME	COLOR	BLOOM
5–8′	*L. auratum var. virginale*		August–September
5–7′	*L. auratum-japonicum*		
	Hybrids		
	White Pearl Strain		August

HEIGHT	NAME	COLOR	BLOOM
6–8'	Aurelian Hybrids		August
	Ivorine	ivory	
	Silver Sunburst	ivory and white	
	Strain	white	
3–4'	*L. candidum*	white	June
2–7'	*L. formosanum* Wallace's Variety		August
2–4'	*L. longiflorum* All varieties and strains		July or for forcing
4'	*L. martagon album*	white	June
5–7'	Olympic Hybrids White Selections		July
3–4'	*L. regale var. album*	white	June
4–6'	*L. speciosum album*		August
4–6'	*L. speciosum* var. White Champion		August

WHITE WITH DARK ACCENTS OR WITH LIGHT COLORS OTHER THAN PINK

HEIGHT	NAME	COLOR	BLOOM
4–8'	*L. auratum var. praecox*	white, gold banded	August–
	L. auratum platyphyllum	as above but with maroon spots	September
5–7'	Black Dragon	white, purple-brown reverse	August
	Black Magic Strain	as above	
4–5'	*L. browni*	white-purplish-brown reverse	July
	L. browni australe	white, maroon-brown reverse, brown anthers	
	L. formosanum	white, purple-brown reverse	September
	Price's Variety	as above	July
	St. Louis Strain	as above	September
	wilsoni	as above	September

HEIGHT	NAME	COLOR	BLOOM
5–7'	Green Mountain Hybrids	ivory to greenish bronze	July
5–7'	New Era	white to chartreuse	July
5–7'	Olympic Hybrids	cream, pink, green, darker reverse	July
4–5'	L. regale	white, rose-purple reverse	July
5–7'	Sargentiae Hybrids	white, darker reverse	August
5–7'	Sentinel Strain	white, gold throat, dark brown pollen	
	Stardust	white, green center	
2–5'	L. taliense	cream, purple spots	July
4–5'	L. washingtonianum	white, changing to purple purple dots	June–July

YELLOW

3'	L. amabile luteum	black spots	June
5–7'	Aurelian Hybrids:		July–Aug.
	Golden Clarion Strain	cream to butter	
	Golden Splendor	deep gold, maroon reverse	
	Golden Sunburst	lemon	
	Lemon Cup	lemon	
6'	Bellingham Hybrid	bright yellow	July
	Buttercup		
3–5'	L. canadense flavum		early July
3'	L. concolor coridion	citron	June–July
4–5'	Fiesta Hybrids:		July
	Citronella Strain	black spots	
	Golden Wedding Strain	golden	
2½–4'	Golden Chalice Hybrids		June
	Golden Wonder	light gold	
	Mogul	orange-yellow, spotted	
5–8'	L. henryi citrinum		August

HEIGHT	NAME	COLOR	BLOOM
3–4'	Marlyn Ross	lemon	
3'	Mega	lemon, maroon spots	June
3–5'	Mid-Century Hybrids		July
	Destiny	lemon, brown spots	
	Prosperity	lemon	
5'	Palomino	buff	June
2½–5'	*L. parryi*	lemon	July
2–3'	*L. pumilum* Yellow Bunting	golden	
4–5'	*L. regale* Royal Gold		July
4–5'	*L. regale* hybrid Red Gold Strain	gold, red veins	July
4–7'	*L. sulphureum*	sulphur	August–September
5–6'	Sulphur Hybrids	pale to sulphur yellow	July
2–3'	*L. wilsoni flavum*	mimosa yellow	August–September

LILIES BY BLOOMING DATES

NOTE: These blooming dates—based on records taken at Oregon Bulb Farms over a ten-year period—indicate the relative time of flowering. Flowering dates vary, of course, with local climatic and seasonal conditions.

MAY	JUNE	JUNE–JULY	JULY	JULY–AUG.	AUGUST	AUG.–SEPT.	SEPTEMBER
L. concolor	Backhouse Hybrids	L. amabile	L. auratum praecox	L. auratum	L. auratum platyphyllum	L. catesbaei	L. browni austrole
L. dauricum	L. hansoni	L. amabile luteum	Aurelian Hybrids	Aurelian Hybrids	L. callosum	Marlyn Ross	L. formosanum wilsoni
Golden Chalice Hybrids	Lemon Queen	Bellingham Hybrids	L. browni	L. bakerianum	L. formosanum Wallace St.	L. nepalense	L. tigrinum
Golden Wonder	L. mackliniae	L. canadense	L. bulbiferum croceum	L. bolanderi	Imperial Crimson	L. papilliferum	
L. pumilum	Marhan	L. candidum	L. chalcedonicum	L. grayi	Imperial Gold	L. primulinum	
L. pumilum	L. monadelphum	L. carniolicum	L. davidi	L. henryi	Imperial Silver	L. speciosum gloriosoides	
Golden Gleam	L. pyrenaicum	L. cernuum	L. duchartrei	Jillian Wallace	Ivorine	L. sulphureum	
		L. columbianum	L. formosanum pricei	L. leichtlini maximowiczi	L. nepalense	T. A. Havermayer	
		L. davidi wilmottiae	Green Mountain Hybrids	Lemon Cup	L. papilliferum	L. tigrinum fortunei	
		Fiesta Hybrids	L. humboldti	New Era	Pink Diamond		
		Harlequin Hybrids	L. japonicum	Pink Beauty	L. tigrinum		
		L. japonicum platyfolium	L. kelloggi	Pink Glory	L. wallichianum		
		L. lankongense	L. leucanthum	L. sargentiae	L. wilsoni		
				L. speciosum album punctatum rubrum	L. wilsoni flavum		

fortunei

Hybrid Strains
of trumpet
lilies

L. rubellum	*L. maculatum*	*L. longiflorum*
L. szovitsianum	*L. martagon*	*L. martagon dalmaticum*
	L. martagon album	Mid-Century Hybrids
	Mid-Century Hyb.	*L. nevadense*
	L. pardalinum	Olympic Hybrids
	L. parryi	*L. pardalinum giganteum*
	L. pomponium	*L. polyphyllum*
	Preston Hybrids	*L. rubescens*
	L. regale	*L. speciosum punctatum*
	Sentinel Hybrids	*L. taliense*
	L. x testaceum	*L. tsingtauense*
		Hybrid strains of trumpet lilies

LILIES BY HEIGHT*

5–7' TALL	4–5' MED. TALL	3–4' MEDIUM	2–3' LOW	1–2' DWARF
Afterglow	Backhouse Hybrids	L. bakerianum	L. amabile	L. amoenum
L. auratum & vars.	L. browni	L. callosum	L. amabile luteum	L. bolanderi
Aurelian Hybrids	L. columbianum	L. bulbiferum	L. bulbiferum	L. catesbaei
Bellingham Hybrids	L. davidi	L. croceum	L. cernuum	L. dauricum
Black Magic Strain	L. dauricum	L. canadense	L. concolor	L. medeoloides
Emerald Strain	L. elegans	L. candidum	L. davidi	L. nobilissimum
L. formosanum wilsoni	L. hansoni	L. chalcedonicum	L. distichum	L. papilliferum
Golden Clarion Hybrids	Jillian Wallace	L. columbianum	L. duchartrei	L. pomponium
Green Dragon	L. kelloggi	Fiesta Hybrids	L. formosanum pricei	L. pumilum & vars.
Green Mountain Hyb.	L. martagon album	L. grayi	Golden Chalice Hyb.	L. rubellum
L. henryi	L. parryi	L. hollandicum	L. japonicum	
L. humboldti	L. polyphyllum	L. humboldti	L. lankongense	
L. leucanthum	L. regale	L. leichtlini	L. longiflorum	
L. leichtlini	L. x Royal Gold	L. maritimum	L. maculatum	
Olympic Hybrids	L. rubescens	L. martagon	Mid-Century Hybrids	
L. pardalinum	L. sargentiae	L. medeoloides	L. neilgherrense	
L. sulphureum	L. speciosum & vars.	Mid-Century Hybrids	L. occidentale	
L. superbum	L. x testaceum	L. monadelphum	L. philadelphicum	
L. taliense	L. wallichianum	L. parvum	L. tsingtauense	
L. tigrinum & vars.	L. washingtonianum	L. ponticum	L. wilsoni	
		Rainbow Hybrids	L. wilsoni flavum	
		L. wardi		

*Metric equivalent: 1 foot = .3048 meter

"LILIES" THAT ARE NOT LILIES

"LILY"	BOTANICAL NAME
Adobe lily	*Fritillaria pluriflora*
Afghan Lily	*Schizostylis*
African corn lily	*Ixia maculata*
African blue lily	*Agapanthus africanus*
Amazon lily	*Eucharis grandiflora*
American wood lily	*Trillium*
Angel's lily	*Ismene*
Arum lily	*Zaniedeschia aethiopica*
Asphodel lily	*Asphodeline lutea*
	Hemerocallis flava
August lily	*Amaryllis belladonna*
Atamasco lily	*Zephyranthes atamasco*
Australia lily	*Blandfordia*
	Eustrephus
Australian Giant lily	*Doryanthes palmeri*
Australian Spear lily	*Doryanthes palmeri*
Australian Sword lily	*Anigozanthos manglesi*
Avalanche lily	*Erythronium*
Aztec lily	*Sprekelia formosissima*
Barbados lily	*Amaryllis belladonna*
Basket lily	*Hymenocallis calathina*
Belladonna lily	*Amaryllis belladonna*
Bengal lily	*Crinum zeylanicum*
Bethlehem lily	*Eucharis grandiflora*
Black lily	*Fritillaria camschatcensis*
Blackberry lily	*Belamcanda chinensis*
Blood lily	*Haemanthus coccineus*
Blue lily	*Ixiolirion pallasi*
Blue lily of the Nile	*Agapanthus umbellatus*
Brisbane lily	*Eurycles*
Brodie's lily	*Brevoortia*
Buddhist lily	*Nelumbium*
Bugle lily	*Watsonia*
Bunchlily	*Melanthera*
Butterfly lily	*Hedychium coronarium*

"LILY"	BOTANICAL NAME
Cabbage Tree lily	*Cordyline australis*
Caffre lily	*Clivia*
Calla lily	*Zantedeschia aethiopica*
Black and Yellow	*Zantedeschia melanoleuca*
Golden	*Zantedeschia elliottiana*
Pink	*Zantedeschia rehmanni*
Camas lily	*Camassia*
Canna lily	*Canna*
Cape lily	*Crinum longifolium*
	Agapanthus africanus
Cape Belladonna lily	*Brunsvigia*
Cape Coast lily	*Crinum*
Caribbean lily	*Ismene or Hymenocallis caribaea*
Celestial lily	*Iris kaempferi*
Chamise lily	*Erythronium grandiflorum*
Chatham Island lily	*Myosotidium nobile*
Checkered lily	*Fritillaria meleagris*
Chicken-gizzard lily	*Crinum*
Chilian lily	*Alstroemeria chilensis*
Chinese Sacred lily	*Narcissus tazetta orientalis*
Chocolate lily	*Fritillaria biflora*
Climbing lily	*Gloriosa*
Club lily	*Kniphofia*
Cluster lily	*Hookera*
Coffee lily	*Schizostylis*
Corfu lily	*Hosta*
Corn lily	*Gladiolus*
	Ixia
Cow lily	*Nuphar advena*
Cowboy lily	*Oenothera*
Crinum lily	*Crinum longifolium*
Crocus lily	*Zephyranthes*
Crown Imperial lily	*Fritillaria*
Cuban lily	*Scilla peruviana*
Curly lily	*Erythronium giganteum*
Custard lily	*Hemerocallis flava*
Daffodil lily	*Amaryllis*
Daylily	*Hemerocallis flava*
Darling lily	*Crinum*

"LILY"	BOTANICAL NAME
Delicate lily	*Chlidanthus fragrans*
Desert lily	*Hesperocallis undulata*
Double Golden Crown	*Hemerocallis Kwanso*
Egyptian lily	*Zantedeschia aethiopica*
Eucharis lily	*Eucharis grandiflora*
Evening lily	*Callirhoe*
Fairy lily	*Zephyranthes*
Fawn lily	*Erythronium albidum*
	Erythronium montanum
Fireball lily	*Haemanthus*
Flax lily	*Dianella*
Fleur-de-lis	*Iris psuedo-acorus*
Football lily	*Haemanthus*
Foxtail lily	*Eremurus*
Fringed Water lily	*Limnanthemum*
Frost lily	*Cooperia*
Ginger lily	*Hedychium*
Glacier lily	*Erythronium parviflorum*
Glory lily	*Gloriosa*
Golden lily	*Lycoris aurea*
Grass lily	*Herpolirion*
Ground lily	*Trillium cernuum*
	Zephyranthes atamasco
Guernsey lily	*Nerine sarniensis*
Gumbo lily	*Pachylophus*
Heartleaf lily	*Maianthemum*
Herb lily	*Alstroemeria pelegrina*
Hidden lily	*Curcuma*
Homer's lily	*Allium nigrum*
Honeysuckle lily	*Hedychium*
Hurricane lily	*Lycoris*
Golden	*Lycoris aurea*

"LILY"	BOTANICAL NAME
Ifafa lily	*Cyrtanthus*
Inca lily	*Alstroemeria pelegrina*
Indian lily	*Camassia*
Ismene lily	*Ismene*
Ixia lily	*Ixiolirion*
Jacobean lily	*Sprekelia formosissima*
Japanese Spider lily	*Nerine*
Japanese Toad lily	*Tricyrtis*
Jersey lily	*Vallota speciosa*
Jerusalem lily	*Montbretia*
Josephine's lily	*Brunsvigia josephinae*
Joss lily	*Narcissus tazetta orientalis*
Kaffir lily	*Schizostylis*
Kings Crown lily	*Fritillaria imperialis*
Knight's Star lily	*Hippeastrum*
Lavender Globe lily	*Allium*
Leafless lily	*Aphyllanthes*
Leek lily	*Allium moly*
Lemon lily	*Hemerocallis flava*
Lent lily	*Narcissus*
Leopard lily	*Lachenalia*
Lily of a Day	*Tradescantia*
Lily-of-the-Desert	*Hesperocallis undulata*
Lily-of-the-Field (Biblical)	probably *Anemone*
Lily-of-the-Field	*Sternbergia lutea*
Lily-of-the-Incas	*Alstroemeria pelegrina*
Lily-of-the-Nile	*Agapanthus africanus*
Lily of Peru	*Alstroemeria*
Lily-of-the-Valley	*Convallaria*
Lilythorn	*Catesbaea*
Lilytree	*Crinodendron*
Lilyturf	*Mondo*
	Liriope
	Ophiopogon
Loddon lily	*Leucojum*
Lotus lily Golden	*Nelumbo lutea*

"LILY"	BOTANICAL NAME
Mabel Island lily	*Arthropodium*
Magic lily	*Lycoris squamigera*
Magnolia lily	*Nuttallia*
Malabar Glory lily	*Gloriosa superba*
Mariposa lily	*Calochortus*
Matthiole lily	*Pancratium maritimum*
May lily	*Convallaria majalis*
Meadow lily	*Amaryllis belladonna*
Mediterranean lily	*Pancratium*
Mexican lily	*Amaryllis belladonna*
Mexican Scarlet lily	*Sprekelia*
Mexican Daylily	*Tigridia*
Milk and Wine lily	*Crinum*
Miracle lily (Naked Lady)	*Lycoris squamigera*
Moreton Bay lily	*Eurycles*
Mound lily	*Yucca gloriosa*
Mountain lily	*Ranunculus lyalli*
Mt. Cook lily	*Ranunculus lyalli*
Mozambique lily	*Gloriosa*
Mystery lily	*Lycoris*
Naked lily	*Amaryllis belladonna*
Natal lily	*Clivia—Imantophyllum*
N. Z. Flax lily	*Phormium tenax*
Onion lily	*Ornithogalum caudatum*
Orange lily	*Hemerocallis*
Orinoco lily	*Crinum*
Oxblood lily	*Habrantus advenum*
Palm lily	*Yucca*
Paradise lily	*Paradisea liliastrum*
Parrot lily	*Alstroemeria pulchella*
Brazilian	*Alstroemeria pulchella*
Parrot Lily of South Africa	*Gladiolus psittacinus*
Persian lily	*Fritillaria persica*
Peruvian lily	*Alstroemeria*
Peruvian Swamp lily	*Zephyranthes*

"LILY"	BOTANICAL NAME
Pineapple lily	*Curcuma*
	Eucomis undulata
Pink lily	*Aphyllanthes*
Pitcher lily	*Amaryllis*
Plantain lily	*Hosta*
Polyanthus lily	*Tuberose*
Pond lily	*Nymphaea*
Prairie lily	*Cooperia or Mentzelia*
Purple Dragon lily	*Dracunculus*
Purple Lily Tree	*Magnolia*
Queen lily	*Amaryllis*
	Curcuma petiolata
Rain lily	*Cooperia*
Red Mint lily	*Monarda didyma*
Resurrection lily	*Kaempferia rotunda, or Lycoris*
Rock lily	*Dendrobium speciosum*
	Mentzelia
Rocket Lily of New Zealand	*Arthropodium cirrhatum*
Royal Brunswick lily	*Brunsvigia*
Rush lily	*Sisryinchium*
Sacred Aztec lily	*Tigridia*
Sacred Lily of China	*Narcissus tazetta orientalis*
Sacred Lily of India	*Amorphophallus*
Sacred Tiger lily	*Tigridia*
Saint Bernard lily	*Anthericum liliago*
Saint Bruno lily	*Anthericum liliastrum*
Saint James lily	*Sprekelia formosissima*
Saint John's lily	*Gladiolus communis*
St. Michael's lily	*Hemerocallis*
Sand lily	*Hypoxis hirsuta*
	Leucocrinum montanum
Scarborough lily	*Valotta purpurea*
Sego lily	*Calochortus nuttalli*
Shepherd's lily	*Ranunculus lyallii*

"LILY"	BOTANICAL NAME
Snake lily	*Fritillaria meleagris*
Snake lily	*Brodiaea volubilis*
Soap lily	*Yucca*
Solomon's lily	*Arum palaestinum*
Spear lily	*Doryanthes and Gladiolus*
Spider lily	*Pancratium maritimum*
	Hymenocallis calathina
Golden	*Lycoris aurea*
Pink	*Lycoris radiata*
White	*Hymenocallis calathina*
Spire lily	*Galtonia candicans*
Spring lily	*Erythronium albidum*
Star lily	*Hypoxis stellata*
	Leucocrinum montanum
	Milla biflora
Swamp lily	*Nymphaea alba*
	Crinum americanum
Sword lily	*Gladiolus*
Tawny lily	*Hemerocallis*
Thong lily	*Clivia—Imantophyllum*
Toad lily	*Fritillaria meleagris*
	Tricyrtis
Toad Cup lily	*Marica*
Torch lily	*Kniphofia*
	Doryanthes excelsa
Tree lily	*Magnolia denudata*
Trinity lily	*Trillium*
	Trillium grandiflorum
Triplet lily	*Brodiaea laxa*
Trout lily	*Erythronium*
Trumpet lily	*Zantedeschia aethiopica*
Two-leaf lily	*Maianthemum bifolium*
Variegated Day lily	*Hosta*
Voodoo lily	*Arum cornutum*

"LILY"	BOTANICAL NAME
Wand lily	*Eremurus*
Water lily	*Nymphaea*
White Bead lily	*Clintonia*
White Globe lily	*Calochortus albus*
White Mountain lily	*Erythronium montanum*
White Star lily	*Milla biflora*
Whitsun lily	*Narcissus poeticus*
Wood lily	*Trillium*
Yellow Bead lily	*Clintonia umbellata*
Yucca lily	*Yucca*
Zephyr lily	*Zephyranthes*

LILY REGISTRATION

At the Fifteenth International Horticultural Congress held at Nice, France, in 1958, The Royal Horticultural Society was appointed as the International Registration Authority for the Names of *Lilium* Cultivars. The chief duties of a Registration Authority have been defined as follows:

(*a*) To compile, maintain and publish a list of names of cultivars (i.e., horticultural varieties) and subsequently to publish such supplements and new editions of the list as circumstances may require.

(*b*) To register names which conform to the rules and recommendations of the International Code for the Nomenclature of Cultivated Plants. A registration fee should be charged and should be fixed by the individual International Registration Authorities in consultation with the national organizations concerned in the various countries.

(*c*) To endeavor to get raisers, introducers and others concerned with the distribution of plants to submit all new names to the Registration Authority and to use only names which conform to the Code.

(*d*) To work in close co-operation with a well-established national organization for the group of plants concerned where such a national organization exists.

This list includes all names which have been found in previous indices and publications. It is realized that a number of plants may no longer be procurable or even existent and that the details available about them are inadequate for a proper description. Nevertheless, it has been thought desirable to include them, and the names of such plants are not at present legitimate for use for new cultivars.

In quite a number of cases the same name has been given for several different plants. This has been due very largely to the lack of an International Register and it is hoped that the publication of this list will help to prevent any further duplication of names.

The Registration of Names

In order to avoid in future the confusion which arises through the use of a given name for more than one *Lilium* cultivar, only registered names should be used. All seedlings of the same parentage are not necessarily good and only the best are worth naming. As soon as it is decided that a seedling is worth naming, and while the whole stock is in one person's hands, a name should be registered for it. In the first instance the International Register should be consulted as any name which is already listed is not available for a new plant. Having chosen a name which appears to be available it should be submitted to:

> The Secretary,
> The Royal Horticultural Society
> Vincent Square
> London, SW 1, England

together with the following particulars:

1) Name of seed parent.
2) Name of pollen parent.
3) Name of raiser.
4) Year of first flowering.
5) Brief description. The colors should, when possible, be matched with the Horticultural Color Chart.

The fee for registration of new name is 2s. 6d. (35¢) and this or its equivalent in local currency should be sent at the same time. These fees contribute a small part only to the cost of preparation and publication of *The International Register*.

Any amendments should also be sent to the above address.

SCHEDULE OF AWARDS ADOPTED BY THE
NORTH AMERICAN LILY SOCIETY, CLEVELAND, JULY 1952

1. Certificate of Commendation
To give recognition to and to encourage the production of new varieties of lilies of superior value.
2. Award of Merit
To give recognition of *Lilium* clones of outstanding quality.

RULES

1. Certificate of Commendation
To be awarded to a new clone of *Lilium* which is sufficiently different from and/or is a distinct improvement upon existing varieties.

2. Eligibility is confined to clones, numbered or named, prior to being offered for sale to the general public as indicated by listing in a commercial catalogue.

3. Three spikes must be submitted for judging. (The spikes may be shown in different classes in the show provided that the entry card indicates their location.)

4. The entry card must show the entry number of the exhibitor, the location of the entry, and the parentage (where known) of the clone.

5. The name, or names, of the exhibitor and originator must be withheld until judging is completed.

6. Where the exhibitor is not the originator, the exhibitor and the originator shall each receive a copy of the certificate.

Award of Merit

1. To be awarded to any *Lilium* clone of outstanding quality.

2. Established or well-known clones may be judged on the submission of one well grown spike.

3. Clones introduced or first offered for sale within a period of 3 years prior to submission must have gained the Certificate of Commendation in a previous year.

4. A new clone must be represented by three spikes. (The spikes may be entered in separate classes in the show provided that their locations are shown on the entry card.)

5. The entry card must show the entry number of the exhibitor, the location of the entry, and the parentage (where known) of the variety.

6. The names of the exhibitor and originator must be withheld until judging is completed.

7. The Certificate shall be awarded to the exhibitor. Where the originator is known he (or she) shall also receive a copy.

Judging

It is recommended that:

1. A special committee of judges be appointed to judge entries for the Awards.

2. The committee shall consist of not less than five (5) judges.

3. The exhibitor or originator of a clone presented for judging shall not judge exhibits entered or originated by him. A substitute judge shall be appointed if necessary.

4. More than one unfavorable vote shall prevent an award being made.

5. At the discretion of the President and Board of Directors, regional committees of qualified judges may be appointed to judge lilies which do not bloom during the time of the Annual Show.

6. Recommendations of judging committees shall be presented to the Awards and Standards Committee and to the President for Approval.

BIBLIOGRAPHY OF BOOKS ON LILIES

As an amateur gardener or professional grower, one of the great pleasures and privileges incident to the growing of lilies is the collecting of books, illustrations and articles pertaining to them. It is only through this literature that one can gain a perspective on the scope and ramifications of the culture of the lily in all countries. The books, while often repetitive, usually have some shrewd personal observations of keen gardeners hidden among less original matter. Nearly all are worth the comparatively low price asked for them. While many lily books are now out of print, they can often be found in catalogs from book sellers both here and abroad. To discover these books and collect them is as interesting a hobby as the growing of the lilies themselves. The following list covers the more important recent publications.

ADAMS, H. S. (1913). *Lilies—A Flower Monograph.* 116 pages. New York.
BOTKE, J., Ph.D. and VAN DER SLIKKE, C. M. (1942). *Lelies en Leliecultuur.* 155 pages. Illus. The Hague. A very fine, well-illustrated Dutch text.
CRAIG, W. N. (1928). *Lilies and Their Culture in North America.* 146 pages. Illus. Chicago.

DE GRAAFF, JAN (1951). *The New Book of Lilies.* 176 pages. New York. Illus.

ELWES, H. J. (1877–80). *A Monograph of the Genus Lilium.* Illus. London. This magnificent work contains folio hand-colored illustrations by W. H. Fitch.

ELWES, H. J. (1877–80). *Supplement.* See Grove, A. and Cotton, A. D. (1934–40).

FOX, HELEN M. (1928). *Garden Cinderellas; How to Grow Lilies in the Garden.* 269 pages. Illus. New York.

GOLDRING, W. (1905). *The Book of the Lily* (Handbooks of Practical Gardening Series). 98 pages. Illus. London.

GREEN, SVEN. (1945). *Liljor.* 128 pages. Illus. Copenhagen, Denmark.

GREY, C. H. (1938). Hardy Bulbs, 3., Liliaceae, 368–420, 459–462. Illus. London.

GRIFFITHS, D. (1928). "A Score of Easily Propagated Lilies." United States Department of Agriculture Circular no. 23. 35 pages. Illus. Washington, D.C.

—— (1930). "The production of lily bulbs." United States Department of Agriculture Circular no. 102. 56 pages. Illus. Washington, D.C.

—— (1933). "Some Hybrid Martagon Lilies." United States Department of Agriculture Circular no. 299. 14 pages. Illus. Washington, D.C.

GROVE, A. (1911). *Lilies* (Present-day Gardening series). 116 pages. Illus. London.

GROVE, A. and COTTON, A. D. (1934–40). *A Supplement to Elwes' Monograph of the Genus Lilium.* Illus. London.

HOLZHAUSEN, AXEL. *Akta Liljor Svardsliljor* (1935). 147 pages. Illus. Stockholm, Sweden.

HOLZHAUSEN, AXEL. *Boken om Liljor* (1927). 227 pages. Illus. Stockholm, Sweden.

LAKE, ALEXANDER. (1947). *The Past and the Future of the Croft Easter Lily.* 94 pages. Lompoc, California.

MACFIE, D. T. (1939). *Lilies for the Garden and Greenhouse.* 143 pages. Illus. London.

—— (1947). 2nd Ed. 151 pages. Illus. London.

MACNEIL, A. and MACNEIL, ESTHER (1946). *Garden Lilies.* 226 pages. Illus. New York.

MARSHALL, W. E. (1929). *Consider the Lilies.* 92 pages. Illus. New York.

MAXWELL, ALICE C. (1953). *Lilies in Their Homes.* 256 pages. London.

NORTH AMERICAN LILY SOCIETY. *The Lily Yearbooks of the North American Lily Society.* Illus. Geneva, New York.

PRESTON, ISABELLA (1929). *Garden Lilies.* 126 pages. Illus. New York.

—— (1947). *Lilies for Every Garden.* 160 pages. Illus. New York.

QUINT, I. GEORGE. (1953). *How to Grow Lilies in the Garden.* 96 pages. New York.

ROYAL HORTICULTURAL SOCIETY. *The Lily Year Books.* Illus. London.

SALIWSKI, I. L. (1952). *Lilies.* (In Russian language.)

SALIWSKI, I. L. (1955). *Lilien.* (Same text as above, translated in German. Both give a report on what has been done in the Soviet Union and on the lilies found there.)

SLATE, G. L. (1939). *Lilies for American Gardens.* 258 pages. Illus. New York and London.

STEFFEN, DR. ALEXANDER. (1953). *Unsere Lilien im Garten.* 120 pages. Illus. Berlin, Germany.

STOKER, F. (1943). *A Book of Lilies* (King Penguin, no. 14). 32 pages. Illus. London and New York.

TAYLOR, G. M. (1947). *Lilies for the Beginner.* 72 pages. London.

TEUTSCHEL & CO. (1873). *Notes on Lilies and Their Culture.* 109 pages. Colchester, England.

WALLACE, A. (1879). *Notes on Lilies and Their Culture.* 2nd ed. 215 pages. Illus. Colchester, England.

A collection of papers and letters by various authors, including Burbidge's "On Lily Bulbs," reprinted from *The Garden.* II. 111–17, 131–38, 155–59 (1877), and Baker's "Synopsis of All the Known Lilies" from *The Gardeners' Chronicle,* 1871.

WARE, ROMAINE B. (1956). *Success with Lilies.* 51 pages. Illus.

WILSON, E. H. (1925; reprinted 1929). *The Lilies of Eastern Asia, a Monograph.* 110 pages. Illus. London.

LILY SOCIETIES

The Auckland Lily Society
Miss M. Crighton, Hon. Secretary
90 Kohimarama Rd.
Auckland, E. 1, New Zealand

New England Regional Lily Group
Ernest F. Stokes, President
21 Oakland Street
Lexington 73, Massachusetts

New Zealand Lily Society, Inc.
S. G. Prebble, Secretary
Box 1394
Christchurch, New Zealand

North American Lily Society
Ernest F. Stokes, Treasurer
21 Oakland Street
Lexington 73, Massachusetts

Puget Sound Lily Society
Mrs. Hollis N. Phillips
7550 39th N.E.
Seattle 15, Wash.

Vereniging "De Lelie"
Secretary
Wilhelminastraat 45
Haarlem, Holland

Index

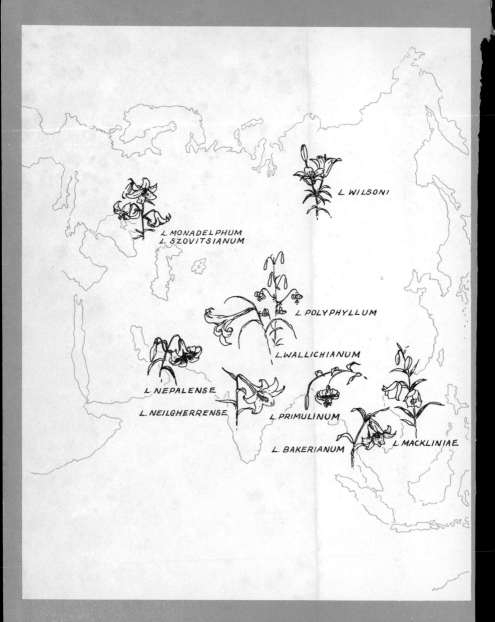

WHERE LILIES

ASIA India—Burma—Caucasus, Russia